Intellectual Property
&
Information Control

*Philosophic Foundations and
Contemporary Issues*

Adam D. Moore

Transaction Publishers
New Brunswick (U.S.A.) and London (U.K.)

Copyright © 2001 by Transaction Publishers, New Brunswick, New Jersey 08903.

This book is printed on acid-free paper that meets the American National Standard for Permanence of Paper for Printed Library Materials.

Library of Congress Number: 2001027885
ISBN: 0-7658-0070-5
Printed in the United States of America

Library of Congress Cataloging-in-Publication Data

Moore, Adam D.
  Intellectual property and information control : philosophic foundations and contemporary issues / Adam D. Moore.
        p. cm.
  Includes bibliographical references and index.
  ISBN 0-7658-0070-5 (alk. paper)
        1. Intellectual property—United States. 2. Computer systems—Law
     and legislation—United States. 3. Data transmission systems—Law
     and legislation—United States   I. Title.

KF2979 .M66 2001
346.7304'8—dc21   2001027885

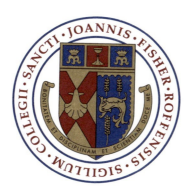

Intellectual Property

&

Information Control

Dedicated to Kimberly, Alan, and Nancy

Contents

List of Tables

Preface

This work contains numerous arguments, sketches, views, and theories and not all are central to the main thesis. I have tried to make the model of intellectual and intangible property presented in these pages accessible while maintaining a fair amount of rigor and depth. I thus skirt the line of boring the expert and overwhelming the novice. My hope is that I have done neither.

After gaining the overview offered in chapter 1, the reader who wishes to move rapidly may want to skim or omit certain sections or chapters. Chapters 3-6 are the argumentative core of the book while chapters 7-11 contain applications of the theory. Sections of chapters are appropriately titled so that the reader can quickly surmise if skimming or omission would be appropriate. For example, experts in moral theory may want to skip the second section of chapter 3 entitled *A General Overview of Utilitarian Theory* while those well versed in intellectual property law (copyrights and patents) may want to omit the first few sections of chapter 2.

The claim that "there is room for words on subjects other than last words" is certainly true of this work. I do not pretend to offer a complete theory that is unassailable and neatly packaged — the moral, legal, and political issues discussed herein are resistant to easy answers. What you will find is an intuitive model of intangible property that is both clearly presented and well reasoned. The tensions between intellectual property, information access, privacy, free speech, and accountability have been highlighted with the coming of the networked world. My hope is that this work will add to what has become a lively area of philosophical debate.

A.D.M.

Acknowledgments

I would like to thank Don Hubin (Ohio State University) and Peter King (Ohio State University) for reading and commenting on the first draft of the manuscript. Their comments and criticisms have profoundly influenced this work. Thanks to David T. Wasserman (University of Maryland, College Park), Ken Itkowitz (Marietta College), Jim Swindler (Wittenberg University), Earl Spurgin (John Carol University), Avery Kolers (University of Arizona), Richard Garner (Ohio State University), Nancy Snow (Marquette University), Dan Farrell (Ohio State University), and John Moser (Institute for Humane Studies) for commenting on specific chapters or sections.

Chapters 3, 4, 5, 8, 9, and 10 benefited significantly from being presented at various conferences and colloquia series including: Pacific Division Meeting of the American Philosophical Association (April 2000); 27th Conference on Value Inquiry (April 1999); Mid-South Philosophy Conference (March 1999); Ohio Philosophical Association Conference (April 1998); Central Division Meeting of the American Philosophical Association (1997); and the Mountain Plains Philosophy Conference (1997). My gratitude to those conference participants who provided helpful comments and suggestions.

Parts of chapters 1, 4, and 6 appear in "Introduction to Intellectual Property" and "Toward a Lockean Theory of Intellectual Property" in my edited anthology, *Intellectual Property: Moral, Legal, and International Dilemmas* (Rowman and Littlefield, 1997). Earlier versions of sections of chapters 4 and 7 appear in "A Lockean Theory of Intellectual Property" found in the *Hamline Law Review* 21 (Fall 1997). Chapter 8 draws directly from material that originally appeared in "Intangible Property: Privacy, Power, and Information Control," *American Philosophical Quarterly* 35 (October 1998). Material from an earlier version of chapter 9 was published in *Business Ethics Quarterly* 10 (July 2000) entitled "Employee Monitoring and Computer Technology: Evaluative Surveillance v.

Privacy." Chapter 10 contains material published in *Bioethics* 14 (Spring 2000) entitled "Owning Genetic Information and Gene Enhancement Techniques." Chapter 11 draws from an article, "Privacy and the Encryption Debate," in *Knowledge, Technology, and Policy* 12 (Winter 2000). I thank editors of these publishers for allowing me to present this material here.

A special thanks to my friends and loved ones who have supported me throughout the writing process—Scott Rothwell, Mark VanHook, Walter James, Bill Kline, Nick Morse, James Summerford, Nancy Moore, Alan Moore, and Kimberly Moore.

I also would like to thank Nancy Moore for reading, editing, and commenting on an early draft and the Institute for Humane Studies (George Mason University, Fairfax, VA) for a summer fellowship (1997) that provided much needed support during the initial writing stages.

1

Introduction and Overview

"I would like to leave you with the impression that if you make a single illegal copy of our software, you will spend the next five years in court, the following ten in prison, and forever after your soul will suffer eternal damnation."
—V. Rosenburgh, "Copyright and the New Technology"[1]

Introduction

Access to ideas, and to the physical embodiments of ideas, fundamentally shapes our opportunities, goals, and lifelong projects. The explosion of computer technology and the proliferation of digital networks has radically altered the way that ideas and information are gathered and manipulated. New models of information access and control promise profound changes for each of us—as life-altering as the changes that flowed from the introduction of Gutenberg's press, Darwin's theory of evolution, or Pasteur's germ theory of disease.

In modern times the debate over the control and ownership of digital information and intellectual property has been waged by two factions. Standing in the way of the cyber-punks, hackers, and net surfers who claim that "information wants to be free" and that intellectual property rights give undue credit to authors and inventors, are the collected cannons of Anglo-American copyright, patent, and trade secret law. Defenders of these institutions typically argue that granting rights to authors and inventors is necessary for the optimal production of intellectual works and the corresponding gains in social utility. Information, like any other commodity, can be bought and sold on the open market. Following Nathaniel Shaler many defenders of intellectual property argue that "there is no property more peculiarly a Man's own than that which is produced by the Labour of his mind"[2] or "[I]t will be clearly seen that intellectual property

1

is, after all, the only absolute possession in the world. . . The man who brings out of nothingness some child of his thought has rights therein which cannot belong to any other sort of property."[3]

Conversely, opponents argue that intellectual property rights give undue credit to authors and inventors and serve to restrict the free flow of information that would otherwise benefit everyone. Another reason why many individuals find it difficult to recognize intellectual property rights is that they see ideas as part of one's common culture. Ideas are not to be corralled or hoarded up—they are the common currency of thought, speech, and language.[4] Thomas Jefferson wrote:

> If nature has made any one thing less susceptible than all others of exclusive property, it is the action of the thinking power called an idea, which an individual may exclusively possess as long as he keeps it to himself; but the moment it is divulged, it forces itself into the possession of everyone, and the receiver cannot dispossess himself of it. Its peculiar character, too, is that no one possesses the less, because every other possesses the whole of it. He who receives an idea from me, receives instruction himself without lessening mine; as he who lights his taper at mine, receives light without darkening me. That ideas should freely spread from one to another over the globe, for the moral and mutual instruction of man, and improvement of his condition, seems to have been peculiarly and benevolently designed by nature, when she made them, like fire, expansible over all space, without lessening their density at any point, and like the air in which we breathe, move, and have our physical being, incapable of confinement or exclusive appropriation. Inventions then cannot, in nature, be a subject of property.[5]

Jefferson was impressed with the non-rivalrous nature of intellectual property—intellectual works can be used and consumed by many individuals concurrently. He was certainly opposed to granting intellectual property rights to ideas already in the public domain. While Jefferson's metaphor of passing light or fire along to others is a strong one, I wonder if he would defend this view if the creator of the light had labored ten years to produce it. In subsequent chapters I will argue that the non-rivalrous nature of intellectual works leads in a different direction—toward intellectual property rights.

Modern day disciples of Shaler and Jefferson push further and argue in a similar fashion as exhibited by the quote that begins this chapter and the following view expressed in the Bellagio Declaration:

> In general, systems built around the author paradigm tend to obscure or undervalue the importance of "the public domain," the intellectual and cultural commons from which future works will be constructed . . . [w]e declare that in an era where information is among the most precious of all resources, intellectual property rights cannot be framed

by the few to be applied to the many . . . We must reimagine the international regime of intellectual property.[6]

Moreover, international treaties like Trade Related Aspects of Intellectual Property, known as TRIPS, seek to pattern the global information infrastructure after Anglo-American copyright law. Defenders of rights to intellectual property find this agreement promising in that the rights of authors and inventors can be protected internationally. Many hackers, cyber-punks, programmers, net surfers, and others, support "idea anarchy" and argue for complete access to all kinds of information. This latter view is echoed by the policies of many developing countries who hold that intellectual works are social, not individual, products. It is claimed that the result of these latter attitudes about intellectual property has led to an explosion of copyright violations and international piracy. Consider the following table which focuses on international computer software piracy.

Table 1.1
Worldwide Software Piracy Table

Country	% falling to piracy, 1992/1999	US $ losses (million), 1992/1999
Australia	45/32	160/150
Denmark	48/29	67/59
France	73/39	1200/548
Germany	62/27	1000/652
Italy	86/44	550/421
Japan	92/31	3000/975
Korea	82/50	648/197
Singapore	41/51	24/61
Spain	86/53	362/247
Sweden	60/35	171/131
Taiwan	93/54	585/122
Thailand	99/81	181/82
UK	54/26	685/679
United States	35/25	1900/3191

Source: Business Software Alliance, 1992/1999

". . . a 36 percent global piracy rate (1999) is still substantial. Currently more than one out of every three software applications installed in the world is pirated. This translates into $12 billion lost due to software piracy. In the U.S. alone, software piracy cost 109,000 jobs . . . "[7] While this overstates the case because it is assumed that those who obtain goods from software pirates would have purchased legal copies, these numbers in the area of software ownership are alarming to those who would defend institutions of intellectual property.[8]

Things may be even worse for the recording industry where music swap sites like Napster make piracy easy and cost free. "Napster allows you to search for almost any song . . . finds the song on a fellow enthusiast's hard drive and then permits you to get the song for yourself, *right now*."[9] You can then burn your own CD, download the song to an MP3 player, or simply cue it up on your own computer. Millions of college students and music junkies have been flocking to Napster or similar sites and amassing huge music libraries—for free. One artist manager claimed, "Basically they're saying our art is worthless . . . music used to be collectable now it is disposable."[10] Lars Ulrich, the drummer for Metallica, put the point the following way. "This is an argument about intellectual property . . . where does it end? Should journalists work for free? Should lawyers? Engineers? Plumbers?"[11]

Even so, many argue that the information age has passed by the old, and now outdated, copyright paradigm. Where institutions of copyright may have worked well for the written page they cannot be retrofitted to accommodate the bit streams of digitized intellectual works. John Perry Barlow, a writer for *Wired Magazine*, echoes this view:

> This vessel, the accumulated canon of copyright and patent law, was developed to convey forms and methods of expression entirely different from the vaporous cargo it is now being asked to carry. It is leaking as much from within as from without . . . Legal efforts to keep the old boat floating are taking three forms: a frenzy of deck chair rearrangement, stern warnings to the passengers that if she goes down, they will face harsh criminal penalties, and serene, glassy-eyed denial . . . Intellectual property law cannot be patched, retrofitted, or expanded to contain digitized expression any more than real estate law might be revised to cover the allocation of broadcasting spectrum (which, in fact, rather resembles what is being attempted here). We will need to develop an entirely new set of methods as befits this entirely new set of circumstances.[12]

The problem generated by the digitization of intellectual property for copyright and patent is that these institutions protect durable physical expressions, but digital property is hardly physical or durable in the same way as books, movies, or processes of manufacture. Intellectual property law has always sought to separate the idea from its physical expression, granting ownership rights to the latter but not to the former: "the rights of invention and authorship adhered to activities in the physical world. One didn't get paid for ideas, but for the ability to deliver them into reality."[13] Many within the Anglo-American tradition claim that ideas are public property while physical embodiments of ideas may be privately owned. A major problem for an online age is that there may be no way to separate idea from expression. If so, modern Anglo-American institutions of intellectual property will have to be reworked, or maybe even abandoned altogether.

Complicating things still further are the issues that surround individual privacy, public accountability, free speech, and information control. There is an obvious tension between privacy and free speech. While thought, expression, and a free press are recognizably beneficial they are not always so—not when what is expressed unjustifiably invades private domains. The balance struck in the last century between privacy and free speech is being overturned by digital networking and information trading. For example, with the right kind of computer savvy, I can now go online and find out intimate personal details about almost anyone and offer it all up for public consumption. Moreover, if I am sly enough I may be able to do this anonymously.

Information gathering technology is promising to turn our work environments and public streets into an Orwellian nightmare. Video surveillance, genetic screening, global positioning systems, and purchasing profiles may leave us with little privacy. Information about our medical histories, phone numbers, addresses, and eating preferences is owned and traded by information brokers, including our government. Computer technology and digital networks such as the Internet or World-Wide-Web have changed the game, so-to-speak.

These issues raise deep philosophical problems. What is intellectual property and can rights to intellectual works be justified? Are abstract ideas and information, even sensitive personal information, the proper subjects of ownership? Can computer software and other digital information be protected? How should legal systems accommodate the ownership of intellectual property in an information age and what role should privacy rights play? Should protection extend to the electronic frontier of the Internet and the World Wide Web? What is the moral position of those who violate the intellectual property rights of others and how does this compare to the violation of physical property rights?

Throughout this work I develop answers to these questions or at least try to provide strategies for answering them. As we move further into what many call "the information age," clarity is needed at the philosophical level so that morally justified policies and institutions can be adopted with respect to intellectual property and information control. It is my hope that this work will facilitate and further philosophical inquiry in this important area.

Overview of a Theory

In the broadest terms my goal in this work is to justify rights to intellectual and intangible property. Some think that this goal is easily attained and offer the following argument. Control should be granted to authors and inventors of intellectual property because granting such control provides incentives necessary for social progress. Society ought to maximize social utility; therefore, temporary rights to intellectual works should be granted. This strategy for justifying rights to intellectual property is typically given as the primary basis for Anglo-American copyright, patent, trademark, and trade secret institutions. Nevertheless, I think the argument is fundamentally flawed. With this in mind, I proceed on two fronts. First, a negative argument is given that undermines the aforementioned widely supported rule-utilitarian case for intellectual property. The hope is upon eliminating rule-utilitarian incentives-based arguments, the way will be cleared for a new Lockean justification.

My positive argument begins with an account of Locke's proviso that justified acquisitions of unowned objects must leave "enough and as good" for others.[14] One way to interpret Locke's requirement is that it ensures the position of others is not worsened. This can be understood as a version of weak Pareto-superiority. If the possession and exclusion of an intellectual work makes no one worse off, then the acquisition ought to be permitted. In clarifying the issues that surround a Pareto-based proviso on acquisition, I defend an account of bettering and worsening and offer a solution to the baseline problem—what two situations do we compare to determine if someone has been worsened.

I argue that rights to intellectual works can be justified at both the level of acts and at the level of institutions. At both levels my argument turns on two features of intellectual property. First, intellectual works are non-rivalrous, meaning that they can be created, possessed, owned, and consumed by many individuals concurrently. Second, including allowances for independent creation, I argue that the frontier of intellectual property is practically infinite. Locke hints at this kind of practical infinity when he writes: "Nobody could think himself injured by the drinking of another man, though he took a good draught, who had a whole river of the same water left him to quench his thirst."[15] If I am correct, the case for Locke's water-drinker and the author or inventor are quite alike.

Finally, in light of the expansion of the Internet and the World Wide Web, a Lockean account of copyright, patent, and trade secret is developed along with an analysis of privacy, power, and the ownership of information. As already noted, governments as well as private companies are compiling digital profiles of us and selling this information to advertising agencies, insurance companies, private investigators, and the like. While it is true that this information could be used for our benefit, history is replete with examples of the converse.

In the simplest terms, the problem I address is one of information control. Moreover, it does not matter what form the information takes —it could be a poem, a novel, a new invention, a computer program, military data, or sensitive personal information. The following quote from a Chinese military newspaper applies a number of these issues to information war:

> After the Gulf War, when everyone was looking forward to eternal peace, a new military revolution emerged. This revolution is essentially a transformation from the mechanized warfare of the industrial age to the information warfare of the information age. Information warfare is a war of decisions and control, a war of knowledge, and a war of intellect. The aim of information warfare will be gradually changed from 'preserving oneself and wiping out the enemy' to 'preserving oneself and controlling the opponent.' Information warfare includes electronic warfare, tactical deception, strategic deterrence, propaganda warfare, psychological warfare, network warfare, and structural sabotage.[16]

Our reliance on digital technology and computer networks has left us vulnerable to viruses, worms, programming miscalculations, and information war. Putting information war aside, it seems true to claim that the shift from an industrial economy to an information-based economy has raised the stakes concerning the control of information and ideas. The claim is not that controlling information used to be unimportant and now it is important—alas, censorship in various forms has always been with us. What I think is true, however, is that computer networks coupled with digitally stored information is significantly changing the way we interact and communicate. We will have to be much more careful about what we do and say in the future both publicly and privately. Any information or ideas that we disclose, including inventions, recipes, or sensitive personal information, might soon be bouncing around cyberspace for anyone to access. The stakes are high indeed.

Notes

1. Quoted in Robert P. Benko's, *Protecting Intellectual Property Rights* (Washington, DC: American Enterprise Institute for Public Policy Research, 1987).
2. Copyright Law, State of Massachusetts, 1782.
3. Nathaniel Shaler, *Literary Property*.
4. Spooner notes that "One obstacle to the universal acknowledgment of property in ideas, has been this. Mankind *freely give away* so large a portion of their ideas, and so few of their ideas are of sufficient value to bring anything in the market, (except in the market of common conversation, where men mutually exchange their ideas) that persons, who have not reasoned on the subject, have naturally *fallen into the habit of thinking*, that ideas were not subjects of property; and have consequently been slow to admit that, as a matter of sound theory or law, men had a strict right of property in *any* of their ideas." Lysander Spooner, *The Law of Intellectual Property* (Weston, MA: M & S Press, 1971), 37-38 (Originally published in 1855).
5. Thomas Jefferson, "Letter to Isaac McPherson, Monticello, August 13, 1813," in *XIII The Writings of Thomas Jefferson*, edited by A. Lipscomb (Washington, DC Issud under the auspices of the Thomas Jefferson Memorial Association of the United States, 1904), 326-38.
6. James Boyle, *Shamans, Software, and Spleens* (Cambridge MA: Harvard University Press, 1996), Appendix.
7. Business Software Alliance, http://www.nopiracy.com.
8. For an illuminating account of how software is cracked, re-packaged, and uploaded for distribution, see David McCandless, "Warez Warz," *Wired Magazine* 5.04 (April 1997).
9. Steven Levy, "The Noisy War Over Napster," *Newsweek*, June 5, 2000, p. 48.
10. Ibid., *Newsweek*, June 5, 2000, p. 52. The manager was Ron Stone.
11. Lars Ulrich, "It's Our Property," *Newsweek*, June 5, 2000, p. 54.
12. J. P. Barlow, "Everything You Know About Intellectual Property Is Wrong," in *Intellectual Property: Moral, Legal, and International Dilemmas*, edited by A. Moore (Lanham, MD: Rowman & Littlefield, 1997), chapter 15, 350.
13. Barlow, "Everything You Know About Intellectual Property Is Wrong," 351.
14. John Locke, *The Second Treatise of Government,* edited by Peter Laslett (New York: New American Library, 1965), chapter 5, § 33.
15. Locke, *Second Treatise of Government,* chapter 5, § 33.
16. *Jiefangjun Bao,* Chinese Army Newspaper, cited by John Carlin, "A Farewell to Arms," *Wired Magazine* (May 1997).

2

The Domain of Intellectual Property

"What is it that we want to protect? First is the brilliant invention, the idea, the notion that makes a new product and the insight that makes a whole new industry. The second thing we want to protect is the investment and the hard work. This is the grunt work. This is the pick-and-shovel engineering that turns the idea, the prototype, into a reliable, distributable, maintainable, documented, supportable product."

—Robert Spinrad, Xerox Corp.[1]

Introduction

Apart from allowing individuals to own cars, computers, land, or other tangible goods, intellectual property law enables individuals to obtain ownership rights to control works of literature, musical compositions, processes of manufacture, computer software, and the like. This latter form of ownership is typically called intangible or intellectual property.[2] Setting aside questions of justifying ownership, which shall be a primary concern in the next few chapters, there are questions concerning the nature and scope of intellectual property. These latter questions focus on the domain or subject matter of non-tangible systems of property protection. Before explicating the domain of intellectual property it would be helpful to briefly consider the historical origins of copyright and patent institutions. By reviewing the historical origins and mapping modern institutions we will arrive at a fairly clear picture of intellectual property.

Historial Overview of Intellectual Property

One of the first known references to intellectual property protection dates from 500 B.C. when chefs were granted year-long monopolies for creating culinary delights in the Greek colony of Sybaris. Phylarchus, a Greek historian wrote:

[i]f any caterer or cook invented a dish of his own which was especially choice, it was his privilege that no one else but the inventor himself should adopt the use of it before the lapse of a year, in order that the first man to invent a dish might possess the right of manufacture during that period, so as to encourage others to excel in eager competition with similar inventions.[3]

Perhaps one of the best known cases of intellectual property piracy comes from this period as well. I am referring to Hermodorus' theft and subsequent sale of Plato's speeches. It seems that even Ancient Greece had "bootleg" problems!

There are at least three other notable references to intellectual property in ancient times—these cases are cited in Bruce Bugbee's formidable work *The Genesis of American Patent and Copyright Law.*[4] In the first case Vitruvius, another Aristophanes (257-180 B.C.), known as a critic from Greek Byzantium, is said to have revealed intellectual property theft during a literary contest in Alexandria. While serving as judge in the contest, Vitruvius exposed the false poets who were then tried, convicted, and disgraced.[5]

The second and third cases come from Roman times. Although there is no known Roman law protecting intellectual property, "Roman jurists discussed theoretical problems regarding its ownership, as, for example, the conflicting interests of the artist and of the owner of a table upon which the former had painted a picture."[6] There is also reference to literary piracy by Martial the Roman epigrammatist:

Rumor asserts, Fidentinus, that you recite my works to the crowd, just as if they were your own. If you wish they should be called mine, I will send you the poems gratis; if you wish them to be called yours, buy my disclaimer of them.[7]

These examples are generally thought to be atypical, for as far as we know, there were no institutions or conventions of intellectual property protection in Ancient Greece or Rome. In fact the Romans generally scorned monopolies of any sort as exhibited by Zeno's decree in 483 A.D. that no monopoly pertaining to food or clothing, even if ordered by another emperor, was to be permitted.

From Roman times to the birth of the Florentine Republic there were many franchises, privileges, and royal favors granted. Bugbee distinguishes between franchises or royal favors and systems of intellectual property in the following way: "The term monopoly connotes the giving of an exclusive privilege for buying, selling, working or using a thing which the public freely enjoyed prior to the grant. Thus a monopoly takes something from the people. An inventor deprives the public of nothing which it enjoyed before his discovery, but gives something of value to the community by adding to the sum of human knowledge."[8] One of the first statutes that protected author's rights was issued by the Republic of Florence on June 19, 1421, to Filippo Brunelleschi a famous architect.[9] This statute not only recognized the rights of authors and inventors to the products of their intellectual efforts, it built in an incentive mechanism that became a prominent feature of Anglo-American intellectual property protection. For several reasons, including Guild influence, the Florentine patent statute of 1421 was stillborn, issuing only the single patent to Brunelleschi.

The first lasting patent institution of intellectual property protection is found in the Venetian Republic of 1474. Proposed by committee the general patent statute passed the Venetian Senate by a vote of 116 to 10.[10] The statute read as follows:

> We have among us men of great genius, apt to invent and discover ingenious devices; and in view of the grandeur and virtue of our City, more such men come to us every day from divers parts. Now, if provision were made for the works and devices discovered by such persons, or that others, who may see them could not build them and take the inventor's honor away, more men would then apply their genius, would discover, and would build devices of great utility and benefit to our commonwealth . . . Therefore: Be it enacted that, by the authority of this Council, every person who shall build any new device in this City, not previously made in our Commonwealth, shall give notice of it to the office of our General Welfare Board when it has been reduced to perfection so that it can be used and operated. It being forbidden to every other person in any of our territories and towns to make any further device conforming with and similar to said one, without the consent and license of the author, for a term of 10 years. And if anybody builds it in violation hereof, the aforesaid author and inventor shall be entitled to have him summoned before any magistrate of this City, by which magistrate the said infringer shall be constrained to pay him hundred ducats; and the devise shall be destroyed at once.[11]

This statute appeared 150 years before England's Statute of Monopolies and provided the foundation of the world's first lasting institution of intellectual property protection. Moreover, the system was remarkably mature and sophisticated. The rights of inventors were recognized, an incentive mechanism was included, compensation for infringement was established, and a term limit on inventor's rights imposed. Shortly thereafter, in 1486, one of the first true copyrights was granted to Marc' Antonio Sabellico, a historiographer, giving him exclusive rights to his *Decades rerum Venetarum*.[12]

For the most part though, American institutions of intellectual property protection are based on the English system that began with the Statute of Monopolies (1624) and the Statute of Anne (1709). Although many changes have since been made, the Statute of Monopolies is considered the basis of the British and American patent systems today:

> Generally regarded as the foundation of the present British patent system, the Statute of Monopolies—in keeping with its name—was concerned mainly with the problem of ending royally granted, monopolistic privileges. Those minor portions of the Statute relating directly to inventive property provided for the exemption and limitation of grants for innovations in the Realm . . . .The Statute of Monopolies, therefore, represented no advance over its Venetian predecessor of 1474, under which an inventor received his patent as a matter of right[13]

Nevertheless, the statute granted fourteen-year monopolies to authors and inventors and ended the practice of granting rights to "non-original/new" ideas or works already in the public domain.

In contrast to patent institutions in Europe, literary works remained largely unprotected until the arrival of Gutenberg's printing press in the fifteenth century. And again there were few true copyrights granted—most were grants, privileges, and monopolies.[14] Bugbee notes, "Other . . . cities enacted legislation to promote their publishing trade, but Venice was foremost in this respect. . . . she supported rights of literary proprietorship in the world's first known copyrights and produced a crude from of copyright law in the decree of 1544-1545 . . . ."[15]

The Statute of Anne (1709) is considered the first statute of modern copyright. The statute began, "Whereas printers, booksellers, and other persons have lately frequently taken the liberty of printing, reprinting, and publishing books without the consent of the authors and proprietors . . . to their very great detriment, and too often to the ruin of them and their families: for preventing therefore such practices for the future, and for the encouragement of learned men to compose and write books, be it enacted . . ." The law gave protection to the author by granting fourteen-year copyrights, with a second fourteen-year renewal possible if the author was still alive. The act also stated:

> And . . . if any bookseller, printer, or other person whatsoever, shall print, reprint, or import any such book or books, without the consent of the proprietor . . . then such offender shall forfeit such book or books to the proprietor of the copy thereof, who shall forthwith damage and make wastepaper of them; and farther, that every

such offender shall forfeit one penny for every sheet which shall be found in his custody.

In the landmark case *Miller v. Taylor* (1769) the inherent rights of authors to control what they produce, independent of statute or law, was affirmed. While this case was later overruled in *Donaldson v. Becket* (1774), the practice of recognizing the rights of authors had begun.[16] Other European countries followed the example set by England and the influence of Napoleon helped to expand this practice to many countries on the continent including Belgium, Holland, Italy, and Switzerland. At the time, these ideas strongly influenced the American colonies and provided the foundation upon which American institutions of intellectual property were constructed.

A Working Definition of Intellectual Property

Intellectual property is generally characterized as non-physical property that is the product of cognitive processes and whose value is based upon some idea or collection of ideas.[17] The *res*, or object, of intellectual property just is an idea or group of ideas. Typically, rights do not surround the abstract non-physical entity; rather, intellectual property rights surround the control of physical manifestations or expressions. Intellectual property protects rights to ideas by protecting rights to produce and control physical instantiations of those ideas.[18] It should be noted that in producing or marketing physical manifestations of an idea, rights to physical resources must be acquired—in order to benefit from my idea through production I must first secure the resources that will constitute the physical product. On this view, intellectual property is non-tangible property that takes the form of abstract designs, patterns, ideas, or collections of ideas. Intellectual property rights are rights that surround control of the physical manifestations of these ideas.[19]

Two features that distinguish the Anglo-American systems of copyright, patent, trademark, and trade secret are the subject matter or domain of each system and the bundle of rights granted to property holders. In the first part of this chapter, I will explicate each of these regimes in terms of subject matter and rights conferred on property holders. Included will also be an examination of continental doctrine of moral rights or *droits morals*. As will be seen, this mapping exercise is, in a sense, limited, because many of the restrictions on the domain of intellectual property and the limitations on the rights of property holders are intimately tied to how these systems are justified. The second part of the chapter will consist of offering a new "justification-neutral" model of the domain of intellectual property.

Ownership Rights and the Domain of Intellectual Property

Following Hohfeld and others, the root idea of a "right" can be expressed as follows:

> To say someone has a right is to say that there exists a state of affairs in which one person (the right-holder) has a claim on act or forbearance from another person (the duty-bearer) in the sense that, should the claim be exercised or in force, and the act or forbearance not done, it would be justifiable, other things being equal, to use coercive measures to extract either the performance required or compensation in lieu of that performance.[20]

This broad characterization holds of both moral rights and legal rights. Property is a bundle of rights associated with an owner's relation to a thing where each right in the bundle is distinct. A.M. Honoré has provided a lucid account of full legal ownership or property—the moral rights that underlie systems of intellectual property will be presented and defended in chapters 4-6. Full ownership includes:

1.   the right to possess—that is, to enjoy exclusive physical control of the thing owned;

2.   the right to use—that is, to personal enjoyment and use;

3.   the right to manage—that is, to decide how and by whom the object shall be used;

4.   the right to income—that is, to enjoy the benefits derived from personal use;

5.   the right to the capital—that is, the power to alienate the thing and to consume, waste, modify, or destroy it;

6.   the right to security—that is, immunity from expropriation;

7.   the power of transmissibility—that is, the power to bequeath the object;

8.   absence of term—that is, the indeterminate length of one's ownership rights;

9.   prohibition of harmful use—that is, one's duty to forbear from using the thing to harm others;

10.   liability to execution—that is, liability to having the thing taken away for repayment of debt, and;

11.   residuary character—that is, the existence of rules governing the reversion of lapsed ownership rights.[21]

It is conceded that there are various restricted forms of ownership which omit one or more of these incidents from the bundle of owner's rights. Nevertheless, it should be noted that property rights are conceptually complex—they are complex sets of duties, obligations, and claims. Rights are not free floating moral entities—they are complex sets of moral claims, duties, obligations, powers, and immunities. Some have argued that if this is the case then we should dispense with talk of rights and merely talk of duties, obligations, etc. We could do this but then tedium has its costs, too, and there is nothing wrong with talking in terms of rights so long as we do not lose sight of the fact that they are conceptually complex.

Intellectual property regimes are explicit about the sticks contained in the bundle of rights constituting copyright,[22] patent,[23] trademark,[24] and trade secret.[25] As each domain or subject matter is mapped out, the bundles of rights conferred on property holders found in each regime will be introduced as well.

The Domain of Intellectual Property

At the most practical level the subject matter of intellectual property is largely codified in Anglo-American copyright, patent, and trade secret law, as well as in the moral rights granted to authors and inventors within the continental European doctrine. Although these systems of property encompass much of what is thought to count as intellectual property, they do not map out the entire landscape.[26] Even so, Anglo-American systems of copyright, patent, trademark, and trade secret law, along with certain continental doctrines, provide a rich starting point. We'll take them up in turn.

Copyright

The domain of copyright is expression. Section 102 of the 1976 Copyright Act determines the subject matter of copyright protection:

§ 102: (a) Copyright protection subsists, in accordance with this title, in original works of authorship fixed in any tangible medium of expression, now known or later developed, from which they can be perceived, reproduced, or otherwise communicated, either directly or with the aid of a machine or device.

Works of authorship include the following categories:

1.   literary works, including computer software[27];

2.   musical works, including any accompanying words;

3.   dramatic works, including any accompanying music;

4.   pantomimes and choreographic works;

5.   pictorial, graphic, and sculptural works;

6.   motion pictures and other audiovisual works;

7.   sound recordings;

8.   architectural works;[28] and

§ 102 (b) In no case does copyright protection for an original work of authorship extend to any idea, procedure, process, system, method of operation, concept, principle, or discovery, regardless of the form in which it is described, explained, illustrated, or embodied in such work.[29]

Pamela Samuleson has argued that software, similar to semiconductor chips, should receive a *sui generis* form of protection.[30] One of the problems with protecting software is what to protect. Do we protect the source code or the behavior of a program or the look and feel. Samuleson and others propose and defend a multi-layered model of protection—in brief, copyright protects the source code and short-term (three years) anti-cloning laws that block product entry protect software behavior and maybe look and feel as well.

To continue, the scope or subject matter of copyright, as protected under federal law or the Copyright Act, is limited in three important respects. First, for something to be protected, it must be *original*. Thus, the creative process by which an expression comes into being becomes relevant. Even so, the originality requirement has a low threshold. "Original" in reference to a copyrighted work means that the particular work "owes its origin" to the author and does not mean that the work must be ingenious or even interesting. Minimally, the work must be the author's own production; it cannot be the result of copying.[31] In *Feist Publications, Inc. v. Rural Telephone Service Company*[32] (1991) the United States Supreme Court made it clear that the originality requirement is a crucial prerequisite for copyrightability. "The *sine qua non* of copyright is originality. To qualify for copyright protection, a work must be original to the author . . ." When deciding the issues of originality and copyright infringement courts examine expressions and not the abstract ideas from which the expressions are derived.[33]

A second requirement that limits the domain of what can be copyrighted is that the expression must be "non-utilitarian" or "non-functional" in nature. Utilitarian products, or products that are useful for work, fall, if they fall anywhere, within the domain of patents. As with the originality requirement, the non-utilitarian requirement has a low threshold because the distinction itself is contentious. An example of an intellectual work that bumps against the non-functional requirement is copyright protection of computer software.[34] While a computer program as a whole is functional and useful for producing things, its object code and source code have been deemed to be protectable expressions. In response to the seemingly difficult task of defining the functional aspects of intellectual works, the courts have invoked this requirement infrequently.[35]

Finally, the subject matter of statutory copyright is concrete expression, meaning that only expressions as fixed in a tangible and permanent medium can be protected.[36] The crucial element is that there be a physical embodiment of the work. Moreover, within the system of copyright, the abstract idea, or *res*, of intellectual property is not protected.[37] Author's rights only extend over the actual concrete expression and the derivatives of the expression—not to the abstract ideas themselves. For example, Einstein's Theory of Relativity, as expressed in various articles and publications, is not protected under copyright law. Someone else may read these publications and express the theory in her own words and even receive a copyright for her particular expression. Some may find this troubling,[38] but such rights are outside the domain of copyright law. The individual who copies abstract theories and expresses them in her own words may be guilty of plagiarism, but she cannot be held liable for copyright infringement.

The distinction between the protection of fixed expressions and abstract ideas has led to the "merger doctrine": If there is no way to separate idea from expression, then a copyright cannot be obtained. Suppose that I create a new recipe for spicy Chinese noodles and there is only one way, or a limited number of ways, to express the idea. If this were the case, then I could not obtain copyright protection, because the idea and the expression have been merged. Granting me a copyright to the recipe would amount to granting a right to control the ideas that make up the recipe.[39]

The Copyrights

There are five exclusive rights that copyright owners enjoy and three major restrictions on the bundle. The five rights are:[40]

1.   the right to reproduce the work,

2.   the right to adapt it or derive other works from it,

3.   the right to distribute copies of the work,

4.   the right to display the work publicly, and

5.   the right to perform it publicly.

Each of these rights may be parsed out and sold separately. "The owner of any particular exclusive right is entitled, to the extent of that right, to all of the protection and remedies accorded to the copyright owner by this title."[41] Moreover, it is important to note the difference between the owner of a copyright and the owner of a copy (the physical object in which the copyrightable expression is embodied). Although the two persons may be the same they typically are not. Owners of copies or particular expressions who do not own the copyright do not enjoy any of the five rights listed above. The purchaser of a copy of a book from a publisher may sell or transfer that book, but may not make copies of the book, prepare a screenplay based on the book, or read the book aloud in public.

The three major restrictions on the bundle of rights that surround copyright are fair use, the first sale doctrine, and limited duration.[42] Although the notion of "fair use" is notoriously hard to spell out, it is a generally recognized principle of Anglo-American copyright law. Every author or publisher may make limited use of another's copyrighted work for such purposes as criticism, comment, news reporting, teaching, scholarship, and research. The enactment of fair use, then, restricts the control that copyright holders would otherwise enjoy.

The first sale doctrine as codified in section 109(a) limits the rights of copyright holders in controlling the physical manifestations of their work after the first sale.[43] "[O]nce a work is lawfully transferred the copyright owner's interest in the material object (the copy or the phonorecord) is extinguished so that the owner of that copy or phonorecord can dispose of it as he or she wishes."[44] The first sale rule prevents a copyright holder who has sold copies of the protected work from later interfering with the subsequent sale of those copies. In short, the owners of copies can do what they like with their property short of violating the copyrights mentioned above.

Finally, the third major restriction on the bundle of rights conferred on copyright holders is that they have a built-in sunset, or limited term. All five rights lapse after the lifetime of the author plus seventy years—or in the case of works for hire, the term is set at ninety-five years from publication or 120 years from creation, whichever comes first.[45]

Patents

Patent protection is the strongest form of protection, in that a twenty-year exclusive monopoly is granted over any expression or implementation of the protected work.[46] The domain or subject matter of patent law is the invention and discovery of new and useful processes, machines, articles of manufacture, or compositions of matter. There are three types of patents recognized by patent law: utility patents, design patents, and plant patents. Utility patents protect any new, useful, and nonobvious process, machine, article of manufacture, or composition of matter, as well as any new and useful improvement thereof. Design patents protect any new, original, and ornamental design for an article of manufacture. Finally, the subject matter of a plant patent is any new variety of plant.

As with copyright, there are restrictions on the domain of patent protection. The Patent Act requires usefulness, novelty, and nonobviousness of the subject matter. The usefulness requirement is typically deemed satisfied if the invention can accomplish at least one of its intended purposes. Needless to say, given the expense of obtaining a patent, most machines, articles of manufacture, and processes are useful in this minimal sense.

A more robust requirement on the subject matter of a patent is that the invention defined in the claim for patent protection must be new or novel. There are several categories or events, all defined by statute, that can anticipate and invalidate a claim of a patent.[47] In general, the novelty requirement invalidates patent claims if the invention was publicly known before the applicant for patent invented it.[48] The following statutes determine novelty:

1. The invention was publicly known in the United States before the patentee invented it.

2. The invention was publicly used in the United States either (a) before the patentee invented it, or (b) more than one year before the patentee filed the patent application.

3. The invention was described in a printed publication anywhere in the world either (a) before the patentee invented it, or (b) more than one year before the patentee filed the patent application.

4. The invention was patented in another patent anywhere in the world either (a) before the patentee invented it, or (b) more than one year before the patentee filed the patent application.

5. The invention was on sale in the United States more than one year before the patentee filed the patent application.

6. The invention was invented by another person in the United States before the patentee invented it, and such other person did not abandon or conceal the invention.

7. The invention was described in a patent granted on a patent application filed in the United States before the patentee made the invention.[49]

If any of these statutes hold then the application for patent protection fails the novelty test and is not granted.[50]

In addition to utility and novelty, the third restriction on patentability is non-obviousness. United States patent law requires that the invention not be obvious to one ordinarily skilled in the relevant art at the time the invention was made. A hypothetical individual is constructed and the question is asked, "Would this invention be obvious to her?" If it would be obvious to this imaginary individual then the patent claim fails the test.[51]

Patent Rights

In return for public disclosure and the ensuing dissemination of information the patent holder is granted the following rights:

1. the right to make;

2. the right to use;

3. the right to sell the patented item, and;

4. the right to authorize others to sell the patented item.[52]

The bundle of rights conferred by a patent exclude others from making, using, or selling the invention regardless of independent creation. For twenty years the owner of a patent has a complete monopoly over any expression of the idea(s). Like copyright, patent rights lapse after a given period of time. But unlike copyright protection, these rights preclude others who independently invent the same process or machine from being able to patent or market their invention. Thus, obtaining a patent on a new machine excludes others from independently creating their own machine (similar to the first) and securing owner's rights.[53]

Trade Secret

The subject matter of trade secret is almost unlimited in terms of the content or subject matter that may be protected and typically relies on private measures, rather than state action, to preserve exclusivity:

> A trade secret is any information that can be used in the operation of a business or other enterprise and that is sufficiently valuable and secret to afford an actual or potential economic advantage over others.[54]

As long as certain definitional elements are met, virtually any type of information or intellectual work is eligible for trade secret protection. It may be a formula for a chemical compound; a process of manufacturing, treating, or preserving materials; a pattern for a machine or other device; or a list of customers.

The two major restrictions on the domain of trade secrets are the requirements of secrecy and competitive advantage. Secrecy is determined in reference to the following three rules of thumb. An intellectual work is not a secret if:

1. it is generally known within the industry,

2. it is published in trade journals, reference books, etc., and,

3. it is readily copyable from products on the market.

If the owner of a trade secret distributes a product that discloses the secret in any way, then trade secret protection is lost. Imagine that Coke's secret formula could be deduced from a chemical analysis of a sample. If this were the case, then Coke Inc. would lose trade secret protection for its recipe. Competitive advantage is a weaker requirement and is satisfied so long as a company or owner obtains some benefit from the trade secret.

Although trade secret rights have no built-in sunset they are extremely limited in one important respect. Owners of trade secrets have exclusive rights to make use of the secret but only as long as the secret is maintained.[55] If the secret is made public by the owner, then trade secret protection lapses and anyone can make use of it. Moreover, owner's rights do not exclude independent invention or discovery. Within the secrecy requirement, owners of trade secrets enjoy management rights and are protected from misappropriation. This latter protection is probably the most important right given the proliferation of industrial espionage and employee theft of intellectual works.

Trademark

The domain or subject matter of trademark is, generally speaking, the good will or good name of a company. A trademark is any word, name, symbol, or device, or any combination thereof adopted by a manufacturer or merchant to identify her goods and distinguish them from goods produced by others[56] (e.g., the "Energizer bunny"). The Federal Trademark act notes that trademark law has two purposes:

> One is to protect the public so it may be confident that, in purchasing a product bearing a particular trade-mark which it favorably knows, it will get the product which is asked for and wants to get. Secondly, where the owner of a trademark has spent energy, time, and money in presenting to the public the product, he is protected in his investment from its misappropriation by pirates and cheats.[57]

A major restriction on what can count as a trademark is whether or not the symbol is used in everyday language. In this respect, owners of trademarks do not want their symbols to become too widely used because once this occurs the trademark lapses. An example of this restriction eliminating a word from trademark protection is "aspirin"—as the word became a part of the common culture rights to exclusively use the trademark lapsed.

Ownership of a trademark confers upon the property holder the right to use a particular mark or symbol and the right to exclude others from using the same (or similar) mark or symbol. The duration of these rights is limited only in cases where the mark or symbol ceases to represent a company or interest, or becomes entrenched as part of the common language or culture.

Protecting Mere Ideas

Outside of the regimes of copyright, patent, trademark, and trade secret, there is a substantial set of case law that allows individuals to protect mere ideas as personal property. This system of property is typically called the law of ideas.[58] A highly publicized case in this area is *Buchwald v. Paramount Pictures*[59] concerning the Eddie Murphy movie *Coming to America*. Buchwald approached Paramount Pictures with a movie idea and it was agreed that if a movie was made following Buchwald's premise he would receive compensation. After several years of false starts and negotiations Paramount notified Buchwald that the movie based on his idea was not going to be produced. Shortly after this notification, *Coming to America* was released and credit was given to Eddie Murphy. Even though the movie lost money, Buchwald sued and received compensation.

The law of ideas is typically applied in cases where individuals who are unaffiliated with companies produce ideas and submit them to corporations expecting to be compensated for any use thereof. In certain cases, others who use these ideas without authorization have misappropriated property and can be prevented from using or disclosing the ideas until they have compensated the idea owners. Before concluding that an author has property rights in her idea(s), courts require the idea(s) to be novel or original[60] and concrete.[61] Compensation is offered only in cases of misappropriation.[62]

Ideas do not have to meet a high standard of novelty to merit protection as property. Minimally, the idea must demonstrate a degree of novelty and originality sufficient to show that it was not copied and that it is of value to the idea originator. The requirement of concreteness limits the domain of what can be protected as property by requiring the idea to be fixed in tangible form and mature. Fixation is easily understood along the lines of the fixation requirement in copyright law but maturity is another matter. This system of property does not protect ideas that are broad, vague, or ideas that require extensive investigation and research—these ideas would not be "mature." Generally, what counts as a protectable idea is decided on a case by case basis with reference to these restrictions.

Property holders in this system have complete control over their property with the exception of excluding others from obtaining rights to the same idea through independent creation. Thus the rights conferred on property holders in this system are similar to the conjunction of rights conferred on holders of copyrights and trade secrets.

Comparing Systems

This general framework of subject matter, rights, and full ownership provides a useful set of tools for comparing different forms of intellectual property within the Anglo-American tradition. Consider the following tables.

Table 2.1
Systems of Property[63]

Property Regime	Subject Matter	Restrictions on Subject Matter	Rights Conferred on Property Holders	Limitations on Rights
Copyright	expression: writings, photos, music, computer software, etc.	fixation, originality, non-utility	the rights to: reproduce, adapt, distribute copies, display, and to perform publicly	limited term, allows independent creation, fair use, first sale rule
Patent	inventions, processes, compositions of matter, articles of manufacture	usefulness, novelty, non-obviousness	the exclusive rights to: make use of, sell, and produce, excludes	limited term (rights lapse after twenty years)
Trade Secret	expressions, inventions, processes, compositions of matter, articles of manufacture, words, ideas	secrecy, competitive advantage	rights to: use, manage, derive income, capital, and absence of term -rights against misappropriations	does not exclude independent creation
Trademark	words, symbols, marks, or combinations thereof	common use restriction (i.e. generic or merely descriptive symbols are excluded)	the exclusive rights to: use, manage, security, transmissibility, absence of term	no limitations on rights so long as the word or symbol does not become generic
Law of Ideas	ideas or collections of ideas	novel and original, mature or concrete	rights to: use, manage, derive income, security, transmissibility, absence of term	owner's rights lapse when idea becomes common knowledge, does not exclude independent creation
Tangible/ Physical Property	individual physical or tangible items	separable or distinctness, dangerous weapons, hazardous materials, etc.	full ownership rights, including liability to execution, etc.	eminent domain, taxation on income, inheritance tax, etc.

Table 2.2

Simplified Relationships Between Patents, Copyrights,
Trademarks, and Trade Secrets[64]

Types of Protection	Functional Patent	Design Patent	Copyright	Trademark	Trade Secret
What is protected?	Functional features of process, machine, manufactured item or composition of matter	Ornamental designs for article of manufacture	Writings, photos, music, labels, works of art, software	Words, names, symbols or devices	Processes, designs, writings, software, devices, etc.
Criteria for protection?	New and "non-obvious"	New and "non-obvious"	Originality	Used to identify and distinguish goods or services	Secrecy
How to obtain rights?	Granted only by Federal Government (U.S. Patent and Trademark Office)	Granted only by Federal Government (U.S. Patent and Trademark Office)	Automatic upon creation and fixation	Common law: Adoption & Use Federal/State Registration: compliance with statutes	
Term of rights	20 years from date of Federal Grant	14 years from date of Federal Grant	Copyrighted before 1978: 28 years with renewal for add'l 47. Copyrighted 1978 or after: (By author) life of the author plus 70; (By employer or unnamed author) 120 years from creation or 95 years from publication, whichever comes first	Common Law: As long as properly used as a mark. Federal Registration: 20 years - renewable for 20 year periods	No term limit
Test of infringement	Making or selling devices embodying the claimed invention	Designs look alike to eye of ordinary observer	Substantial portion copied? Similarity?	Likelihood of confusion	Misappropriation

Trade secret subject matter is broader than the subject matter or domain of other forms of intellectual property and does not include a fixation requirement. Aside from the secrecy and competitive advantage requirements, potentially anything can become the subject of a trade secret. Thus in many respects the domain of trade secrets includes that of copyright, patent,[65] trademark, and the law of ideas.

The duration of rights to trade secret, trademark, and the law of ideas, like the duration of rights in real or tangible property, is potentially unlimited. Rights to absence of term distinguishes these regimes of property from that of copyright and patent. Generally, copyrights lapse after the lifetime of the author plus seventy years and patent rights lapse after twenty years.

Of all of the forms of intellectual property, patents provide the most extensive set of rights for the property holder within the limited term requirement. Patent protection grants inventors of new and useful processes, machines, articles of manufacture, and compositions of matter[66] the "right to exclude others from making, using or selling" the invention[67] and the right to prevent the importation of products made with a patented process.[68] Thus, the bundle of rights that surround patent protection allow property holders exclusive monopoly rights. Unlike copyright, trade secret, and the law of ideas, and similar to trademarks, a patent permits the owner to exclude others from marketing or using any implementation of the patented invention. Patent rights even allow owners to sue for damages when users know nothing of the patented idea and use it by accident. In this last respect the rights conferred on patent holders are more like the rights that surround ownership of physical goods.

Droits Morals: Continental Systems of Intellectual Property

Article 6 *bis* of the Berne Convention articulates the notion of "moral rights" that are included in continental European intellectual property law:

> Independently of the author's economic rights, and even after the transfer of the said rights, the author shall have the right to claim authorship of the work and to object to any distortion, mutilation or other modification of, or other derogatory action in relation to, the said work, which would be prejudicial to his honor or reputation.

The doctrine protects the personal rights of creators, as distinguished from their economic rights, and is generally known in France as "droits morals" or "moral rights." These moral rights consist of the right to create and to publish in any form desired, the creator's right to claim the authorship of his work, the right to prevent any deformation, mutilation or other modification thereof, the right to withdraw and destroy the work, the prohibition against excessive criticism, and the prohibition against all other injuries to the creator's personality.[69] Much of this doctrine has been incorporated in the Berne Convention:

> When the artist creates, be he an author, a painter, a sculptor, an architect or a musician, he does more than bring into the world a unique object having only exploitive possibilities; he projects into the world part of his personality and subjects it to the ravages of public use. There are possibilities of injury to the creator other than merely economic ones; these the copyright statute does not protect.[70]

It should be noted that granting moral rights of this sort goes beyond a mere expansion of the rights conferred on property holders within the Anglo-American tradition. While many of the moral rights listed above could be incorporated into copyright and patent law, the overall content of these moral rights suggests a new domain of intellectual property protection. This new domain of moral rights stands outside of the economic– and utilitarian– based rights granted within the Anglo-American tradition. This is to say that independent of social and economic utility, and sometimes in conflict with it, authors and inventors have rights to control the products of their intellectual efforts.

A Generic View of Intellectual Property

To this point, the domain of intellectual property has been mapped by focusing on the Anglo-American systems of copyright, patent, trademark, trade secret, the law of ideas, and the European doctrine of moral rights. But with respect to Anglo-American institutions this mapping exercise has been, in a sense, limited. Many of the afore-mentioned restrictions on the domain of intellectual property and the limitations on the rights of property holders are intimately tied to how these systems are justified.[71] It follows that a rejection of how these systems are justified will lead to a rejection of many utility-based limitations placed on subject matter and owner's rights. It may be the case that an alternative justification of intellectual property will also justify similar limitations. This remains to be seen.

Although modern Anglo-American systems of intellectual property have been "justified" on rule-utilitarian grounds, it is possible to filter out the utilitarian components and arrive at a more generic model.[72] In a sense we are working backwards so that upon reject-ing rule-utilitarian attempts to justify systems of intellectual property we have a generic model that is largely "justification" neutral. First, a new model will be presented and second, each regime of intellectual property will be reexamined with an eye towards a "jus-tification" neutral exposition. Sadly as will be seen, this generic "jus-tification" neutral model will be sketchy precisely because restrictions on subject matter and owner's rights are so intimately tied to the method of justification.[73]

Intellectual property is generally characterized as non-physical property where owner's rights surround control of physical mani-festations or tokens of some abstract idea or type. As we shall see this general definition of intellectual property may be inadequate in cases where there is no type/token distinction possible—e.g., where the expression and the idea are merged. Even so it will be argued that as a general model the type/token distinction is plausible. Ideas or collections of ideas are readily understood in terms of non-physical types, while the physical manifestations of ideas can be modeled in terms of tokens. Intellectual property rights surround control of physical tokens, and this control protects rights to types or abstract ideas.[74] For example, the ownership of Windows grants Microsoft a level of control over every physical embodiment of a certain kind— over every token of the type.

The intellectual property regime of trademark is easily modeled in terms of a type/token distinction. Each individual mark or symbol affixed to some product is a token of the quality and good will of a company. For instance, the mark " 🍎 " is a token of a type that is affixed to many products and represents the quality and good will of Apple Incorporated.

Moreover, it is easy to imagine how this system of property would be without the restriction of common use which is justified on utilitarian grounds.[75] The restriction of common use eliminates owner's rights when the symbol or mark becomes part of the culture or language. The general rule-utilitarian justification given for this restriction is that allowing exclusive control over symbols and marks that are commonly used leads to a decrease in overall utility. Although an alternative justification of the Anglo-American system of trademark may yield a similar restriction, this need not be the case.

As with trademark, trade secret fits well with our type/token distinction given the subject matter that is protected. Formulas, patterns, designs, and compilations of information are easily understood as types and their physical instantiations as tokens. An example is Coca Cola's secret recipe where the tokens are individual cans of coke and the type is the recipe itself.

The property system of trade secret protects formulas, patterns, designs, and compilations of information from misappropriation.[76] The major restriction placed on owner's rights is the requirement of secrecy. The primary issue involved in trade secret protection is one of privacy and the rights of individuals and companies to control their own private ideas from wrongful invasion and seizure. The restriction of secrecy is an essential element of trade secret because protection from misappropriation is the extent of owner's rights and others cannot misappropriate things that are commonly known. In this way the restriction stands or falls with the system of property. Alternative justifications of the system would then seem to automatically justify the restriction.

Patents protect the invention and discovery of new and useful processes, machines, articles of manufacture, or compositions of matter.[77] In terms of a type/token distinction, types are the collection of ideas that make up new and useful processes, machines, or compositions of matter and tokens are any physical manifestations thereof.

The restrictions of functionality, novelty, and non-obviousness are all justified along utilitarian lines. Patents are granted to inventors when their inventions are functional, novel, and non-obvious because restricting the domain of patent law in these ways typically leads to an increase in overall utility. Rights are granted as incentive for the production of intellectual works and the following dissemination of information. Once again, although an alternative justification of the Anglo-American system of patent may yield similar restrictions, this need not be the case.

As noted before, in one important respect the rights conferred on owners of patents are more robust than the rights granted to property holders of copyrights and trade secrets. Unlike copyright and trade secret, patents exclude the possibility of independent invention as grounds for granting rights. As with the previously mentioned restrictions, these monopoly rights are typically justified in terms of promoting the common good. Owners of patents, and to some extent trademarks, are given exclusive control over an intellectual work even to the extent of excluding others who independently create the same invention.[78] Thus those who hold patents are in a position of great power—for example, consider the "land grab" that is currently happening with DNA information. Obviously, alternative justifications of this particular system of property may not grant such robust rights to property holders.

The intellectual property system of copyright protects any original expression fixed in a tangible medium. As with the other regimes of intellectual property, copyright fits well with a type/token model. Expressions are tokens of ideas or collections of ideas and ideas just are types of which there can be many expressions. An example would be Einstein's Theory of Relativity which, as a type, can have many physical instantiations or tokens. And in fact this is exactly the case. Many books (i.e., concrete tokens) have been printed explaining, augmenting, and challenging the Theory of Relativity (i.e., non-physical type).

Now things get messy very fast when one tries to map all copyright in terms of a type/token distinction.[79] Imagine art that has been traditionally protected, yet has no underlying idea or collection of ideas that can be considered a separable distinct type. For example, a hastily shot photograph, a modern painting where paint is haphazardly splashed on canvass, or freeform blues or jazz, etc. Maybe there are brute expressions with no underlying idea(s). Moreover, what is important in some protectable intellectual work is not the abstract idea or type, but the style of the expression itself. In these latter cases the idea and the expression of the idea have been merged. It may be argued that it is not the plot or the characters that make Hemingway's *The Sun Also Rises* but rather his distinct style of expression. So it would seem that mapping all of copyright in terms of a type/token distinction would be a mistake.

As noted before, copyright protects original expressions from being copied and this includes any expression that is substantially similar.[80] What this means is that individuals cannot merely copy an expression and change a few things around. If someone were to copy *The Sun Also Rises* and change the sentences slightly they would still infringe Hemingway's copyright. The rights conferred on the owners of a copyright allow them to control exact copies of their work and any copies that are substantially similar. In this way physical expressions become type-like and can thus be modeled in terms of a type/token distinction. For example, within the domain of copyright, Hemingway's book *The Sun Also Rises* is both a type and a token. It is a type because Hemingway can control any exact copy of it and any copy that is substantially similar. Moreover, it is a token because it is a physical manifestation of something that could take many physical forms. Also, while it may be impossible to separate an idea from its mode of expression—maybe the specific way in which the idea is expressed is integral to the idea itself—we can still draw a type/token distinction.

Within the Anglo-American tradition the restrictions of originality, non-usefulness, and fixation on the subject matter of copyright are given both utilitarian-based justifications and alternative justifications. Given this, I will put off considering these restrictions until some alternative justification is offered.

Finally, a type/token distinction fits well with the subject matter that constitutes the law of ideas. Property holders within this system retain rights to the abstract ideas themselves by controlling physical manifestations of those ideas. The restrictions of novelty, maturity, and misappropriation are typically given rule-utilitarian based justifications.[81] A system of intellectual property protection for particular ideas is necessary for an optimal amount of social progress. Moreover, a system that includes these restrictions is better than one with some other set of restrictions or no restrictions. It remains to be seen whether or not an alternative justification of the law of ideas will retain these restrictions.

Conclusion

In mapping out the domain or subject matter of intellectual property, I have relied heavily on the modern Anglo-American systems of copyright, patent, trademark, trade secret, and the law of ideas. Although these systems include much of what we think should count as intellectual property, they do not map out the entire landscape. Consider the following case.

Imagine an individual investing a large amount of time and resources in developing a new and revolutionary theory of literary critical assessment only to find that his market share (assuming there is a market share) has been gobbled up by someone who has copied his abstract ideas and created a second, less expensive, yet different expression. As noted, Anglo-American copyright law only protects particular expressions not abstract ideas or theories, so the usurper may express his own version of aesthetic critical assessment and obtain a copyright in his original expression. Surely something has gone awry in this case given that if anything should be protected, it should be the creator's rights to his/her theories. We say *Einstein's* Theory of Relativity because it is his theory, his creation, no matter how it is expressed. In this respect there is a rather large hole in modern Anglo-American theories of intellectual property.

As was discussed earlier and in contrast to the Anglo-American system, the continental Europeans have a more inclusive system of copyright protection centered around creator's rights.[82] Notice that such rights would make copyrights more like patents in that the totality of the idea and expression could be protected. Thus by including author's rights into the bundle of rights that surround copyright, we obtain a more robust domain of intellectual property. In 1988 the United States became the seventy-eighth nation to join the Berne

Copyright Convention. Along with the economic rights previously mentioned, the Berne Convention grants authors rights of paternity and integrity. In recent years, to reflect statutes found in the Berne Convention Treaty, the United States has moved to expand copyright protection to include creator's rights.

It may be argued that the domain of intellectual property is still impoverished in certain respects. But the purpose of this chapter has not been to exhaustively present and examine the entire domain of intellectual and intangible property. Rather, the goal has been to examine a good portion of the domain in the hopes not only of clarifying what counts as intellectual property, but laying the foundation for alternative justifications.

Notes

1. Quoted in Robert P. Benko's, *Protecting Intellectual Property Rights* (Washington, DC: American Enterprise Institute for Public Policy Research, 1987).
2. Actually, I will use intangible property as a broader notion than intellectual property—the former includes the latter as well as other kinds of property like personality rights (owning one's public image, etc.), information, and stock options.
3. Quoted by Athenaeus, *The Deipnosophists* (New York:G.P. Putman's Sons, 1927), translated by C. Burton Gulick, 348-49.
4. B. Bugbee, *Genesis of American Patent and Copyright Law* (Washington, DC: Public Affairs Press, 1967). For other works tracing the historical foundations of intellectual property see, Nathaniel S. Shaler, *Thoughts on the Nature of Intellectual Property and Its Importance to the State* (Cambridge, MA: Welch Bigelow, and Company, 1877); Frank D. Prager, "A History of Intellectual Property from 1545 to 1787" *Journal of the Patent Office Society*, XXVI (November 1944) and "The Early Growth and Influence of Intellectual Property" *Journal of the Patent Office Society*, XXVII (February 1952); Allan Gomme, *Patents of Invention: Origin and Growth of the Patent System in Britain* (London, Longmans Green, 1946); Giulio Mandich, "Venetian Origins of Inventors' Rights" trans. Frank D. Prager, *Journal of the Patent Office Society*, XLII (June 1960); W. S. Holdsworth, *A History of English Law* (London, Methuen Company, 1903); and W. Hulme "The History of the Patent System under the Prerogative and at Common Law" *Law Quarterly Review* XII (1896).
5. For references to intellectual or literary piracy see Plato, *Apology*; translated by H. North Fowler (London, W. Heinemann, 1917), 98-99, *The Frogs* in Aristophanes, translated by B. Rogers (London, 1927) II, 302-305; G. H. Putnam, *Authors and their Public in Ancient Times* (New York:G.P. Putman's Sons,1894), 202; H. L. Pinner, *The World of Books in Classical Antiquity* (Leiden, A.W. Sijthoff,1948), 25, 38-43. Cited in B. Bugbee, *Genesis*, 167, n13.
6. Bugbee, *Genesis*, 167, n16.
7. Martial, *Epigrams*, trans. Walter C. A. Ker (London and New York, 1920-25, Cambridge MA: Harvard University Press, 1943) I, 46-47. Cited in Bugbee, *Genesis*, 167, n15.
8. Bugbee, *Genesis*, 7.

9. The preamble read: "Considering that the admirable Filippo Brunelleschi, a man of the most perspicacious intellect, industry and invention, a citizen of Florence, has invented some machine or kind of ship, by means of which he thinks he can easily, at any time, bring in any merchandise and load on the river Arno and on any other river or water, for less money than usual,. . . ; and that he refuses to make such machine available to the public, in order that the fruit of his genius and skill may not be reaped by another without his will and consent; . . . And desiring that this matter, so withheld and hidden without fruit, shall be brought to the light, to be of profit both to said Filippo and to our whole country and others; and that some privilege be created for said Filippo, as hereinafter described, so that he may be animated more fervently to even higher pursuits, and stimulated to more subtle investigations, . . ." F. Peager, "Brunelleschi's Patent," *Journal of Patent Office Society* (herafter JPOS), XXXVIII (February 1946), 127.

10. See Bugbee, *Genesis*, 22.

11. G. Mandich, Venetian Inventors' Rights," translated by F. Prager, JPOS, XXX (March, 1948): 172-73.

12. Bugbee, *Genesis*, 45.

13. Bugbee, *Genesis*, 39.

14. For example, in 1469 John Speyer was granted the right to conduct all printing in Venice for a term of five years.

15. Bugbee, *Genesis*, 47.

16. *Miller v. Taylor* (1769), 4 Burr. 2303; *Donaldson v. Becket* (1774), 4 Burr. 2408.

17. For a similar view, see J. Hughes "The Philosophy of Intellectual Property" in *Intellectual Property: Moral, Legal, and International Dilemmas*, edited by A. Moore (Lanham, MD: Rowman & Littlefield, 1997), chapter 6. Also note that the proposed working definition does not distinguish between owing *ideas* and owning *expressions* of ideas—as we shall see, copyright protection does not extend to mere ideas but only to fixed expressions. Trade secret protection and what is commonly known as the "law of ideas" do extend to cover ideas.

18. I use the term "idea" loosely meaning theories, abstract designs, and theoretical constructs.

19. For a discussion of discovered intellectual property compared to created intellectual property see the relevant section of chapter 5.

20. Lawrence Becker, *Property Rights, Philosophic Foundations* (London: Routledge & Kegan Paul, 1977). Hohfeld distinguishes four types of rights, claim-rights, liberty-rights, power-rights, and immunity-rights. See W. N. Hohfeld, "Fundamental Legal Conceptions," *Yale Law Journal* (New Haven, CT: Yale University Press, 1919). Note that we are considering moral rights here, not legal rights.

21. Following Honoré, 107-47 and Becker, *Property Rights, Philosophic Foundations*, 19. It should be noted that Honoré giving an analysis of *full legal ownership*.

22. 17 U.S.C. § 106 (1988) (enumerating rights belonging to copyright owner).

23. 35 U.S.C. § 261 (1988) (enumerating rights belonging to patent owner).

24. 15 U.S.C. § 1174 (1988) (enumerating rights belonging to trademark owner).

25. As codified in various state statutes.

26. Personality ownership, stock options, and the like, are areas of intellectual property not included in this overview.

27. Copyright Act, 17 U.S.C. § 102 (1988).

28. The 1990 Architectural Works Copyright Protection Act amended the 1976 Copyright Act to afford explicit protection to works of architecture.

29. 17 U.S.C § 102 (1988).

30.   See P. Samuleson, "A Manifesto Concerning the Legal Protection of Computer Programs," *Columbia Law Review* 94 (1994): 2308. See also, "Innovation and Competition: Conflicts over Intellectual Property Rights in New Technologies" in *Owning Scientific and Technical Information*, ed J. Snapper & V. Weil (New Brunswick, NJ: Rutgers Press, 1989), 173.

31.   See *Bleistein v. Donaldson Lithographing Co.*, 188 U.S. 239 (1903), and *Time Inc. v. Bernard Geis Associates,* 293 F. Supp. 130 (S.D.N.Y. 1968).

32.   *Feist Publications, Inc. v. Rural Telephone Service Company* 499 U.S. 340 (1991).

33.   Infringement is determined often by substantial similarity tests. See *Nichols v. Universal Pictures Corp.*, 45 F.2d 49 (2d Cir. 1930), and *Sheldon v. Metro-Goldwyn Pictures Corp.*, 81 F.2d 49 (2d Cir.), *cert .denied*, 298 U.S. 669 (1936).

34.   For a more detailed discussion of this see P. Samuleson, "Innovation and Competition," 173.

35.   See *Kieselstein-Cord v. Accessories By Pearl, Inc.* U.S.C. of Appeals, Second Circuit, 1980, *Carol Barnhart Inc. v. Economy Cover Corporation,* U.S.C. of Appeals, Second Circuit, 1985, and *Brandir International, Inc. v. Cascade Pacific Lumber Co.* U.S.C. of Appeals, Second Circuit, 1987.

36.   See *Baltimore Orioles, Inc. v. Major League Baseball Players Ass'n,* 805 F.2d 663 (7th Cir. 1986), *cert. denied*, 480 U.S. 941 (1987), and *National Football League v. McBee & Bruno's, Inc.*, 792 F.2d 726 (8th Cir. 1986). It should be noted that State, or common law copyright, still protects unfixed works — for example, the choreography of a play in production.

37.   See 17 U.S.C. § 102(b) (1988).

38.   This kind of worry is, in part, the basis for the moral rights championed by the European continent. See the section *Droits Morals* below.

39.   For more about the merger doctrine, see *Morrissey v. Procter & Gamble Company,* 379 F.2d 675 (1st Cir. 1967), and *Kregos v. Associated Press,* 937 F.2d 700 (2d Cir. 1991).

40.   17 U.S.C. § 106 Copyright Act.

41.   17 U.S.C. § 201(d).

42.   The proposed UCC Article 2B/UCITA is threatening to undermine "first sale" and "fair use." Article 2B provides a contractual framework for controlling certain kinds of information and services. The worry is that "shrink wrap," "click wrap," and similar licensing arrangements will allow rights holders to circumvent the free use zones of "first sale" and "fair use." See Amy M. Harris, "The Proposed UCC Article 2B," *Intellectual Property Update* (1998): 5; and Robert L. Oakley, "UCC Article 2B: Some Preliminary Comments on a New Issue for the Library Community." Presented at the Annual Meeting of the Association of Research Libraries, October 16, 1997. Some version of Article 2B is expected to be adopted by July of 1999 and then presented to each state for consideration.

43.   See 17 U.S.C. § 109(a).

44.   S. Halpern, D. Shipley, H. Abrams, *Copyright: Cases And Materials* (St. Paul, MN: West Publishing, 1992), 216.

45.   The limited term of copyright, and patent as well, is required by the Constitution. Article I, Section 8 empowers Congress to "promote the Progress of Science and useful Arts, by securing *for limited Times* to Authors and Inventors the exclusive Right to their respective Writings and Discoveries" (emphases mine).

46.   Patent Act, 35 U.S.C. § 101 (1988). The 1995 version of the Patent Act has added three years to the term of patent protection—from seventeen to twenty. See 35 U.S.C. § 154(a)(2).

47. 35 U.S.C. § 101 (1988).
48. 35 U.S.C. § 101-104 (1988). See also *Christie v. Seybold*, 55 Fed. 69 (6th Cir. 1893) and *Hull v. Davenport*, 24 C.C.P.A. 1194, 90 F.2d 103, 33 USPQ 506 (1937).

49. 35 U.S.C § 101-104 (1988).
50. See *Christie v. Seybold* (United States Court of Appeals, Sixth Circuit, 1893), *Hull v. Davenport* (United States Court of Customs and Patent Appeals, 1937), and *Kimberly-Clark corp. v. Procter & Gamble Distributing Co., Inc.* (United States Court of Appeals, Federal Circuit, 1992).
51. See 35 U.S.C. sec 103. See also *Ryko Manufacturing Co. v. Nu-star, Inc.*, 950 F.2d 714 (Fed. Cir. 1991, *Environmental Designs, LTD. v. Union Oil Company of California*, 713 F.2d 693 (Fed. Cir. 1983), *ACS Hospital Systems, Inc. v. Montefiore Hospital*, 732 F.2d 1572 (Fed. Cir. 1984), and *In Re Oetiker*, 977 F.2d 1443 (Fed. Cir. 1992).
52. 35 U.S.C. § 154 (1984 and Supp. 1989).
53. In chapter 7 I argue that this rule should be eliminated.
54. The Restatement (Third) of Unfair Competition, § 39 (1995).
55. See *Forest Laboratories, Inc. v. Pillsbury Co.*, 452 F.2d 621 (7th Cir. 1971), and *E.I. duPont deNemours & Co., Inc. v. Christopher*, 431 F.2d 1012 (5th Cir. 1970).
56. 15 U.S.C. § 1127 (1988).
57. 15 U.S.C. § 1174 (1988).
58. Throughout this section I follow M. Epstein's *Modern Intellectual Property*, 2nd ed. (Englewood Cliffs, NJ: Prentice Hall Law and Business, 1992), 259-88.
59. *Buchwald v. Paramount Pictures*, 13 U.S.P.Q. 2d 1497 (Cal. Super. Ct. 1990).
60. See *Murry v. National Broadcasting*, 844 U.S. F2d 988 (Second Cir. 1988) ("[N]on-novel ideas are not protectable as property..."), *Davies v. Carnation Co.* (9th Cir. 1965) ("A mere idea without novelty is not a property right to which one may claim exclusive ownership"), *Puente v. President and Follows of Harvard College* (1st Cir. 1957), and *Hamilton Nat'l Bank v. Belt* (D.C. Cir. 1953).
61. See *Hamilton Nat'l Bank v. Belt* (D.C. Cir. 1953). ("In addition to being new, novel or original, an idea to be legally protected must also be concrete. The law shies away from according protection to vagueness") and *O'Brian v. RKO Radio Pictures Inc.* ("It is well-settled law that an author has no property rights in his ideas unless the same are given embodiment in a tangible form").
62. See *Sellers v. American Broadcasting Co.* (11th Cir. 1982) and *McGhan v. Ebersol* (1985) ("A plaintiff cannot recover for misappropriation of ideas unless the ideas are actually used by a defendant").
63. Obviously, within the Anglo-American tradition there are number of exceptions to the subject matter, rights, and limitations found in these tables. For example, a corporation may receive a patent on a nuclear devise but not obtain a right use the device. For a more precise account of the rights conferred on property holders within each system, please see the relevant statute or code along with Hohfield and Honoré's analysis of rights.
64. Adapted from W. Borchard, "A Trademark is not a Patent or a Copyright," USTA Executive Newsletter No. 39 (1986), 186.
65. Although it is possible to obtain a copyright and trade secret for the same expression, it is not possible to obtain a patent and a trade secret in the same intellectual property. Patent law requires disclosure which would run up against the secrecy requirement for trade secrets.

66. 35 U.S.C. § 101 (1988).
67. 35 U.S.C. § 271 (1988).
68. 35 U.S.C. § 154 (1988).
69. Generally these moral rights have not been recognized within the Anglo-American tradition. See *Crimi v. Rutgers Presbyterian Church*, 194 Misc. 570 (N.Y.S. 1949). Recently, given the inclusion of the United States in the Berne Convention treaty, there has been a move toward indirect recognition. See *Gilliam v. American Broadcasting Companies, Inc.*, 538 F. 2d 14 (2d Cir. 1976), *Wojnarowicz v. American Family Association*, 745 F. Supp. 130 (S.D.N.Y. 1990), and the Berne Convention Implementation Act of 1988. See also 17 U.S.C. § 106A (1998) Rights of certain authors to attribution and integrity.
70. Roeder, "The Doctrine of Moral Right: A Study in the Law of Artists, Authors and Creators," *Harvard Law Review* 53 (1940): 554.
71. Anglo-American systems of intellectual property are justified along rule-utilitarian lines. See chapter 3.
72. Foreshadowing things to come—the rule-utilitarian typically argues in the following way. Society ought to adopt a system or institution if it leads to the maximization of overall social utility. A system or institution that confers limited rights to authors and inventors over what they produce is necessary for the production of intellectual works. Promoting the creation and dissemination of intellectual works is necessary (or nearly so) for an optimal amount of social progress. It follows that a system of intellectual property should be adopted. It will be argued in chapter 3 that rule-utilitarian attempts to justify Anglo-American systems of intellectual property protection fail—i.e., if intellectual property rights are to be defended they will have to be defended on different grounds.
73. After providing a Lockean justification for intellectual property in chapters 4-6, I will return to these issues in chapter 7.
74. Please note the generality here. It is intentional given that I am offered a working definition of intellectual property that will range across all of the types canvassed above—including trade secrets, the law of ideas, and the moral rights of authors and inventors recognized in Europe.
75. Restatement of Torts § 757.
76. Restatement of Torts § 757.
77. 35 U.S.C § 101 (1988).
78. 35 U.S.C. § 271 (1988).
79. It has been suggested to me that the type-token distinction is 'messy' because intellectual property protection is really about ideas and their reduction to practice (patents) or ideas and their expressions (copyrights). This, however, simply begs the question against trade secrets, the law of ideas, and the moral rights recognized in Europe. I acknowledge that protecting ideas or types will require the control of physical goods or tokens and that there many different levels of control. Thus, you may be able to think about some set of ideas yet be prohibited from broadcasting them.
80. For more about the actual application of the substantial similarity test, see *Computer Assocs. Int'l v. Altai*, Inc. 2nd Cir. 1992 and *Herbert Rosenthal Jewelry Corp. v. Kalpakian* (9th Cir. 1971).
81. See *Murry v. Paramount Pictures* (Cal. Super. Ct. 1990).
82. The differences between Anglo-American and French systems of copyright largely stem from how the systems are justified. See "A Tale of Two Copyrights: Literary Property in Revolutionary France and America" in *Of Authors and Origins*, edited by B. Sherman and A. Strowel (Oxford: Clarendon Press, 1994).

3

Against Rule-Utilitarian Intellectual Property

> "No one can doubt, that the convention for the distinction of property, and for the stability of possession, is of all circumstances the most necessary to the establishment of human society, and that after the agreement for the fixing and observing of this rule, there remains little or nothing to be done towards settling a perfect harmony and concord."
>
> —David Hume, *Treatise of Human Nature*

Introduction

Anglo-American systems of intellectual property are typically justified on utilitarian grounds. Limited rights are granted to authors and inventors of intellectual property "to promote the progress of science and the useful arts."[1] Beginning with the first Patent Act of 1790 and continuing through the adoption of Berne Convention standards in 1989, the basis given for Anglo-American systems of intellectual property is utilitarian in nature and not grounded in the natural rights of the author or inventor. Thomas Jefferson, a central figure in the formation of American systems of intellectual property, expressly rejected any natural rights foundation for granting control to authors and inventors over their intellectual work. "The patent monopoly was not designed to secure the inventor his natural right in his discoveries. Rather, it was a reward, and inducement, to bring forth new knowledge."[2] Society seeks to maximize utility in the form of scientific and cultural progress by granting rights to authors and inventors as an incentive toward such progress. This approach is, in a way, paradoxical. In order to enlarge the public domain permanently, society protects certain private domains temporarily. In general, patents, copyrights, and trade secrets are devices, created by statute, to prevent the diffusion of information before the author or inventor has recovered profit adequate to induce such investment.

This view is echoed by the committee report that accompanied the 1909 Copyright Act:

> In enacting a copyright law Congress must consider . . . two questions: First, how much will the legislation stimulate the producer and so benefit the public, and, second, how much will the monopoly granted be detrimental to the public? The granting of such exclusive rights, under the proper terms and conditions, confers a benefit upon the public that outweighs the evils of the temporary monopoly.[3]

The justification typically given for Anglo-American systems of intellectual property "is that by slowing down the diffusion of information . . . it ensures that there will be more information to diffuse."[4] Moreover, utilitarian-based justifications of intellectual property are elegantly simple. Control is granted to authors and inventors of intellectual property because granting such control provides incentives necessary for social progress. Coupled with the theoretical claim that society ought to maximize social utility, we arrive at a simple yet powerful argument.[5]

In this chapter I will examine the rule-utilitarian approach to justifying systems of intellectual property protection. Along with a brief explanation of utilitarian moral theory, the first part will consist of an analysis and dismissal of two of the most widely supported rule-utilitarian justifications for intellectual property. It will be argued that internally, on its own grounds, rule-utilitarianism fails to justify the Anglo-American systems of patent, copyright, trade secret, and trademark. Note that this internal attack, if successful, will only present a problem for those rule utilitarians who want to justify the present system. The second part of this chapter will consist of an external examination and rejection of rule-utilitarian moral theory. Thus, if the internal or the external critique is successful, then the rule-utilitarian approach for justifying current systems of intellectual property protection will be eliminated as a plausible contender and the way will be cleared for alternative justifications.

A General Overview of Utilitarian Theory[6]

"Utilitarianism" is not a single theory, but rather a cluster of theories that center around the following three components:

i.   the consequent component—the rightness of actions is determined by the consequences;

ii.   the value component—the goodness or badness of consequences is to be evaluated by means of some standard of intrinsic value;

iii.   the range component—it is the consequences of an act (or class of actions) as
         affecting everyone, and not just the agent himself, that are to be considered in
         determining rightness.

This way of characterizing utilitarianism is purposefully ambiguous between act-utilitarianism and rule-utilitarianism depending on the notion of "action" used in (i) and (iii). I begin this way, because I don't want to beg any questions as to the exact type of utilitarianism that justifies Anglo-American systems of intellectual property.

Act-utilitarianism is a theory which holds that an individual act is morally right if, and only if, it produces at least as much utility as any alternative action when the utility of all is counted equally. For example, classical act-utilitarianism is the view that individual acts are right or wrong solely in virtue of the goodness or badness of their consequences. The value component is identified in terms of pleasure and pain and the range or scope of the theory touches everyone affected by an act. Modern utilitarians have generally rejected the crude hedonistic account of value in favor of an interest satisfaction view. For our purposes, a precise utilitarian account of value will not be needed and thus "utility" will be used as a blanket term to stand for that which is intrinsically good.

Act-utilitarians view rules that govern behavior as mere rules of thumb[7] that serve as helpful guides when there is no time to calculate the probable consequences of our actions or when personal biases cloud judgment.[8] The rightness or wrongness of following some rule on a particular occasion depends only on the goodness or badness of the consequences of keeping or breaking the rule on that particular occasion. If the goodness of the consequences of breaking the rule is greater than the goodness of the consequences of keeping it, then we must abandon the rule. On this view, rules may serve as useful guides but when it is clear that following them leads to bad consequences, then we must break the rule.

If granting an author or inventor limited rights over what she produce maximizes net utility for everyone affected by the act, then intellectual property rights have been justified on act-utilitarian grounds. But it should be obvious that this is not an accurate model of how intellectual property rights are justified within Anglo-American systems. Individual acts of conferring rights to each author and inventor are not tested to see if they will maximize overall expected utility for everyone affected. Moreover, the rules that comprise Anglo-American systems of intellectual property are not taken as mere rules of thumb. Even in cases where it is known beforehand that conferring rights to an inventor will lead to bad consequences, intellectual property rights are granted nonetheless. This point is echoed by J. Robinson:

> Since it is rooted in a contradiction (long term benefits verses short term incentives), there can be no such thing as an ideally beneficial patent system, and it is bound to produce negative results in particular instances, impeding progress unnecessarily even if its general effect is favorable on balance.[9]

It is for these reasons and others that, in terms of the justification typically given, Anglo-American systems of intellectual property are rule-utilitarian in nature.

Rule-utilitarians hold that moral rules are more than just rules of thumb that are to be broken when following them produces less utility than some other act. For the rule-utilitarian, the rightness of an act is not to be judged by comparing its consequences to the consequences of alternative acts, but only by considering whether or not it falls under a correct moral rule. Rules themselves are judged by considering the consequences of everyone following the rule.[10] If adopting a rule, set of rules, or institution maximizes net utility for everyone affected, then the rule, set of rules, or institution is morally justified. Generally, actions are to be judged in reference to rules and rules in reference to the consequences. The only time particular acts are tested directly is when there is no rule which covers the act or when two rules conflict.

In terms of "justification," modern Anglo-American systems of intellectual property are easily modeled as rule-utilitarian.[11] Typically, it is argued that adopting the systems of copyright, patent, trademark, trade secret, and the law of ideas, leads to an optimal amount of intellectual works being produced and a corresponding optimal amount of social utility. These systems or institutions are not comprised by mere rules of thumb. In particular cases, conferring rights to authors and inventors over their intellectual products may lead to bad consequences. Justification, in terms of social progress, occurs at the level of the system or institution. B. Robinson (1890) concludes that the institution of patent protection is fully justified because, in general, adopting such a system leads to good consequences for society as a whole:

The granting of a patent privilege at once accomplishes three important objects; it rewards the inventor for his skill and labor; it stimulates him, as well as others, to still further efforts in the same or different fields; it secures to the public an immediate knowledge of the character and scope of the invention. Each of these objects, with its consequences, is a public good, and tends directly to the advancement of the useful arts and sciences.[12]

What follows is an explication of two of the most plausible rule-utilitarian "justifications" offered for intellectual property and a dismissal of each in turn. Criticisms will be leveled in a somewhat general way so that neighboring theories to the ones presented will fall prey as well.[13] The claim is that rule-utilitarian justifications of intellectual property fail. I will go on in later chapters to defend a Lockean-based justification of intellectual property, but this does not entail that there are no other ways to justify intellectual property rights.

The Internal Critique—The Incentives Argument

Given that intellectual works can be held by everyone at the same time, cannot be used up or easily destroyed, and are necessary for many lifelong goals and projects, it would seem that we have a prima facie case against regimes of intellectual property that would restrict such maximal use. Tangible property, including concrete expressions of intellectual works, is subject to exclusive physical domination in a way that intellectual or intangible property is not. Smith's use of a car excludes my concurrent use, whereas his use of a theory, process of manufacture, or recipe for success, does not. Thus intellectual works can be seen as non-rivalrous commodities.[14] If this is true, we have an immediate prima facie case against rule-utilitarian justifications of intellectual property rights.

The rejoinder, typically given, is that granting rights to use, possession, and control of both ideas and expressions of ideas is necessary as incentive for the production of an optimal amount of intellectual works. Ideas themselves may be independently valuable but when use, possession (in some cases), and control are restricted in a free market environment, the value of certain ideas increases dramatically. Moreover, with increased value comes increased incentives, or so it is argued.

On this view, a necessary condition for promoting the creation of valuable intellectual works is granting limited rights to authors and inventors. "Without the copyright, patent, and trade secret property protections, adequate incentives for the creation of a socially optimal output of intellectual products would not exist."[15] The claim is that without certain guarantees, authors and inventors would not engage in producing intellectual property. Although success is not guaranteed by granting rights, failure certainly is, if others who incur no investment costs can seize and produce the intellectual effort of others. Generally, under conditions of no protection, it would be in a company's interest to let others create products and then merely reverse engineer the product, thereby forgoing investment and research costs. In this case, social progress slows and overall social utility suffers.

Many rule-utilitarians argue that private ownership of *physical* goods is justified because of the tragedy of the commons or problems with efficiency. Systems of private property are more efficient, or so it is argued, than systems of common ownership. It should be clear that this way of arguing is based on providing incentives. Owners of physical goods are given an incentive to maintain or increase the value of those goods, because the costs of waste, and the like, are internalized. It is commonly argued that in the case of physical goods, granting rights generates incentives to efficiently use those goods, and this policy thereby optimizes social utility.

The incentives-based, rule-utilitarian argument for systems of intellectual property protection is very similar. In this case, rights are granted as incentive for the production of intellectual works, and rule-utilitarians argue that production of this sort, in turn, maximizes social utility.

It is important to note, that on this view, rights are granted to authors and inventors, not because they deserve such rights or have some natural right to their creations, but because this is the only way to ensure that a optimal amount of intellectual products will be available for society.[16] A more formal way to characterize this argument is,

P1. Society ought to adopt a system or institution if and only if it leads to or, given our best estimates, is expected to lead to the maximization of overall social utility.[17]

P2. A system or institution that confers limited rights to authors and inventors over what they produce is expected to serve as incentive for the production of intellectual works.

P3. Promoting the creation and dissemination of intellectual works produces an optimal amount of social progress.

Therefore, C4. A system of intellectual property should be adopted.

The first premise—or the theoretical premise—is supported by rule-utilitarian arguments that link theories of the good and theories of the right in a particular way. For the rule-utilitarian, a correct moral rule is determined in reference to the consequences of everyone adopting it. By following a rule-based component it is argued that the problems that face act-utilitarianism—problems of justice,[18] special obligations,[19] integrity,[20] and excessive demands[21]—are circumvented. Moreover, by grounding the theory solely in a consequent component, unlike deontic theories, rule-utilitarians argue that the theory is given firm footing. In combining the most promising aspect of act-utilitarianism (consequences are all that matter) with the most promising aspect of deontology (its rule following component), rule-utilitarians hope to arrive at a defensible moral theory.

The second premise, P2, is an empirical claim supported by the aforementioned considerations concerning incentives. The view is that it is an empirical fact that authors and inventors will not engage in the appropriate activity unless certain guarantees are in place. What keeps authors and inventors burning the midnight oil, and thereby producing an optimal amount of intellectual works, is the promise of massive profits. The third premise is supported by general arguments to the effect that cultural, technological, and industrial progress are necessary for an optimal amount of social utility.[22] It follows that a system of intellectual property should be adopted.

Problems for the Incentives Argument

Putting aside general attacks leveled at rule-utilitarianism which will concern us in a latter section, a serious challenge may be raised by questioning the truth of the second premise (hereafter P2). It will be argued that P2 is false or at least highly contentious, and so even granting the truth of the first and third premises, the conclusion does not follow.[23] Given that the truth of P2 rests on considerations of incentives, what is needed are cases which illustrate better ways, or equally good ways, of stimulating production without granting private property rights to authors and inventors. It would be better to establish equally powerful incentives for the production of intellectual property which did not also require initial restricted use. Here I am not denying that copyright and patent-based incentives work. In good consequentialist fashion, I am asking can we do better? Furthermore, I argue that even if P2 is assumed true the resulting system of intellectual property would be markedly different from modern Anglo-American systems of intellectual property. Note that this latter worry only affects those rule-utilitarians who want to justify the present system or closely related systems.

One alternative to granting initial restricted control to authors and inventors as incentive is government support of intellectual labor.[24] The cases I have in mind are ones where the government funds research projects and the results immediately become public property. It is obvious that this sort of funding can and does stimulate the production of intellectual property without allowing initial restricted control to authors and inventors. The question becomes can government support of intellectual labor provide enough incentive to authors and inventors so that an equal or greater amount of intellectual products are created compared to what is produced through incentives created by conferring limited property rights?[25] If so, then P2 is false and intellectual property rights should not be granted on grounds of utility.[26]

In response to this kind of charge, defenders of the argument based on incentives have claimed that government support of intellectual labor does not and will not create the requisite incentives. It is only by holding out the promise of huge profits that society obtains maximal progress for all. Governments may be able to provide some incentives by paying authors and inventors in advance, but this kind of activity will never approach the incentive created by adopting a system that affords limited monopoly rights to intellectual property.

Another reply typically given is the standard utilitarian argument against centralized planning. Governments are notoriously bad in the areas of predicting the demand of future markets, research and development, resource allocation, and the like. Maximizing social utility in terms of optimizing the production of intellectual works is best left in the hands of individuals, businesses, and corporations.

The problem with these kinds of replies is that they are misleading. Certainly the promise of huge profits is part of what drives authors and inventors to burn the midnight oil, but the promise need not be guaranteed by ownership. Fritz Machlup, in *Production and Distribution of Knowledge in the United States,* argues that patent protection is not needed as incentive for corporations, in a competitive market, to invest in the development of new products and processes. "The short-term advantage a company gets from developing a new product and being the first to put it on the market may be incentive enough."[27] Consider, for example, the initial profits generated by the sales of certain software packages. The market share guaranteed by initial sales, support services, and the like, may provide adequate incentives without granting governmental protection. Moreover, given the development of advanced copy-protection schemes, software companies can protect their investments and potential profits for a number of years. Sidney Winter's more recent research supports this view. "In our book, Nelson and I present a simulation study of innovation in an industry model; the results suggest rather strongly that *unimpeded imitation* need not yield inferior results from a social standpoint."[28]

Jack Hirshleifer uses Eli Whitney's invention of the cotton gin as an example of how non-rights based incentives are available.[29] Suppose Whitney, armed with the knowledge of a superior method of processing cotton, invested in cotton producing. Whitney could buy stock in cotton-based companies as well as businesses that benefited from the cotton industry. Profiting on the use of this information may be all the incentive that Whitney needed to invent. If this is so, granting property rights to inventors may entail overall costs in utility rather than net gains.

Machlup also suggests that large corporations (who own the majority of patents) can, in some cases, hinder general technological progress by controlling entire industries. An obvious example would be Microsoft's control of computer operating systems. Microsoft has captured approximately 60 to 80 percent of the world market and has patented and copyrighted its operating systems. Any software company that wants to produce a product must first obtain licensing agreements with Microsoft and construct new software so that it runs on top of the Microsoft platform. It has been argued that granting such patents and copyrights, in effect, allows Microsoft to maintain a stranglehold on the market. This in turn has a detrimental effect on social progress.

Moreover, in some cases, "[T]he patent position of the big firms makes it almost impossible for new firms to enter the industry."[30] Alas, if the groundwork of a certain technology is patented, then the company that owns the patent may control who enters the market. Potential worthy competitors are not granted licensing agreements and are thus prohibited from competing in a particular area. If

Machlup's empirical observations are correct, then patent protection cannot be justified in this way.[31]

Machlup is actually undecided about the costs and benefits associated with patent institutions. "Such net effects are impossible to estimate, because they presuppose answers to unanswerable questions: How many inventions would not be made and developed if no promises were given that the inventor or his assignee or licensee would be protected against competition from imitators? How much output is not produced when competitors are not allowed to use the superior production processes or to make and sell the novel products protected by patents? Both the benefits society stands to gain and the losses it stands to suffer can be appraised only by comparing actual with fictitious situations, with no clues, let alone evidence, available for such comparisons."[32] This seems to me to be overstating things a bit. What good rule-utilitarians ought to do is to make their best guess given the information available and then adopt the institution that will most likely maximize utility. This might require tinkering with the current system, for example, a study could be done that tests the costs and benefits of having mere anti-piracy protection for software. Moreover, if the jury is out, so-to-speak, then the rule-utilitarian can hardly appeal to the known or likely benefits of the patent system for justification.

Trade secret falls prey to similar objections. Given that no disclosure is necessary for trade secret protection, there are no beneficial trade-offs between promoting behavior through incentives and long term social benefit.[33] From a rule-utilitarian point of view the most promising aspect of allowing intellectual property rights is the widespread dissemination of information and the resulting increase in social progress. Trade secret protection allows authors and inventors the right to slow the dissemination of protected information indefinitely—a trade secret requires secrecy.[34] Unlike other regimes of intellectual property, trade secret rights are perpetual. This means that so long as the property holder adheres to certain restrictions, the idea, invention, product, or process of manufacture may never become common property.[35]

The truth of P2 is also in doubt when considering certain kinds of Anglo-American copyright protection. Many authors, poets, musicians, and other artists would continue to create works of intellectual worth without proprietary rights being granted. A number of musicians, craftsman, poets, and the like simply enjoy the creative process and need no other incentive to produce intellectual works. For example, a musician friend of mine creates and performs songs simply for the joy of creation, prestige, and community support.

Conversely, though, it may be argued that the production of many movies, plays, and television shows is intimately tied to the limited rights conferred on those who produce these expressions. But this kind of reply is subject to the same problem that befell patent protection. The short-term advantage a production company gets from creating a new product and being the first to market, coupled with copy-protection schemes, may be incentive enough. And even if the production of movies is more dependent on copyright protection than academic writing or poetry readings, all that can be concluded is that incentives may be needed for the optimal production of the former but not the latter.[36] The system or institution that distinguishes between these kinds of expressions and only granted rights where incentives are necessary would be better, on rule-utilitarian grounds, than our current system. This kind of problem represents a general objection to rule-utilitarianism that will be explored in a later section.[37]

If these observations reach beyond the scope of patent, copyright, and trade secret protection to other forms of intellectual property, the general falsity of P2 will have been established. The upshot is that if P2 is false we will have found that the incentives-based, rule-utilitarian argument, far from justifying intellectual property rights, actually becomes an argument against allowing the rights guaranteed by Anglo-American systems of intellectual property protection. Notice that incentives-based, rule-utilitarian argument for intellectual property protection becomes even more strained when viewed from a global perspective. It is an open question as to whether or not these systems of property are beneficial in the long run when compared to the immediate needs of developing countries. With no conclusive evidence to decide the issue either way (following Machlup), it would seem that the rule-utilitarian would have to take seriously the benefits that would occur with an immediate transfer of information and technology from developed countries to developing countries.[38]

But suppose for the sake of argument that these charges can be answered. Even granting the truth of P2, it seems that the incentives-based argument would lead to a radically different system of intellectual property than is currently exhibited by modern Anglo-American systems. The claim is that society could provide the necessary incentives without granting such robust rights to authors and inventors. If conferring a more limited set of rights would lead to an equal or greater amount of worthwhile intellectual products, then the dissemination of information may be increased and overall social utility augmented. And if Machlup's and Winter's observations are even partially correct, this seems obviously the case. Granting exclusive twenty-year patent monopolies is not necessary as incentive to get companies to produce an optimal amount of intellectual products. In most industries a five-year *non-exclusive* monopoly may provide the necessary incentives.[39] Similarly, copyright protection need not extend past the lifetime of the author. It can be argued that novels, movies, music, and other works of art would still be produced in equal amounts with more limited incentives.

The justification typically given for the "fair use" rule is that limiting the rights of authors in this way causes no decrease in incentives to produce. My suggestion is that more limitations could be justified in this way—maybe all that is needed is a prohibition against piracy and bootlegging.[40] Furthermore, is seems that far from justifying the regime of trade secret protection, the incentives-based (trade-off) argument would require its elimination. As noted before, so long as holders of trade secrets adhere to certain restrictions they never have to divulge the information to the public, and so there is no trade-off of short-term property protection for long-term social progress. Needless to say, even if the incentives argument is correct, the resulting system or institution would be quite different from modern Anglo-American systems of intellectual property.[41]

In response, my critic may charge that a system with too many exceptions will be unworkable. If this is true, such a system could not be defended by a rule utilitarian. But our system is fairly unworkable currently—a brief review of the relevant sections of chapter 2 and current case law would indicate this. Many of the issues are so murky some companies merely work out deals rather than litigate. Company A accuses company B of intellectual property infringement. B makes several counter claims against A. Rather than litigate, A and B work out a deal and drop all infringement claims.[42] This could be a way in which the system "works" although it is doubtful, given that large companies are generally benefited—if B is a small company with few patents, then the counter infringement claims will be hollow at best.

Moreover, I do not think that it is beyond the conceptual ability of judges and attorneys to distinguish between pharmaceutical products and movies or computer software. Considering each intellectual work on a case by case basis to determine the optimal package of rights and limitations offered is clearly unworkable. This is not my suggestion. The evidence noted above indicates that it may be possible to offer fewer rights while maintaining the current level of incentives. If so, then we are giving away too much to authors and inventors and modifications are in order.

To summarize, my general position against the incentives-based argument is that institutions of intellectual property are not necessary as incentive for the production of intellectual works, and even if some system is necessary, the argument still fails to justify anything remotely close to Anglo-American systems of intellectual property. Both of these points can be considered part of an internal critique of the incentives-based, rule-utilitarian argument. Although I will now move on to present and critique (internally) a second rule-utilitarian argument for intellectual property, I will return in a later section to give an external critique of rule-utilitarian moral theory. The general attack against rule-utilitarianism is given at the end, because it applies to the theoretical components of both arguments presented.

A Traditional Rule-Utilitarian Argument

Lawrence Becker examines a second rule-utilitarian argument for property rights and concludes that the argument is, in part, successful. Although Becker's reconstruction of the argument is aimed at justifying rights to tangible property, with minor modifications it can be used to justify a system or institution of intellectual property. In general, the claim is that a system or institution of intellectual property is a necessary means for human flourishing and well-being. Hume reminds us in the quote that prefaces this chapter that stability of possession and the distinction of property are necessary for the establishment of society. Coupled with the assumption that the formation and long-term establishment of a stable, secure society is a requirement of human well-being, we arrive at a simple, and seemingly powerful, argument for institutions or systems of intellectual property protection. Consider a more formal version of this argument:[43]

1.   Society ought to adopt a system or institution if and only if it leads to or, given our best estimates, will lead to the maximization of overall social utility.

2.   Some institutions are necessary for the achievement of human flourishing and well-being and these institutions are determined by an examination of the social conditions which are required for human well-being, but which cannot exist without rule-governed institutions.

3.   How those necessary institutions are to be defined is to be determined by how well the rules constitutive of their various possible definitions, when applied to cases, meet the demands which make the institution necessary.

4.   People need individually to possess, use, and control intellectual works in order to achieve (the means to) a reasonable degree of well-being.

5.   Security in possession and use of intellectual property is impossible (given society as we know it) unless enforced modes of acquisition are controlled. Such enforcement amounts to the administration of a system of intellectual property rights.

6.   It follows that a system of intellectual property rights is necessary (or nearly so) if individuals are to achieve (the means to) even a reasonable degree of well-being and ought to be adopted.

As with the incentives-based argument, the first premise of the traditional argument is supported by rule-utilitarian arguments that link theories of the good and theories of the right in a particular way.

There are many arguments used to establish the truth of the second premise, that some social institutions are necessary in order to achieve a reasonable degree of human well-being. One such argument, offered by David Hume, is given the "numberless wants and necessities" that humans have, and the "slender means" nature has provided for the satisfactions of these wants and necessities, certain social institutions are needed:

By the conjunction of forces, our power is augmented: by the partition of empolyments, our ability increases. And by the mutual succour we are less expos'd to fortune and accidents. 'Tis by this additional force, ability, and security, that society becomes advantageous.[44]

Stable systems or institutions that decide property relations, legal and illegal behavior, societal obligations, and the like, all seem prerequisites for human flourishing and well-being. As rational lifelong project pursuers, humans need certain stable systems or institutions that allow such behavior. Hume argues along similar lines claiming that "the internal satisfaction of our minds, the external advantages of our body, and the enjoyment of such possessions as we have acquir'd by our industry and good fortune" are three kinds of goods that are necessary for human well-being. The chief advantage of society is the improvement of these goods and, therefore, the institutions that create, maintain, and stabilize society would seem necessary. All things considered, the second premise seems fairly uncontroversial.

The third premise, the definition of the necessary institutions, provides a way to determine which institutions are necessary and what rules or practices should make up those necessary institutions. "[t]he particular character of a necessary institution must itself be submitted to the test of utility. If property is found to be necessary, then questions will arise not only about the various ways of defining and limiting the scope of the incidents of 'full or liberal ownership,' but about including each of the incidents at all."[45]   If the argument is to do any work it must indicate which institutions are necessary for human flourishing and which set of rules will constitute those institutions deemed necessary.

The fourth premise, the claim that people need individually to acquire, possess, and use intellectual products in order to achieve a reasonable degree of well-being may be defended the following way. As rational lifelong project pursuers, humans need to use and possess things, including intellectual property. Many purposeful activities require the use of both physical goods and intellectual products. To the extent that these items are unavailable or unsecure, humans are frustrated in their pursuits; and finally, frustration of this sort diminishes overall social utility.[46]

Premise five is typically justified on empirical grounds. Given humans as they are, and as they have been, certain coercive institutions are necessary for security of possession and use of intellectual products. This seems obviously the case when considering institutions of intellectual property. Given the ease of theft and the prevailing attitudes concerning intellectual property, it seems plausible to maintain that coercive institutions are necessary.

It follows that a system of intellectual property rights is necessary, or nearly so, if individuals are to achieve the means to a reasonable degree of well-being and ought to be adopted. The specific rules that constitute each regime of intellectual property will be determined in reference to overall social progress; and, if premise four is correct, each of these regimes will include limited rights to use, possess, and control intellectual works.

Problems for the Traditional Rule-Utilitarian Approach

Consider, once again, the prima facie case against allowing the ownership of intellectual works. Given that intellectual works can be held by everyone at the same time, cannot be used up or easily destroyed, and are necessary for many lifelong goals and projects, it would seem that we have a prima facie case against regimes of intellectual property that would restrict such maximal use.

As noted before, the rejoinder is that granting rights to use, possession, and control of both ideas and expressions of ideas is necessary as incentive for the production of an optimal amount of intellectual works. But this takes us back into the incentives-based argument that has been shown to be problematic at best. It would seem then, that premise two in the traditional argument would not likely pick out systems or institutions of intellectual property protection as best promoting human flourishing.

A second problem, one that arises in relation to premise three, is that the resulting systems of intellectual property would be radically different than current regimes. If conferring a more limited set of rights would lead to an equal or greater amount of worthwhile intellectual products, then the dissemination of information may be increased and overall social utility augmented. As noted before in the incentives argument, granting exclusive twenty-year patent monopolies is not necessary as incentive to get companies to produce an optimal amount of intellectual products. Copyright protection need not extend past the lifetime of the author. The regime of trade secret protection could be eliminated or severely limited with no loss in overall social utility. So even if true, the third premise would most likely support institutions of intellectual property protection that are much less robust than current Anglo-American systems.

Thirdly, in order to justify intellectual property rights, premise four must be modified in such a way that it becomes implausible. As it stands, premise four states that people need individually to possess, use, and control intellectual products in order to achieve a reasonable degree of well-being. But this claim may well be true with no *exclusive* rights to intellectual property being granted. Given the non-exclusive nature of intellectual works it is possible for everyone to concurrently possess, use, and control (non-exclusively) the same intellectual work. To justify anything akin to intellectual property rights, the premise must be recast to include an exclusivity or semi-exclusivity component. People need individually to possess, use, and control intellectual products exclusively or semi-exclusively in order to achieve a reasonable degree of well-being. But surely this will not do either because exclusivity need not be guaranteed by legal rights. Keeping one's ideas a secret is one way to ensure exclusivity that does not depend on government protection. Finally, if we recast the premise to include that exclusivity or semi-exclusivity is to be guaranteed by rights, then the latter formulation seems wildly implausible.[47]

Finally, there are various utility based anti-property arguments that if sound would call for the elimination of current institutions of intellectual property. Consider the following argument:[48] Systems of intellectual property rights which permit private ownership of the means of production and exclusive monopolization of intellectual works inevitably produce inequality in wealth of a sort that increases over generations, hardens the social order into classes, and leads to an unjustifiable amount of poverty and social instability. It is not necessary to permit exclusive or semi-exclusive ownership of intellectual works given that these items are not necessary for survival or the full development of personality. And finally, since it is not obvious that people need to exclusively control intellectual works, and allowing such control leads to poverty and social instability, we should not adopt such institutions. If successful, such an argument undermines premise three in defining institutions of intellectual property as necessary or utility maximizing.[49]

Becker criticizes this argument on the grounds that there is no way to accurately determine the empirical claim that certain kinds of property institutions lead to poverty and instability:

> But whether the institution of property rights always must produce poverty and social instability just seems to me to be beyond anyone's power to determine. One can, after all, imagine circumstances in which it would not, and those circumstances are not all utopian fantasies.[50]

Becker admits that this is indeed how things have often turned out, but thinks that such an admonition is far from granting the claim that the one necessarily leads to the other. But surely this misses the point. If property theorists can summon historical empirical facts to support their claims that adopting systems of intellectual property will *likely* maximize general utility, then the door has been opened for the anti-property theorist to appeal to similar historical facts. The anti-property theorist does not need to claim that institutions of intellectual property will *necessarily* lead to poverty and instability, only that they *likely* will. Moreover, we do not require that the rule-utilitarian property theorist show that institutions of intellectual property will *necessarily* lead to an optimal amount of social progress, so it is presumptuous to require the anti-property theorist to show instability and poverty follows of necessity.

Digitized Intellectual Works—A Final Worry

A basic rule of rule-utilitarian copyright and patent law is that while ideas themselves cannot be owned, the physical or tangible expressions of them can.[51] Ideas, as well as natural laws and the like, are considered to be the collective property of humanity.[52] It is commonly assumed that allowing authors and inventors rights to control mere ideas would diminish overall social utility and so an idea/expression distinction has been adopted.

But digital technology and virtual environments are detaching intellectual works from physical expression. The "bit streams" that inhabit the World Wide Web seem to be much less tangible than paper and ink or machines and processes of manufacture. This tension between protecting physical expressions and the status of online intellectual works leads to a deeper problem. Current Anglo-American institutions of intellectual property are constructed to protect the efforts of authors and inventors and, at the same time, to disseminate information as widely as possible. But when intellectual works are placed online there is no simple method of securing both protection and widespread access. Once I have access to a work that is placed online, I can download it or send copies to my friends.

Note also, that in a networked world it is possible for artists, who produce for fun rather than profit, to reach a worldwide audience. Thus information may be distributed independent of a publishing industry driven by incentives and profits. As this kind of distribution increases, the need for incentives-based distribution models may be further undermined.[53]

In light of these problems the rule-utilitarian could merely reevaluate the consequences of adhering to certain intellectual property rules and try to better the overall system. Maybe adopting an idea/expression distinction will not yield the best results, or maybe further restrictions on the rights granted to authors and inventors will increase information flow and yet still provide adequate incentives.

Imagine though, that circumstances arise where granting authors and inventors limited control over what they produce is not needed as incentive for an optimal production of intellectual works. Suppose that a policy of granting rights to intellectual works diminishes overall social utility compared to not granting rights. Are those who defend rule-utilitarian intellectual property prepared to deny all rights to control intellectual works in this case? Suppose we conclude, according to our best utility calculations, that no one should be able to exclusively control any idea or collection of ideas. Imagine a world where all would be best off if everyone were required to disclose any new idea that they had—maybe appropriately placed digital cameras equipped with sensitive listening devices could capture all of this information. Suppose further that new computer technology disseminated these ideas in a logical and efficient fashion.

In cases such as this, rule-utilitarians may be forced to an unsavory position. In principle their theory may advocate almost any atrocity—so long as the rules adopted yield the best long-term utility. That such a case would, in fact, never happen is beside the point.

Summary of Internal Critique

Before turning to an external critique of rule-utilitarian based arguments for systems of intellectual property protection, I would like to summarize the main points of the internal critique. The general position leveled against the incentives-based argument is that granting rights to authors and inventors as incentive is either giving away too much or would justify systems foreign to current Anglo-American institutions of intellectual property. The traditional rule-utilitarian argument falls prey to these problems as well, insofar as a likely defense of the second and third premise would focus on incentives. Moreover, where premise four seems true when considering tangible property, it is most likely false with respect to intellectual property.

The External Critique[54]

So far, I have given an internal critique by arguing that, even on its own terms, the rule-utilitarian approach fails to justify intellectual property rights. In the remainder of this chapter, I will turn to an external critique of rule-utilitarian moral theory. The first premise of both rule-utilitarian arguments given as justification for systems of intellectual property is that society ought to adopt an institution if and only if it leads to or, given our best estimates, will lead to the maximization of overall social utility. As we shall see, this approach to moral theory is beset with difficulties.

The Problem of Act Description

Rule-utilitarians determine the rightness or wrongness of actions by appealing to moral rules. In general, actions are to be tested in reference to rules and rules in reference to the consequences. One problem for the rule-utilitarian is that without an adequate account of act description, the theory cannot be applied. Since the evaluation of rules is dependent on the consequences, and acts not rules have consequences, we must decide how to describe actions in order to justify rules. Consider the following example. Some action I perform may be described in a number of ways. For instance, a particular action might be described in any of the following ways:

- copying the intellectual works of another;

- copying the intellectual works of another when no one else will;

- copying the intellectual works of another when no one else will, and when doing so will save lives of fifty children; and,

- copying the intellectual works of another when no one else will, and when doing so will save lives of fifty children who have been genetically engineered to grow into Hitlers and Stalins.[55]

Since the consequences of everyone doing actions of these different types would be very different, the rule utilitarian must give us a theory of act description before we can apply the theory. The difficulty is solving the problem in such a way that doesn't lead rule-utilitarianism to collapse into act-utilitarianism. If we determined kinds of actions (action types) by giving a maximally specific description of each action (action tokens), then the type will only cover one specific act and hence the collapse.[56]

Eric D'Arcy and David Lyons both independently develop answers to the problem of act description.[57] In general their theories distinguish between acts, circumstances, and consequences. The solution that both seem to advocate is that we use moral norms to determine the relevant description of a particular act. Since utilitarians are concerned with the goodness of consequences, we should describe an act in such a way that all the relevant consequences are included.

The problem with this solution is that it is circular. We need to describe acts so that we can determine moral norms but the only way to adequately determine the appropriate act description is to appeal to moral norms. Moreover, there can be no moral norms outside of the moral theory in question—it is not as if the rule utilitarian can appeal to deontological considerations to determine the appropriate act description.[58] Crudely put, act descriptions are necessary to determine moral norms yet moral norms are necessary to determine appropriate act descriptions. Let us assume, however, that the rule utilitarian can give an adequate account of act description. As we shall see, there are other, possibly more serious, problems to consider.

Adoption and Adherence

Although the first premise of both arguments call for the *adoption* of certain institutions, rule-utilitarians have also defended an *adherence* view. On the adherence view the correctness of an institution or set or rules is dependent on the results of everyone actually conforming to the rules, whereas on the adoption view, the correctness of an institution is dependent on the results of everyone adopting, but not necessarily actually adhering to, the rules. The adoption model takes into account the possibility of misapplications of the rules as part of the consequences of adoption. The adherence model does not.

There are two versions of the adherence view that have been defended by rule-utilitarians. The restricted model of adherence limits the descriptions of action types by not allowing references to the actions of others as part of the description. Restricted adherence, then, would not allow describing the act of taking another's intellectual property as "taking another's intellectual property *when no one else will*":

> The intuition behind this restriction is that if you are allowed to make reference to the actions of others in describing your action, then rule-utilitarianism will allow the same kind of unfairness that act-utilitarianism will in these cases. In particular, it will allow what is called free-riding: receiving benefits from the cooperative sacrifices of others without making those sacrifices oneself.[59]

The second version of the adherence model is unrestricted in that, outside of the limitations required by a theory of act description in answer to the preceding problem, there are no restrictions on act descriptions.

The problem with the restricted version of the adherence model is that it requires us to follow moral rules even when doing so will lead to bad results. Suppose we had a justified moral rule of the following sort: "Don't copy or pirate the intellectual works of others." Imagine that if everyone were to follow this rule that social utility would be maximized and wealth, peace, and prosperity would visit everyone. Suppose though, that you are a member of a community of radical communists and that no one else follows the rule. The only thing that will be accomplished by following the rule is that you will be put at a disadvantage compared to your fellows. You respect their intellectual property but they simply copy and pirate anything you produce. Even if it were true that no one else will follow the rule, the restricted version of the adherence model of rule-utilitarianism will say of an individual citizen that she has a moral obligation to do so. This leads to what some have called "rule futility" not "rule utility." Alas, it seems in some cases that considering what actions others will perform does make a difference in terms of moral obligation.

This problem can be circumvented by allowing the descriptions of actions to refer to the actions of others. When considering what the consequences of adhering to a rule would be, we are allowed to include references to the actions of others. We can now describe the action in the previous case as "not violating the intellectual property of others when everyone else will." Given that this would be futile, it is not obligatory. The problem with this unrestricted version of the adherence model is that it looks like it will collapse into act-utilitarianism. Consider the following example given by J. J. C. Smart in "Extreme and Restricted Utilitarianism":

Suppose there is a rule R and that in 99% of cases the best possible results are obtained by acting in accordance with R. Then clearly R is a useful rule of thumb; if we have no time or are not impartial enough to assess the consequences of an action it is an extremely good bet that the thing to do is to act in accordance with R. But is it not monstrous to suppose that if we *have* worked out the consequences and if we have perfect faith in the impartiality of our calculations, and if we *know* that in this instance to break R will have better results than to keep it, we should nevertheless obey the rule?[60]

The answer to this problem cannot be to change R to include the exception because the final result of including each exception would be to collapse rule-utilitarianism into act-utilitarianism—i.e., this form of rule-utilitarianism would prescribe the same actions as act-utilitarianism. But surely, R with the exception is a better rule on consequentialist grounds than R with no exceptions. It would seem that the rule-utilitarian is forced to include the exception that makes R a better rule—and the collapse ensues.[61] If this is correct, then either version of the adherence model of rule-utilitarianism is ruled out as a correct and workable moral theory.

Putting adherence to rules aside, there is also the adoption model to consider. On this view, strict conformity is not required when considering the consequences of adopting a rule. Individuals may make mistakes when applying the rule and these mistakes may have bad consequences. The adoption model, but not the adherence model, allows these latter consequences to be considered when deciding the moral correctness of a rule or set of rules. The problem with the adoption model is that it makes the correctness of moral rules or sets of rules dependent on the rule following capacities of those who will adopt the rule. Consider the following case adapted from Hubin's society of dolts example:

Imagine that one lives in a society of dolts. These people are so stupid that they can't apply rules that have any exceptions at all. Their rules must be simple statements. Suppose further that you are trying to decide if you should copy and pirate the intellectual works of another given that in doing so you will save hundreds of children from a new deadly virus. You might think this is morally permissible—that a good moral rule would treat this case as an exception to the rule "don't copy or pirate the intellectual works of another." But, on the adoption model, this is not so. If others adopted the rule "Don't copy or pirate the intellectual property of another except when doing so will save the lives of hundreds of children (or lead to really bad consequences)" they would be so confused in applying it that they would pirate all kinds of intellectual property and cause a general decrease in overall utility. Therefore, the best rule to have adopted in this society of dolts is the rule, "Never copy or pirate the intellectual works of another"; and that rule prohibits your copying even when lives are at stake.

If misapplications of a rule are to be factored in when considering the consequences of everyone adopting a rule, then the rule following capacities of individuals may play an important role in determining the correctness of moral rules. But this seems unacceptable.

But why is this unacceptable? Why shouldn't the rule following capacities play an important role in determining which moral rules are justified? The answer cannot be that this would lead to bad consequences given the assumption that in a society of dolts exceptionless rules are best. But different individuals have different rule following capacities and this leads to a problem. Suppose we introduce into Hubin's society of dolts, one expert rule follower who correctly follows complex rules that have multiple exceptions. This individual recognizes that the rule "Never copy or pirate the intellectual works of another" is not as good as the rule "Never copy or pirate the intellectual works of another except when you can save the lives of hundreds of children." The question now becomes, why shouldn't the expert rule follower adopt the latter rule rather than the former? The worry becomes apparent when, in the same circumstances, one individual is morally required to do X while another individual is morally required to not do X—given our example, the average dolt is required to not steal the intellectual property of another while the expert rule follower is required to do the opposite. An odd kind of moral relativism looms.

Moreover, the view that the rule following capacities of individuals are important in determining correct moral rules leads back to a conception of rules as rules of thumb or strategic rules. We follow these latter kinds of rules when we can't be sure of our utility calculating abilities. Maybe the issue before us is too near and dear, or the consequences stretch too far into the future, or our judgment is clouded for some other reason. In cases like these we follow rules because they have in the past maximized utility for everyone affected. But if we know better, if our judgment is clear, or if our *capacities* change, then we must abandon the rule or add the exception. Thus rules become fluid and a collapse of rule-utilitarianism into act-utilitarianism may occur.

Finally, it is not as if this more sophisticated utilitarian theory will allow the consequentialist to side-step the problems that befall the act-utilitarian. Adherence models or adoption models of rule-utilitarianism may still, in theory, advocate almost any atrocity. If following some rule maximizes utility, then we ought to follow the rule no matter what its content. Suppose the capacities of the dolts, assuming an adoption model, leads them to conclude that others—the ones who have a different skin pigmentation, or religion, or eye color, or gender—lack freewill and are really just simple animals. The dolts adopt the rule "Do what you want with your property or animals" because they figure that following this rule will maximize utility for everyone affected. And assume it would given their capacities. Have we just justified racism or sexism for the dolts? Would we have to say of such a culture that, given their capacities, they ought to follow such a rule?

The answer, it could be argued, lies in the difference that Joel Feinberg notes between "(1) What (speaking most generally) are the correct moral principles for use by a private individual in guiding his own personal conduct (including that part of his conduct that falls within the scope of public rules)? (2) Which public rules or regulations of the kind that control private conduct by imposing duties and conferring rights should be adopted by a given community?"[62] This latter notion is sometimes called "actual practice rule-utilitarianism" and concerns public rules, maybe laws, already in force.[63] Actual practice rule-utilitarianism need not collapse into act-utilitarianism because while certain exceptions will be built into the rules, the general act-utilitarian exception—follow rule R unless acting otherwise would maximize net utility—will almost never be invoked because of the difference between adherence and adoption. Public rules will almost never allow an act-utilitarian exception because citizens are apt to misapply the exception.

While this may allow the actual practice rule-utilitarian to avoid a collapse into act-utilitarianism the society of dolts case may still have force and there is now a further problem. What justifies an actual practice rule viewed as a public rule or law? If an actual practice rule is to be justified by utility in relation to the capacities of citizens, then we again have a rule that could have almost any content. If the rule is intended to allow for the maximization of social utility bounded by certain rights of individuals, then an important question has been begged—why think that intellectual property rights are not like other individual rights? I take this latter worry to also apply if we view the rules of Anglo-American intellectual property to be what John Rawls calls constitutive practice rules:[64]

the rules of practices are logically prior to particular cases. This is so because there cannot be a case of an action falling under a rule of a practice unless there is the practice . . . We may think of the rule of a practice as defining offices, moves, and offenses. . . Striking out, stealing a base, balking . . . are all actions which can only happen in a [baseball] game. [Furthermore,] if one wants to play a game, one doesn't treat the rules of the game as guides . . .[65]

While this view may be helpful in solving the problem of act description and it may be useful when thinking about the action of registering a copyright, I take that it leaves open the possibility that intellectual property rights may exist prior to and independent of copyright, patent, and trade secret practices.[66]

Conclusion

In conclusion, I would like to mention one final problem with rule-utilitarian justifications of intellectual property. The problem I have in mind is not a difficulty with rule-utilitarianism as a correct moral theory, but how it fits with other rights generating moral theories found in the Anglo-American tradition.

Consider a common variation of the incentives argument and the traditional argument that incorporates the notion of a contract between the author or inventor and the government. This view is accurately captured in *Fried. Krupp Akt. v. Midvale Steel Co.*:

Tersely stated, an American patent is a written contract between an inventor and the government. This contract consists of mutual, interrelated considerations moving from each party to the other for such contract. The consideration given on the part of the inventor to the government is the disclosure of his invention is such plain and full terms that any one skilled in the art to which it pertains may practice it. The consideration on the part of the government given to the patentee for such disclosure is a monopoly . . . .[67]

Here the idea is that mutual benefit can be had between creators and the government ultimately maximizing social utility. Authors and inventors gain by having their works protected for a limited time and society gains by the free flow of information and the ensuing progress.[68]

If an inventor has no claims to control a particular intellectual work independent of a contract with society, then the subsequent contract seems at best suspect. When two parties contract about what will happen with some good, for the contract to be binding, one of the parties must be entitled to the relevant kind of control over the good in question. Without any prior claims or commitments why not pick someone at random and give them title? The answer typically given is that we would then lose the incentive structure needed to drive the entire system—needless to say we are back in the incentives argument.

But what if, somehow, we could maintain the incentives to burn the midnight oil while picking intellectual property owners by lottery? What if this system and the contracts that fall out of it maximized overall social utility? Here I am driving at what I call a "global inconsistency problem."

Life rights, privacy rights, and tangible property rights are typically given a deontic base that stand athwart utilitarian concerns. Even if following the rule "don't violate rights" were to diminish overall social utility, the dominant Anglo-American tradition would be to follow the rule anyway.[69] This is not to say that rights are absolute and can never be overridden by bad consequences. The point here is about the grounds of rights not their relative strength. If systems of intellectual property rights are indeed justified on rule-utilitarian grounds and life rights and the like are deontic in nature, then there is a kind of global inconsistency within the Anglo-American tradition.[70] Why, for instance, are rights to rocks, cars, and houses justified on different grounds than books, works of art, and processes of manufacture? Why is it the case that my ownership of a copy of your book compared to your ownership of the intellectual work is more resistant, in a deep way, to considerations of consequentialist value maximization? Those of us who find this troubling and agree that the aforementioned internal and external problems with rule-utilitarianism are correct, have good reason to reject rule-utilitarian based justifications of intellectual property rights.

These results, if true, call for revisions in Anglo-American systems of intellectual property protection. Alas, these institutions are shot through with rules, tests of rules, statutes, provisions, exemptions, limitations, and the like, that have been justified because the rules and systems supposedly maximize overall social utility.

Finally as noted in later chapters, I am not opposed to "social utility arguments" at the governmental level when such activity is restrained by individual "natural" rights. The American system of government can be understood as a method of maximizing social utility within certain constraints. Thus it may be the case that some rights exist independent of governments or institutions while others are simply created by governments and institutions. I will argue in the following chapters that intellectual property rights can exist independent of governments or other rights granting agencies. Intellectual property rights are essentially no different than our rights to life, liberty, and physical property. Upon rejecting traditional rule-utilitarian justifications of copyright, patent, trademark, and trade secret, the path is cleared for a new Lockean justification of intellectual property that truly upholds the creative rights of authors and inventors.

Notes

1.   U.S. Constitution, § 8, para. 8.
2.   See W. Francis and R. Collins, *Cases and Materials on Patent Law: Including Trade Secrets - Copyrights - Trademarks*, 4th ed. (St. Paul, MN: West Publishing Company, 1987), 92-93. Prior to the enactment of the U.S. Constitution a number of states adopted copyright laws that had both a utilitarian component and a natural rights component. A major tuning point away from a natural rights framework for American institutions of intellectual property came with the 1834 decision of *Wheaton v. Peters* 33 US (8 Pet.) 591, 660-1 (1834). See "Copyright Enactments of the United States, 1783-1906," in *Copyright Office Bulletin* 3 (1906), 14. "Unquestionable, the 1834 decision marked an important turning-pint, in that it distances American copyright law from the natural law perspectives which were very much in evidence at the end of the eighteenth century." Alain Strowel, "Droit d'auteur and Copyright: Between History and Nature," in *Of Authors and Origins*, edited by Brad Sherman and Alan Strowel (Oxford: Clarendon Press, 1994), 245. See also, Edward C. Walterscheid, "Inherent or Created Rights: Early Views on the Intellectual Property Clause," *Hamline Law Review* 19 (1995). Nevertheless, anomalies still pop up. "In 1984 the Supreme Court cited Locke when it held that intangible 'products of an individual's labor and invention' can be 'property' subject to the protection of the Takings Clause." Wendy J. Gordon, "A Property Right in Self-Expression: Equality and Individualism in the Natural Law of Intellectual Property," *Yale Law Journal* 102 (1993): 1533-609, citing *Ruckelshaus v. Monsanto Co.*, 467 U.S. 986, 1002-03 (1984).
3.   Committee Report: 1909 Copyright Act. See also, *Sony Corp. of America v. Universal Studios Inc.*, 464 US 417, 78, L. Ed 2d. 574 (1984).
4.   See Joan Robinson, *Science as Intellectual Property* (New York: Macmillan 1984), 15.
5.   See the Committee Report accompanying the 1909 Copyright Act, H.R. Rep. No. 2222, 60th Cong., 2nd Sess. 7 1909. The courts have also reflected this theme: "The copyright law . . . . makes reward to the owner a secondary consideration." (*United States v. Paramount Pictures,* 1948) "The limited scope of the copyright holder's statutory monopoly, like the limited copyright duration required by the Constitution, reflects a balance of competing claims on the public interest: Creative work is to be encouraged and rewarded, but private motivation must ultimately serve the cause of promoting broad public availability of literature, music, and other arts." (*Twentieth Century Music Corp. v. Aiken*, 422 U.S. 151, 95 S.Ct. 2040, 45 L.Ed.2d [1974]).
6.   Parts of this section draw directly from R. G. Frey's "Introduction: Utilitarianism and Persons" in *Utility and Rights*, edited by R. G. Frey (Minneapolis, MN: Uni-

versity of Minnesota Press, 1984), 3-19 and J. J. C. Smart's "Extreme and Restricted Utilitarianism, in *Theories of Ethics*, edited by Philippa Foot (Oxford: Oxford University Press, 1967).

7.   Some utilitarians use strategic rules and rules of thumb. Strategic rules are rules that we are almost always more confident in than our calculating abilities. Utilitarians of this sort argue that we should follow the strategic rule even when it looks like violating it will maximize goodness. But when we have strong evidence that breaking a rule in a certain instance will maximize utility, then we should break the rule.

8.   For similar views see J. J. C. Smart "Extreme and Restricted Utilitarianism," and David Lyons, *Forms and Limits of Utilitarianism* (Oxford: Clarendon Press, 1965).

9.   Joan Robinson quoted in D. Nelkin's, *Science as Intellectual Property* (New York: Macmillan Press, 1984), 15 (parentheses mine).

10. This kind of rule-utilitarianism is sometimes called "ideal rule-utilitarianism." In a later section I will address two variants of ideal rule-utilitarianism formulated as Adoption RU (rules that require "acceptance" utility) and Adherence RU (rules that require "ideal conformance" utility). At that time I will also consider a separate view called "actual rule-utilitarianism." For a lucid account of the many forms of utilitarianism see Lyons, *Forms and Limits of Utilitarianism* and Joel Feinberg's review of Lyons, "The Forms and Limits of Utilitarianism," *Philosophical Review* (1967): 368-81.

11. See C. Oppenheim, "Evaluation of the American Patent System" in Journal 33 (Patent Office Society, 1951); National Patent Planning Commission: First Report (1943), 783-84; Report of the President's Commission (1966); Tom Palmer, "Intellectual Property: A Non-Posnerian Law and Economics Approach," in *Intellectual Property: Moral, Legal, and International Dilemmas*, edited by A. Moore (Lanham, MD: Rowman & Littlefield, 1997), chapter 7, 179; and Leonard G. Boonin, "The University, Scientific Research, and the Ownership of Knowledge," *Owning Scientific and Technical Information* (New Brunswick, NJ: Rutgers University Press, 1989), 257-60.

12. B. Robinson, *Robinson on Patents*, § 33. Robinson is considered by many to be the foremost early authority on American systems of intellectual property.

13. For example, see Patrick Croskery's "Institutional Utilitarianism and Intellectual Property" *Chicago-Kent Law Review* 68 (1993): 631.

14. Some intangible property is rivalrous. "This is true, for instance, in the case of knowledge which gives one a competitive advantage (for example, a trade secret) and for information relating to future events, which allows one to speculate on forthcoming price changes (or example, the lifting of a blockade or a projected takeover)." Ejan MacKaay, "Economic Incentives in Markets for Information and Innovation," in *Harvard Journal of Law and Public Policy* 13 (Summer 1990): 892.

15. Edwin C. Hettinger, "Justifying Intellectual Property," in *Intellectual Property: Moral, Legal, and International Dilemmas*, edited by A. Moore (Lanham, MD: Rowman & Littlefield, 1997), chapter 1, 30.

16. This view is echoed in the following denials of a common law right to intellectual property. "Wheaton established as a bedrock principle of American copyright law that copyright, with respect to a published work, is a creature of statute and not the product of the common law." See S. Halpern, D. Shipley, and H. Abrams, *Copyright: Cases and Materials* (Saint Paul, MN: West Publishing, 1992), 6. "There shall be no monopolies granted or allowed among us, but of such new inventions as are profitable to the country, and that for a short time." (General court of Massachusetts, 1641). "The monopoly did not exist at common law, and the rights, therefore,

which may be exercised under it cannot be regulated by the rule of common law. It is created by the act of Congress; and no rights can be acquired in it unless authorized by statute, and in the manner the statute prescribes" (Chief Justice Taney, *Gayler et al. v. Wilder*, 1850).

17.   This premise and the first premise of the next argument (the traditional argument) could be defended by the act-utilitarian in the following way. Consider the adoption of an institution of intellectual property protection as an *act* of Congress or government. Members of Congress, in voting to adopt some set of rules, are acting so that social utility is maximized—they are adopting a set of rules and attaching sanctions for violating these rules. The sanctions change the consequences of many actions and thus may change what is the correct action for others.

This way of defending the first premise of either argument is not without problems. While such a view would provide a way to side-step the external critique of rule-utilitarianism found at the end of this chapter, it would not answer any of the internal problems discussed. Moreover, it is not as if, by moving from rule-utilitarianism to act-utilitarianism, the defender of this view obtains firmer footing—alas there are many damaging criticisms of act-utilitarianism as well. For a lucid account of many of the problems with act-utilitarianism, see Benard Williams, "A Critique of Utilitarianism" in *Utilitarianism: For & Against* (New York: Cambridge University Press, 1973), 75-150; John Rawls, *A Theory of Justice* (Cambridge, MA: Harvard University Press, 1971), 22-34; H. J. McCloskey, "Respect for Human Moral Rights versus Maximizing Good" in *Utility and Rights*, edited by R. G. Frey (Minneapolis, MN: University of Minnesota Press, 1984), 121-36; David Lyons, *Forms and Limits of Utilitarianism*; and footnotes 18-21 below.

18.   Generally speaking, the problem of justice for act-utilitarianism is, what if doing something unjust maximizes overall utility. For example, what if framing an innocent person would lead to the best consequences for everyone affected? Act-utilitarianism would seem to required such an unjust act—i.e., we would have a moral obligation to frame the innocent person and this seems wrong.

19.   The problem of special obligations is that sometimes we have obligations that stand independent of the consequences. For example, it may be best for all concerned that a teacher give everyone A's but the teacher has a special obligation to award grades based on merit.

20.   In general terms, the problem of integrity is that act-utilitarianism requires individuals to treat their own lifelong goals and projects impartially. As a good utility maximizer we each should be willing to abandon our goals and projects for the sake of maximizing overall social utility. The problem is that we cannot be impartial in this way.

21.   The problem of excessive demands is that act-utilitarianism demands too much of us. Since everything we do and don't do has consequences, every action or inaction is moral or immoral. But this seems wrong. Whether I wake up at 10:00 or 10:05 seems to be outside the realm of morality, assuming of course that I have no prior obligations.

22.   For example, consider the advances in medical treatment that are seemingly the result of incentive producing structures.

23.   While I will not challenge the truth of the third premise in this chapter, it seems dubious as well. When we consider other more pressing social needs and wants like, food, health care, housing, education, safety, and the like, the need for the promotion of many/most intellectual works seems to fall well down on the list.

24.   The example comes from Hettinger, "Justifying Intellectual Property," 31, and from Croskery's "Institutional Utilitarianism and Intellectual Property," 637. Croskery's

analysis is particularly useful here in that he discusses five possibilities for the production of intangible goods: government production; private production, government reward; market reward, government fine tuning; market production and fine tuning, government fencing; and market production and fencing. Most of these arrangements deviate from our current systems in some respect and if any offer better prospects for society, then the rule-utilitarian must advocate the appropriate changes.

25. It may even be better, overall, to produce fewer intellectual works if the costs are lower.
26. Michael Polanyi, "Patent Reform," *Review of Economic Studies* 61 (1944) advocates a system where people invent intangible works as they currently do, are paid by the government, and receive no exclusionary rights to the works. An assessment of the economic value is made by those who use the invention and the government would pay some fraction of this approximate value to the inventor.
27. Fritz Machlup, *Production and Distribution of Knowledge in the United States* (Princeton, NJ: Princeton University Press, 1962), 168-69.
28. Sindey Winter, "Patents in Complex Contexts" in *Owning Scientific and Technical Information* (New Brunswick, NJ: Rutger University Press, 1989), 43 (italics mine). The book cited is S. Winter and R. Nelson, *An Evolutionary Theory of Economic Change* (Cambridge, MA: Harvard University Press, 1982).
29. Jack Hirshleifer, "The Private and Social Value of Information and the Reward to Inventive Activity," in the *American Economic Review* 61 (1971): 561.
30. Machlup, *Production and Distribution of Knowledge in the United States*, 170.
31. For other utilitarian based arguments against owning intellectual property see Richard Stallman, "Why Software Should Be Free," in *Intellectual Property: Moral, Legal, and International Dilemmas*, edited by A. Moore (Lanham, MD.: Rowman & Littlefield, 1997), chapter 11; and Arthur Kuflik, "The Moral Foundations of Intellectual Property Rights," in *Owning Scientific and Technical Information* (New Brunswick, NJ: Rutger University Press, 1989), 228-31.
32. Machlup, *Knowledge: Its Creation, Distribution, and Economic Significance* (Princeton, NJ: Princeton University Press, 1984), 164.
33. "In some cases, such as Coca-Cola and Smith's Brothers cough drops, trade secrecy has provided a century of protection far superior to the limited returns which would have been offered by patent law.... Some firms rely on secrecy because they expect a relatively short life for their products. By keeping the product a secret until marketed, the firms gain enough lead time over competitors so that patent protection is not worthwhile. The firms invest in marketing and advertising to protect a share of the market." Roger Miners and Robert Staaf, "Patents, Copyrights, and Trademarks: Property or Monopoly," in *Harvard Journal of Law and Public Policy* 13 (Summer 1990): 927-28.
34. *See* the Restatement (Third) of Unfair Competition § 39-45.
35. The two restrictions on trade secrets are the requirements of secrecy and competitive advantage. See chapter 2.
36. See Hettinger, "Justifying Intellectual Property," 32. It may be argued that only independently wealthy artists or artists who receive grants of some kind can afford to pursue their artistic endeavors independent of copyright. The vast majority of artists, however, are dependent on copyright (directly or indirectly) for their livelihood. But this is the very question at issue — are copyright, patent, and trade secret institutions, with their full complement of rights, necessary? As I have been arguing this seems highly unlikely.

37. See the problem of the collapse of rule-utilitarianism into act-utilitarianism below.

38. See Marci A. Hamilton, "The TRIPS Agreement: Imperialistic, Outdated, and Over-protective" and Hugh C. Hansen, "International Copyright: An Unorthodox Analysis," both in *Intellectual Property: Moral, Legal, and International Dilemmas*, edited by A. Moore (Lanham, MD.: Rowman & Littlefield, 1997).

39. An obvious example is the progress of the computer industry. As things now stand ROM, RAM, and CPU speed doubles every eighteen months (an Internet year is only six months!). With such accelerated turnover it is difficult to understand the need for twenty years of patent protection and a lifetime plus seventy years for copyright protection.

40. Bootlegging is generally understood as the direct copying of some kind of digital information and then the subsequent marketing and sale of the copies. Pirates merely copy, they don't sell.

41. For radical deconstructionist arguments calling for the elimination of copyright and patent protection, see Tom Palmer, "Intellectual Property: A Non-Posnerian Law and Economics Approach" in *Intellectual Property: Moral, Legal, and International Dilemmas*, edited by A. Moore (Lanham, MD.: Rowman & Littlefield, 1997), chapter 7.

42. I first heard of this method from Duane Smith, Vice President, Chief Operating Officer, Vision Quest 2000, Inc. in an interview. It is also mentioned in E. Von Hippel, "Appropriability of Innovation Benefit as a Predictor of the Source of Innovation," *Research Policy* 11 (1982), cited in Winter, "Patents in Complex Contexts," 54.

43. Adapted from Becker's *Property Rights: Philosophic Foundations* (London: Routledge & Kegan Paul 1977), 57-67. Here again, and throughout this section, I am indebted to Becker's analysis.

44. David Hume, *Treatise of Human Nature*, book III, part II, § II.

45. Becker, *Property Rights*, 61.

46. Sometimes a genetic-based defense is given here. Part of human nature is the desire to set personal boundaries, the crossing of which would cause great psychological distress. These intimate personal boundaries naturally extend to one's acquisitions. It is claimed that not only physical, but psychological well-being rests on the protection of these boundaries. A number of empirical studies seem to support such a view. See E. O. Wilson, *Sociobiology* (Cambridge, MA: Harvard University Press 1975); E. T. Hall, *The Hidden Dimension* (New York: Doubleday, 1966); and G. Allport, *Becoming* (New Haven, CT: Yale University Press, 1955).

47. Why, for instance, is the exclusivity of intellectual property guaranteed by legal rights necessary for human flourishing? Why is imposed scarcity *needed?*

48. Adapted from Becker, *Property Rights*, 89.

49. Some have argued, however, that systems of intellectual property have a leveling effect on the distribution of goods and income or that, at least, such institutions are non-elitist. See Justin Hughes, "The Philosophy of Intellectual Property," in *Intellectual Property: Moral, Legal, and International Dilemmas*, edited by A. Moore (Lanham, MD.: Rowman & Littlefield, 1997), chapter 5.

50. Becker, *Property Rights,* 89.

51. 17 U.S.C. § 102(b) (1988) states, "In no case does copyright protection for an original work of authorship extend to any idea, procedure, process, system, method of operation, concept, principle, or discovery, regardless of the form in which it is described, explained, illustrated, or embodied in such work."

52. See 17 U.S.C. § 102(b); *International New Service v. Associated Press* 248 U.S. 215, 39 S.Ct. 68, 63 L.Ed. 211 (1918); *Miller v. Universal City Studios, Inc.* 224

USPQ 427 (1984, CD Cal); and *Midas Productions, Inc. v. Baer* 199 USPQ 454 (1977, DC Cal).

53. I would like to thank Sanford Thatcher for bringing this point to my attention.

54. The problems of act description and with adherence and adoption are advanced by J. J. C. Smart in "Extreme and Restricted Utilitarianism," *Theories of Ethics*, edited by Philippa Foot (Oxford: Oxford University Press, 1967); David Lyons in *Forms and Limits of Utilitarianism* (Oxford: Clarendon Press, 1965); R. B. Brandt in *Ethical Theory* (Englewood Cliffs, NJ: Prentice Hall, 1959), 396-400; "Toward a Credible Form of Utilitarianism, in *Morality and the Language of Conduct*, edited by H. Castanenda (Detroit, MI: Wayne State University Press, 1963), 107-40; and Don Hubin, unpublished manuscripts. The form of the arguments given draw directly from Hubin and indirectly from Lyons and Brandt.

55. Adapted from an example given by Hubin (unpublished manuscripts). See also, Eric D'Arcy, *Human Acts: An Essay in their Moral Evaluation* (Oxford: Oxford University Press, 1963), 3 (Darcy attributes this type of example to J. J. C. Smart) and Johnathan Harrison, "Utilitarianism, Universalization, and our Duty to Be Just," *Proceedings of the Aristotelian Society* (1952-53).

56. This problem is similar to the problem of the sly maxim maker and Kant's first formulation of the categorical imperative.

57. Eric D'Arcy, *Human Acts*. 1-61; Lyons, *Forms and Limits of Utilitarianism*, chapter II.

58. If we constrain utility maximizing arguments through the use of deontic based rights—this is basically how our current constitutional system is arranged—it may be possible to appeal to deontic norms to determine appropriate act descriptions. If the Lockean model presented in chapters 4-7 is correct, though, intellectual property rights will be recast in a deontic light that insulates them from utility maximization arguments.

59. Hubin unpublished manuscripts.

60. J. J. C. Smart, "Extreme and Restricted Utilitarianism," 177. This is also how many act-utilitarians attack rule-utilitarianism. Rule-utilitarianism ends up looking like superstitious rule worship.

61. "If unrestricted adherence RU is to be distinct from AU, there must be some action, call it A_{best}, that produces the best consequences but is prohibited by the best moral rule. Call this rule R_{best}. Imagine that this is so. (Or, try to imagine it, because as it will turn out, it is impossible. This is the key to the argument. If it is impossible for this to be true, then this version of RU is equivalent to AU.) R_{best} requires $A_{not-best}$ instead of A_{best}. Now imagine another rule that is exactly like R_{best} except that instead of requiring $A_{not-best}$ it requires in its place A_{best}. Now compliance with this other rule, will produce all the utility that compliance with R_{best} will at every other time, but, when it comes time to perform A_{best} or $A_{not-best}$, this other rule will produce more utility than R_{best}. So, this other rule produces equal utility to R_{best} at all other times and more utility in the choice of A_{best} over $A_{not-best}$ and, therefore, it produces more utility than R_{best}. But that means that R_{best} isn't the best rule — the other rule is better. This violates our original assumption and shows that it is not possible for the best rule to require anything but the best action at every time." Hubin (unpublished manuscripts).

62. Joel Feinberg, "The Forms and Limits of Utilitarianism," 377.

63. Feinberg notes that a defense of actual practice rule-utilitarianism is given by John Rawls. See J. Rawls, "Two Concepts of Rules," *Philosophical Review* 64 (1955): 3-32, reprinted in *Theories of Ethics*, ed. Phillippa Foot (London: Oxford University Press, 1967), 144-70 (all page citations refer to the reprint).

64. Rawls, "Two Concepts of Rules," 163.
65. Rawls, "Two Concepts of Rules," 163-64.
66. For further worries with Rawls' view and, more generally, with actual practice rule-utilitarianism and ideal rule-utilitarianism, see Lyons *Forms and Limits of Utilitarianism*, chapter V.
67. *Fried. Krupp Akt. v. Midvale Steel Co.* (C.A.3, 1911), 191 Fed. 588, 594. See also, *National Carbon Co. v. Western Shade Cloth Co.* (C.A.7, 1937), 93 F.2d 94, 96 cert. den. 304 U.S. 570, 82 L.ed 1535 (1938); *Tschappat v. Hinderliter Tool Co.* (C.A.10, 1938), 98 F.2d 994 998; *Strong-Scott Mjg. v. Weller* (C.A.8 1940), 112 F.2d 389, 394; *David Airfoils v. United States* (1954), 124 F. Supp. 350, 352, cert. den. 348 U.S. 950, 99 L.ed. 742; B. Bugbee, *The Genesis of American Copyright and Patent Law* (Public Affairs Press, 1967), 10.
68. David Carey, *The Ethics of Software Ownership* (Ph.D. Dissertation, Pittsburgh University) 1988, offers a lengthy defense of this view.
69. It could be argued that the purpose of the Bill of Rights is to protect individuals from utilitarian-type reasoning—we don't want lives, goals, and projects left at the mercy of policies engineered to promote social utility.
70. Palmer argues that this is good reason for revising or eliminating the regimes of copyright and patent. Michael Davis echoes this concern in "Patents, Natural Rights, and Natural Property," *Owning Scientific and Technical Information* (New Brunswick, NJ: Rutger University Press, 1989), 241-44.

4

A Pareto-Based Proviso on Original Acquisition

"Whatsoever then he removes out of the State that Nature hath provided, and left it in, he hath mixed his *Labour* with, and joyned to it something that is his own, and thereby makes it his *Property*. It being by him removed from the common state Nature placed it in, it hath by this *labour* something annexed to it, that excludes the common right of other Men."
—John Locke *The Second Treatise Of Government*[1]

Introduction

One of the most promising strategies for justifying property rights begins with the claim that individuals are entitled to control the fruits of their labor. Laboring, producing, thinking, and persevering are voluntary and individuals who engage in these activities are entitled to what they produce. Subject to certain restrictions, rights are generated when individuals mix their labor with an unowned object. "The root idea of the labor theory is that people are entitled to hold, as property, whatever they produce by their own initiative, intelligence, and industry."[2] The intuition is that the person who clears land, cultivates crops, builds a house, nurtures livestock, or creates a new invention obtains property rights by engaging in these activities.

One version of Locke's famous argument goes as follows.[3] Individuals own their own bodies and labor—i.e., they are self-owners. When an individual labors on an unowned object her labor becomes infused in the object and for the most part, the labor and the object cannot be separated. It follows that once a person's labor is joined with an unowned object, and assuming that individuals exclusively own their body and labor, rights to control are generated. The idea is that there is a kind of expansion of rights. We each own our labor

71

and when that labor is mixed with objects in the commons our rights are expanded to include these goods.

Locke's argument is not without difficulties.[4] Some have argued that the idea of mixing one's labor is incoherent—actions cannot be mixed with objects.[5] The following objections have also been raised. Why isn't mixing what I own (my labor) with what I don't own a way of losing what I own rather than gaining what I don't?[6] Why shouldn't the second labor on an object ground a property right in an object as reliable as the first labor?[7] Why shouldn't mixing one's labor with an unowned object yield more limited rights than rights of full ownership?[8] What constitutes the boundary of one's labor? If one puts up a fence around ten acres of land does one come to own all of the land within or merely the fence and the land it sits on?[9] And finally, if the skills, tools, and inventions used in laboring are social products should not society have some claim on the laborer's property?[10]

Among defenders of Lockean-based arguments for private property, these challenges have not gone unnoticed.[11] My goal in this chapter is not to answer these challenges or to rehearse the various strands of Lockean labor-mixing arguments. What I am particularly interested in is Locke's proviso that justified acquisitions must leave "enough and as good for others." This restriction on acquisitive behavior is what Robert Nozick called "the Lockean proviso."[12] "For this labor being the unquestionable property of the laborer, no man but he can have a right to what that is once joined to, at least where there is *enough and as good left for others*."[13]

The primary focus of this chapter is to examine and clarify a number of important issues that surround the use of Locke's proviso. What does it mean to leave enough and as good for others and can such a requirement, in any way, justify rights to control what is found in the commons? My hope is that by examining the property theories of Robert Nozick and David Gauthier, and in particular their distinct uses of Locke's proviso, we will be able to overcome certain problems that proviso-based theories of property have faced and move toward a defensible theory that justifies the control of both tangible goods and intellectual works.

A Historical and Topical Examination of the Lockean Proviso

Robert Nozick offers a sketch of a theory of justified entitlement incorporating a version of Locke's proviso. Nozick claims that the proviso should be understood as requiring that the situation of others not be worsened by one's acquisitive behavior. Thus, for Nozick, the proviso is a necessary condition for justified appropriation. As each new interpretation of the proviso is offered, I will examine it as a sufficient condition as well as a necessary condition. Hopefully, by preceding this way the strengths and weaknesses of proviso-based property theories will be clarified.

Nozick's Theory of Acquisition

In answering the question, "what counts as being worsened by another's appropriation?" Nozick offers two possibilities. One way a person could be worse-off is,

> by losing the opportunity to improve his situation by a particular appropriation or any one (or any appropriation)14

On this reading, a necessary condition for justified acquisition is that others not lose out in terms of opportunities to improve their situation through appropriation. A proviso incorporating this way to be worsened would be:

> NP1: A process normally giving rise to a property right in a previously unowned thing will not do so if the position of others is worsened in terms of lost opportunities to acquire.

The objection to NP1 is that it leaves us with what Nozick calls the reverse domino problem.[15] Imagine some person, Z, who cannot appropriate anything because everything has been appropriated and is thereby worse-off in terms of lost opportunities to improve his situation. Now person Y, who appropriated the last bit of the commons, has violated the proviso and her acquisition is illegitimate. Y's acquisitions are illegitimate because this will leave Z with no opportunities to improve his situation through appropriation. But if Y's acquisitions violate the proviso because of Z's lost opportunities, then the acquisitions of X (the person who appropriated just before Y) are illegitimate because of Y's lost opportunities. This process continues back to A, who finds his acquisitions in violation of the proviso.

Nozick argues that this proviso is too strong—i.e., it does not capture what it means to be worsened and requires what almost no acquisition could satisfy. If some individual appropriates a grain of sand from an endless beach are others worsened because they cannot now improve their position by using *that* grain of sand? More-over, suppose that a superb manager of resources acquires the whole of an island where ten individuals live. Suppose further that the new owner employs her ten fellows and compensates them beyond the value they produced or could have produced. Have these individu-als been worsened because they cannot acquire unowned objects from the commons? If the answer is no, then this proviso does not adequately account for what it means to be bettered and worsened and thus fails as a necessary condition.

While Nozick did not consider this, suppose we interpret the pro-viso as a sufficient condition rather than a necessary condition for justified appropriation.[16]

> SP1: If no one's position is worsened by an acquisition in terms of lost opportunities to acquire, then an acquisition is justified.

Assuming that when most objects are appropriated others will be excluded from using them, those individuals who did not appropri-ate them will have lost the opportunity to improve their situation by a specific appropriation and will thereby be worse-off. In fact, any singular appropriation will cause others to be worse-off because they will have lost the opportunity to improve their situation by appropri-ating that object. As before, SP1 is violated when Fred appropriates a grain of sand from a endless beach, because Ginger has lost the opportunity to improve her situation by appropriating *that* same grain of sand (assuming of course that Ginger would be better-off by ap-propriating that grain of sand). This objective account of worsening trivializes the notions of bettering and worsening. Consider the wors-ening that arises when Fred takes a drink of water. His fellows have lost the opportunity to improve their situation by drinking that wa-ter. Certainly these kinds of worsenings are trivial or morally irrel-evant (assuming water is abundant, etc.), so it would seem that SP1 is too strong to be interesting as a sufficient condition.

A general problem with SP1 is that the terms of being worsened are too narrow—it focuses *only* on opportunities to improve one's situation through appropriation. Imagine a case where if Ginger ap-propriates some object it will improve her situation n amount, but if Fred appropriates the object it will improve Ginger's situation $n+1$. Now imagine the case where Ginger is made better-off if Fred ap-propriates everything compared to how she would have been had

Fred not appropriated. Although Ginger has lost all of her opportunities to improve her situation through appropriation her position is still better. The upshot of this is that it is not merely opportunities to improve one's situation through appropriation that count; there are other morally relevant factors present. This is to say that SP1 is not sufficient.

Nozick dismisses a proviso based on the first way of being worsened (NP1) and offers a second way that individuals may be worsened by the acquisitive behavior of their fellows. A person could be worsened,

> by no longer being able to use freely (without appropriation) what he previously could[17]

A proviso incorporating this way to be worsened would be:

> NP2: A process normally giving rise to a property right in a previously unowned thing will not do so if the position of others no longer at liberty to use the thing is thereby worsened.

"With the weaker requirement, we cannot zip back so quickly from Z to A, as in the above argument; for though person Z can no longer appropriate, there may remain some for him to *use* as before."[18] Nozick avoids the regress of the reverse domino problem by adhering to NP2. But surely, one reading of NP2 is too stringent as well. The appropriation of any object will make me worse-off in this sense given that I can no longer freely use the object.

Given a more general reading of NP2, one that considers an individual's overall position and not merely how they fare relative to some particular object that has been acquired, in conditions of scarcity it seems plausible to maintain that individuals can justly acquire and not leave their fellows enough to use. Imagine the classic desert island case where there is little food or fresh water. In this case when individuals appropriate, they will worsen their fellows in terms of liberties to use, yet such acquisitions seem permissible. If so, then we have found a case that shows NP2 is not a necessary condition for justified appropriation.[19]

Suppose, however, that we incorporate this way of being worsened into a proviso interpreted as a sufficient condition:

> SP2: If no one's position is worsened by an acquisition in terms of lost freedoms to use, then the acquisition is justified.

SP2, which sets the terms of being worsened as lost freedoms to use, is also problematic. In a narrow sense we consider how Ginger would be in terms of freedoms to use some particular object after Fred has appropriated the object, compared to her freedoms to use the object before Fred's appropriation.

On this reading SP2 is too strong to be interesting because any appropriation will cause others to lose the freedom to use what was appropriated. Once everything has been appropriated everyone will be worse-off in this sense, even those who have appropriated a generous amount of the commons (each will have fewer freedoms to use things).

A defender of SP2 might claim that this is too fast and move to a more general reading of the proviso. Maybe it is not your loss of liberty to use some particular object that counts—what counts is that you have enough and as good left over to use. Nozick implies that at some point appropriation of the commons will stop, leaving individuals in a world where some property remains in the commons and other property is held exclusively. Imagine a world where half of the objects, including land, were held in common (as if it were still in the state of nature) while the other half had been appropriated (maybe it is the proviso itself that halts appropriation). It might be argued that in this case the proviso is satisfied. Those who have appropriated have not made their fellows worse-off because there is plenty left to use. But we may ask why? Given the appropriation of some object by another, there is now something that you cannot use. Why is it the case that this limitation of your freedom does not count as worsening? I will flag this question for later consideration.

There is a case which I call the "exploited worker case" that shows this general version of SP2 to be too weak—i.e., it does not pick out all morally relevant worsenings surrounding legitimate appropriation. It should be clear that this is a problem with the terms of being worsened. Suppose Fred appropriates all of the land on an island and offers Ginger a job at slightly higher earnings than she was able to achieve by living off of the commons. Although Ginger is worse-off in terms of liberties to freely use, she has secured other benefits that serve to cancel out this worsening. So far so good. But now suppose in a few months Ginger would have independently discovered a new gathering technique that would have augmented her earnings fivefold. Having achieved this success she would have gone on

to discover even better techniques, ultimately ending in a fully satiated life in the commons. Instead, Ginger spends her life working in
quiet drudgery and Fred becomes fully satiated.[20]

This is actually a case where SP2 is violated and the compensation offered does not take into account Ginger's opportunities to use
things in the future. Ginger has been compensated for her loss of
freedoms to use things at the time of appropriation but is still worsened in terms of future opportunities to improve her situation by
using things. Part of Ginger's wealth *now* may be her opportunities
to use more things at some future time. The first conclusion to be
drawn from the exploited worker case is that SP2 lacks opportunity
costs and thus allows morally relevant worsenings to occur.

Furthermore, even if opportunity costs to use were incorporated,
SP2 would be unsuitable as a proviso. An individual might be left
unaffected in terms of his opportunities to use things but still be
worsened in terms of lost opportunities to acquire wealth. Certainly
there is a difference between opportunities to use and opportunities
to acquire a particular level of material well-being, for the latter may
only be possible given the security of tenure that is not guaranteed
by mere use.

Consider SP2' where worsening is measured in terms of freedoms
and opportunities to use things. SP2' differs from SP2 only because
SP2' contains opportunity costs surrounding use. Now consider the
exploited worker case again, only this time imagine that Fred has
compensated Ginger for her future opportunities to use things as
well as her current freedoms to use things. Suppose further that Ginger had (before Fred's appropriation) certain opportunities to improve her situation through appropriation above and beyond her
opportunities to improve her situation through mere use.[21] What the
exploited worker case shows (in this context) is that it is not only
opportunities to use things freely that matter, but other opportunities
may count as well. In this case (when we know for certain of Ginger's
future earnings) opportunities to acquire wealth or to earn more seem
relevant to Fred's appropriation. Gauthier echoes Locke and reminds
us of this point:

> Clearly it is not enough to leave others as they were before, able to carry on with their
> present activities and to reap benefits equal to those attained in the past, if one also
> deprives them of opportunities previously available for bettering themselves without
> affording them new alternatives.[22]

In summary, SP2 fails as a sufficient condition for original acqui-sition because it does not incorporate opportunity costs and SP2' (which builds in opportunities to use) is inadequate because it fails to incorporate opportunities to acquire or own. Moreover, what we think is wrong about Fred acquiring so much that it interferes with Ginger's opportunities to use is also present in the case of her oppor-tunities to acquire. Although Nozick correctly identifies the Paretian, or no harm no foul, intuition that grounds the proviso, he neither adequately defines what it means to be better-off or worse-off nor seriously considers the baseline problem—bettered or worsened rela-tive to what? David Gauthier's property theory characterizes the baseline situation and gives an account of bettering and worsening in terms of subjective preference satisfaction that sharply contrasts with Nozick's objective account. We will now turn to Gauthier's theory.

Gauthier's Modified Lockean Proviso

Gauthier uses his version of the Lockean proviso as a general constraint on action to ensure that the initial bargaining position (where we agree about the benefits and burdens of social interac-tion) is fair.[23] The proviso provides a fair bargaining position be-cause it provides for basic rights and thus eliminates prior predation and parasitism from undermining the force of the agreement.[24] If an agreement is made under duress of some sort—suppose a gun is pointed at someone or a forceful threat has been made—then it can hardly be claimed that the obligations generated from the agreement are binding.

Gauthier interprets the Lockean proviso so that it prohibits wors-ening the situation of another, through interaction with that person, except to avoid worsening one's own position. The base point for determining bettering and worsening is how those affected would be in your absence (see P3/B2 in Table 4.1) and the terms of being worsened are determined by preference satisfaction. "We may treat 'better' and 'worse' as unproblematic; one situation is better for some person than another, if and only if it affords him greater expected utility."[25] Expected utility, for Gauthier, is couched in terms of sub-jective preference satisfaction. Consider the following proviso:

P3: If no one's position is worsened (in terms of subjective preference satisfaction) by another's action compared to how they would be were the action-taker absent, then the action is permitted.

Gauthier uses P3 to assign basic rights in the following way. Each individual, in the absence of others, may expect to use his own powers but not theirs. How one would be in the *absence* of others provides the base point of comparison. Continued use of one's own body and capacities in the presence of others may fail to better their situation but it does not in itself worsen their situation (compared to how they would be in your absence). Finally, using the body and powers of another, in interfering with their own use, does worsen their situation and is therefore prohibited:

> Thus the proviso, in prohibiting each from bettering his situation by worsening that of others, but otherwise leaving each free to do as he pleases, not only confirms each in the use of his own powers, but in denying to others the use of those powers, affords to each the exclusive use of his own.[26]

Gauthier concludes that each individual's rights to their body and powers is thus justified.

When Gauthier moves to justify property rights in external objects he switches the baseline and thus we have a new version of P3 (see P3' below). His justification of property rights takes the following form:

> We must ask whether someone, in seeking exclusive use of land or other goods, violates the proviso, bettering her situation through worsening that of others. If not, then we must ask whether some other person, in interfering with a claim to exclusive use, violates the proviso. If so then the proposed right is established.[27]

Gauthier's version of the Lockean proviso for acquisition (P3') holds that Eve cannot better her situation (by acquiring some particular object) through worsening the situation of Adam. The baseline or context is how Adam would be in the acquisitive case (where Eve had appropriated some particular object) compared to the non-acquisitive case (where the object was left in the commons):

> P3': If no one's position is worsened (in terms of subjective preference satisfaction) by another's acquisition compared to how they would be were the acquired object left in the commons, then the acquisition is permitted.

Gauthier points out that, ". . . although Eve intends to better her situation in relation to her fellows, she need not seek to bring this about by worsening their situation."[28] Her fellows do lose the freedom to use the part of the commons that Eve has appropriated, but given that Eve's plot of land is not overly large, they may receive other benefits as well. Gauthier argues:

> Planned intensive cultivation made possible by her security of tenure may well make it possible for her to live better on a part of the island sufficiently small that the others would also be better-off, living without her on the remaining land, than they were when all used the entire island in common . . . . Hence her (Eve's) appropriation may enable everyone to improve her situation, in relation to the base point *set by use in common*, so that it does not violate the proviso.[29]

Generally, Gauthier claims that Eve's fellows are not made worse-off so the appropriation does not run afoul of P3'. Furthermore, once Eve's right to the land has been established, any interference or seizure of her property will violate the proviso because the individual seizing Eve's property is making himself better-off by worsening her position. Gauthier concludes that Eve's right to the plot of land is thus vindicated.[30]

To take stock of our results and to clarify the issues we must consider, I offer the following Proviso/Baseline table. Be aware that this table represents only a small sample of the possible baselines and provisos.

Table 4.1
The Baseline Table

	B1: the acquisitive case compared to the commons (no property rights)				B2: the acquisitive case compared to the case where the appropriator is absent			
	B/W as mere use	B/W as use + opps.	B/W as opps. to acq.	B/W as pref. sats.	B/W as mere use	B/W as use + opps.	B/W as opps. to acq.	B/W as pref. sats.
SP1			X					
SP2	X							
SP2'		X						
P3								X
P3'				X				

SP1-P3' are the different provisos. B1 and B2 are baselines. B1 = the acquisitive case where someone appropriates something compared to the commons where there are no property rights. B2 = the acquisitive case compared to the case where the individual who appropriated is absent. B/W = bettering and worsening. Mere use = current freedoms to use things without opportunity costs. opps. to acq. = opportunities to acquire. pref. sats. = preference satisfaction.

Problems for Gauthier

Suppose Adam, who also inhabits the island where Eve resides, prefers that Eve not own any land. In fact, this preference consumes him and generally centers his world—a world where Eve privately owns a plot of land represents a chaotic nightmare for Adam while the actual world, where Eve owns nothing, is one of bliss.[31] If bettering and worsening are couched in terms of subjective preference, then in seeking exclusive rights to the plot of land, Eve worsens Adam's situation. It seems as if Gauthier has forgotten this part of his theory. In trying to vindicate Eve's appropriation of land Gauthier does not discuss the preferences of her fellows, yet for Gauthier it is preferences that count. Gauthier does consider lost opportunities to improve one's situation in terms of wealth and concludes that Eve betters her fellows in this respect. But if bettering and worsening are couched in terms of subjective preferences it is not clear why Gauthier argues as he does.

There are three general problems with allowing the notion of "worse-off" to be explained in terms of subjective preferences when considering the acquisition of goods.[32] The first two problems are based on examples found in Hubin and Lambeth's "Providing For Rights." (See note 24) First, the manipulation of preferences will artificially allow some to bypass the proviso. Imagine the case where a parent shapes a child so that the child prefers that the parent own everything. Any other situation causes the child to be worse-off in terms of preference satisfaction. The parent then appropriates everything he can, hires his child at subsistence wages and lives a full satiated life. The proviso has been effectively bypassed through the manipulation of preferences.

Second, individuals with quirky or odd preferences will be able to legitimately stop specific appropriations. Given a sufficiently odd preference, one individual may be able to halt all appropriation. Imagine the case where Adam prefers to own everything, and anything less will devastate him psychologically. Upon appropriating a grain of sand from an endless beach Eve violates the proviso making Adam worse-off in terms of subjective preference satisfaction.[33]

Finally, if compensation is allowed to rectify a worsening caused by an appropriation and the compensation must be proportionate to the loss, then those who lose big in terms of subjective preferences will acquire more compensation (maybe lost preferences can be compensated by the fulfillment of other preferences). Suppose the compensation required to rectify the worsening caused by an acquisition must fully compensate—i.e., it must return the individual to his pre-appropriation level of utility. Now, the preference that "Adam gets everything" is very dear to him and Eve's appropriation of a grain of sand causes him great psychological distress calling for considerable compensation. This is a problem for P3' because worsening will be allowed so long as compensation is paid. But if the amount of compensation depends on the value of some subjective preference (and maybe its intensity), then the compensation mechanism of the proviso will be askew in some cases.

Imagine a case where most of us think that a legitimate appropriation of the commons has taken place. Consider the small rock appropriator Fred. Fred has been living in the commons for some time and decides one day to polish a small rock into a marble. He randomly selects a rock from the almost endless supply found on earth and begins laboring. After a week of work Fred finishes, satisfied with his somewhat imperfect but smooth marble.

This example provides a general case against P3'. It might be that Ginger prefers that Fred not appropriate the small rock, so in seeking exclusive rights to the rock Fred violates P3'. Surely this seems an odd conclusion given the abundance of small rocks. Fred *has* left "enough and as good" for his fellows. Our imaginary case finds its force in that there is a sufficient amount of material for others to use and appropriate after the appropriation—i.e., his fellows are left with the same opportunities (in the relevant sense) to improve their situation as they were before Fred's appropriation.

Furthermore, there are a host of problems surrounding the baseline that Gauthier chooses. The baseline or context is how Ginger would be in the acquisitive case (where Fred had appropriated some particular object) compared to the non-acquisitive case (where the object was left in the commons). But how do we characterize the commons? Imagine that if Fred did not appropriate the object Eve would have destroyed it through careless use. Is what Eve does (hypothetically) with the object part of Ginger's baseline situation in the commons? If not, why not? Suppose that if Fred does not appropriate some object it will be appropriated jointly by Ginger and Eve. Is this counterfactual part of Ginger's baseline situation? Naively, we might claim that the only relevant counterfactual situation that counts is where the object in question is forever left in the commons. But this artificially restricts the baseline situation without argument. Suffice it to say, any adequate theory of property rights based on the proviso must clarify the baseline situation while providing an argument for a specific characterization of that context.

In summary, this historical and topical examination of the proviso has shown that neither SP2 nor P3'[34] capture all of the morally relevant worsenings that surround the acquisition of property and therefore neither can serve as a sufficient condition for legitimate acquisition meant to ensure that no one is made worse-off.[35] SP2 lacks a provision for opportunity costs and, even if such a provision were incorporated, SP2 would still be inadequate. An individual might be left unaffected in terms of his opportunities to use things, but still be worsened in terms of lost opportunities to acquire wealth. P3' seems hopelessly mired in preference manipulation problems. These problems surround the terms of being worsened, but there also appear to be equally damaging problems with the context or baseline of P3'— and this point could be made with respect to each version of the proviso that we have covered. Finally, we are left where we started. Although SP1 has its difficulties I will argue in the second part of this chapter it can be salvaged.

Values, Opportunities, and the Baseline Problem

Although fault has been found with Nozick's objective and Gauthier's subjective account of bettering and worsening, an adequate account of bettering and worsening can still be given. As indicated by the cases we have been considering, it seems that any adequate account of bettering and worsening will include as valuable wealth or material well-being and opportunities to better ourselves in terms of material well-being. Wendy Gordon insightfully recognizes that "What needs to be established is not simply whether harm is done, but rather whether there is unjustified or wrongful harm."[36] Here, in the most general terms, I am worried about acquisitions that cause unjustifiable harm.

If "bettering," "worsening," "material standing" (wealth), and "opportunities to increase one's material standing" are to be defined, a theory of value must be adopted and defended. The sketch of a theory of value that follows is not intended to be complete. There are no knockdown arguments forthcoming that illuminate the following sketch as unassailable. Alas, that is another project.[37] What is offered are weak and widely held views about value theory and deeper moral commitments.

A Sketch of a Theory of Value[38]

Human well-being or flourishing is the sole standard of intrinsic value. There are at least two reasons to accept this view. First, happiness or flourishing is what is generally aimed at by everyone and second, it seems absurd to ask what someone wants happiness or well-being for. Although the fact that everyone aims at well-being or flourishing does not establish it as the sole standard of intrinsic value, it does lend credibility to the claim that flourishing is valuable. Moreover, given that well-being is not merely an instrumental good, it is plausible to maintain that it is intrinsically good.[39] Finally, well-being or flourishing is general in scope, meaning that it can accommodate much of what seems intuitively correct about other candidates for intrinsic value (e.g., pleasure, love, friendship).

Human beings or persons are rational project pursuers, and well-being or flourishing is attained through the setting, pursuing, and completion of life goals and projects. Both of these claims are empirical in nature. Humans just are the sort of beings that set, pursue, and complete life goals and projects. Project pursuit is one of many distinguishing characteristics of humans compared to non-humans—this is to say that normal adult humans are, by nature, rational project pursuers. The second empirical claim is that only through rational project pursuit can humans flourish—i.e., a necessary condition for well-being is rational project pursuit. Certainly this view is plausible. A person who does not set, pursue, or complete any life goals or projects cannot be said to flourish in the sense of leading a good life—in much the same way that plants are said not to flourish when they are unhealthy or when they do not get enough sunlight or nourishment.

To say that a life plan or project is rational is to say that it accommodates both general and specific facts about human nature. A general fact about human nature is that humans are project pursuers or that humans covet things. Specific facts are facts about specific individuals like Crusoe cannot jump more than three inches and is under six feet tall. If Crusoe's life plan is to obtain a starting job as a center in the NBA his project is irrational. As things stand, and assuming that he has no other special capacities, Crusoe will not achieve his goals and is therefore not aiming at the good.

My position concerning rationality is clearly anti-Humean. A distinguishing feature of Humean and neo-Humean accounts of rationality, at least as I understand them, is the view that ends, goals, or lifelong projects, are not the proper subjects of rational appraisal. On this view, individuals just have ends, goals, or desires, and rationality is merely a kind of means to ends efficiency. The rational person is one who takes the most efficient steps to satisfy her desires, even if the desires are questionable in certain respects. If your end is to eat chocolate ice cream until a gustatory rejection occurs, then there will be one way, or a number of equally good ways, to satisfy this desire. Preceding, straightway, to the ice cream store and beginning the binge may be the most efficient means to this end. If so, then on the Humean account we would call this person "rational."

In one way I think that Hume was correct. Whatever your ends, there are more efficient and less efficient ways of achieving them. Where I part company with this view is by advocating that ends, goals, or desires can be rationally appraised. This is just to say that means to ends rationality is not the whole of rationality. To call an action or a plan of action rational is also to reflectively endorse the end or goal. Let me give an example that clearly distinguishes my view from the Humean view. Suppose that you wanted to see how long you could survive by consuming nothing but your own body parts. If you carry out this end in an efficient manner, then the Humean will have to call you rational. On my view, while we may call you efficient given your end, the end and your pursuit of it would be considered manifestly irrational—certainly not something which can be reflectively endorsed. Obviously these are contentious issues. My goal here, is not to defend a particular conception of rationality, but to indicate the plausibility of non-Humean accounts.[40]

Lastly, I would like to say something about why one's relations to external physical goods and opportunities to better one's material standing are valuable. Whatever life project or goal is chosen, within the constraints already in place, individuals will need to use physical objects.[41] This should not be taken as an argument for private property, but rather as a claim that material relations and opportunities to better oneself in terms of material relations are objectively valuable. So far, the scope and form of the material relations and opportunities are left open.

Bettering and Worsening

We are now in a position to define "bettering" and "worsening" in terms of material standing or wealth, and opportunities to increase one's wealth. For now, assume a state of nature situation where there are no formal property relations similar to a system of private property. Bettering and worsening are measured in terms of material standing or wealth and opportunities to increase one's material standing. Lysander Spooner voices a similar view:

> The term *wealth* properly includes every conceivable object, idea, and sensation, that can either contribute to, or constitute, the physical, intellectual, moral, or emotional well-being of man. . . On the other hand, if we admit a right of property in incorporeal things at all, then *ideas* are as clearly legitimate subjects of property, as any other incorporeal things that can be named. They are, in their nature, necessarily personal possessions; they have value; they are the products of labor; they are indispensable to the happiness, well-being, and even subsistence of man; they can be possessed by one man, and not by another; they can be imparted by one man to another . . .[42]

As stated, the view that bettering and worsening should be explicated in terms of material well-being is not quite right because any acquisition will cause others to lose the opportunity to use or acquire, assuming that the opportunity is legitimate. Crudely, it is not how you fare *vis-à-vis* some particular object that determines your legitimate wealth, income, and opportunities to obtain wealth.[43] Imagine someone protesting your acquisition of a grain of sand from an endless beach, claiming that she can now no longer use *that* grain of sand and has thereby been worsened. What is needed is an "all things considered view" of material well-being or wealth, income, and opportunities to acquire wealth. A better interpretation of "worsening" and "bettering" is that we are concerned with keeping others at the same *level* of material well-being. To be able to achieve or sustain a certain *level* of material well-being is important because it determines the range of individual physical activity which directly affects project pursuit. Suppose it is the case that before Crusoe's appropriation of some object, Friday's current level of material well-being is Z, and it remains Z after Crusoe's appropriation. Crusoe's appropriation would then be justified on grounds of Friday's current level of well-being. But there are also Friday's future opportunities to achieve a certain level of material well-being to consider. It is only when Crusoe's appropriation leaves Friday no worse-off in both of these senses, or Crusoe pays compensation, that an appropriation is justified. If, in the state of nature, Friday gathered five bushels of apples a day to eat before Crusoe's appropriation of a plot of land and Friday's situation remains the same after the appropriation (Friday still gathers five bushels of apples a day in the same amount of time) and gathering five bushels of apples a day exhausts Friday's opportunities to improve his situation, then Crusoe has not made Friday worse-off and the proviso is satisfied. This would amount to a "no loss" requirement in terms of Friday's level of well-being.

At a specific time each individual has a certain set of things she can freely use and other things she owns, but she also has certain opportunities to use and appropriate things. This complex set of opportunities along with what she can now freely use or has rights over constitutes her position materially—this set constitutes her level of well-being. We can think of an individual's level of material well-being as her standard of living with opportunity costs. An example may be helpful. Imagine Crusoe stranded on a desert island where there is no chance of rescue and no other material except the sand on the island. Crusoe has a very low level of material well-being. His opportunities are extremely limited and there is little available for him to use or appropriate. If someone were to acquire a grain of sand from the island would Crusoe be worsened? The answer is negative given that Crusoe would have the same level of material well-being after the acquisition of the grain of sand as he did before the acquisition (including opportunities). Now, if someone tried to acquire all of the sand on the island Crusoe would be worsened. The one material item (loosely speaking) he has that offers him any advantage is the island itself. Clearly, to take this material away from him worsens his situation.

We find a more complex example of an individual's level of well-being with Fred the small rock appropriator. Suppose Fred is living in the commons on a large island suitably stocked with resources. The only other person around is Crusoe who lives as Fred does. Neither thinks to appropriate anything; they merely use things and then discard them. Given the abundance of resources, Fred and Crusoe have a certain level of well-being. Fred can use things so long as Crusoe is not using them and vice versa. They also have certain opportunities to use things and opportunities to appropriate things. One day Fred appropriates a small rock that is one of many on the island. We may ask, is Crusoe worsened by this taking? Given that he can reach down and pick up a similar rock on practically any part of the island it would appear not. Materially, Crusoe is at same level as he was before the appropriation. Moreover, it could be the case that in terms of his level of well-being, which includes opportunity costs, Crusoe is in a better position. Fred's appropriation might actually augment Crusoe's opportunities to acquire wealth or use things as in Gauthier's example where Eve appropriates a plot of land.

Generally, an adequate proviso on original acquisition will incorporate an "all things considered" or general reading for the following reasons. The particular object is not important, so long as there is an ample supply of other things (that are similar or practically indistinguishable from the item acquired—that are substitutable) that can be used or acquired freely. What difference does it make whether or not you can use some particular object in conditions of abundance? Locke claims, and rightly so, that an acquisition "can be of prejudice to no man" when there is enough and as good left over. It does not count as worsening when someone has been deprived of using or acquiring a particular object provided relative abundance —i.e., her *level* of material well-being might be unchanged. In fact, it would be unreasonable to complain about such supposed worsening. Imagine an individual who claims to have been worsened because you have deprived her of inhaling the air you just inhaled.

Furthermore, even in cases of scarcity, an "all things considered" view is warranted. Recall the case where Ginger is made better-off if Fred appropriates some object compared to how she would have been had Fred not appropriated.[44] Although Ginger cannot improve her situation materially through the appropriation of the object in question, her "all things considered" position is still better. The claim is that in conditions of abundance or scarcity it is not some particular object that is morally relevant, it is an individual's overall level of well-being that counts.

Opportunity Costs

So far, there has been a lot of hand waving about opportunities and the worth of opportunities, but we may ask what are opportunities and what are they worth? Moreover, how would one compensate another for lost opportunities? Given that an adequate account of bettering and worsening will incorporate opportunity costs, an examination of opportunities and opportunity costs is necessary.

Although no precise definition of an opportunity will be provided, the following list of features is what I take to be the root idea of an opportunity:

1. Opportunities are future directed;

2. Opportunities are generally probabilistic, which means that most of them are uncertain or contingent;

3. To say that a person has an opportunity is to say that it is possible for them—e.g., one cannot have an opportunity to fly unaided to the moon;

4. Many opportunities (perhaps most) are dependent on place, time, and the actions or preferences of others;

5. Opportunities represent possible improvements in an individual's situation. Assuming that you love life, it would be odd to say that you have the opportunity to die by suffocation.

So what does it mean to say that Ginger has the opportunity to achieve a certain level of material well-being? Crudely, it is to say that in the future Ginger will be at the right time and place to give her a chance to improve her situation materially. Minimally, for Ginger to have an opportunity to do or obtain something, we require that it be possible for her. Furthermore, an opportunity to do or obtain something is not the same as doing it or obtaining it. To say that Ginger has the opportunity to work in a law firm is not to say that she *is* working in a law firm, rather it is to say that if she chooses to take that path she might, one day, work in a law firm. It is also to say that she is in the right place at the right time. If there were no law firms now or in the future there would be no opportunities to work in them.

If a semi-deterministic world and a "God's eye view" is assumed (everything is determined except Ginger), the "chance" element of opportunities can be eliminated. This is basically the view of opportunities found in modern economic theory. Assuming Ginger is the only agent with freewill, the pay-offs of each of her opportunities would be known with certainty. Suppose choosing B yields her n material benefit (compared to the situation she finds herself in before choosing), while choosing C yields her $n+1$ material benefit. For Ginger, choosing B has an opportunity cost attached—she loses the $n+1$ benefit that she would have obtained. Opportunity costs are, for the economist, simply the disadvantages associated with choice among outcomes, where the outcomes are known with certainty. If Ginger chooses B then she loses the opportunity to do C and the benefits C would have given her. If she chooses C then she loses the opportunity to B and the benefits B would have given her.[45] This as an odd result because if both B and C yield the same result (suppose the outcome for both is n) and are mutually exclusive, what is lost? The outcomes are the same, so if B is chosen it seems the only thing that is lost is the bare opportunity to do C. But given the exclusivity of B and C, we cannot even claim to have lost a bare opportunity, because we never had the opportunity to do both. Minimally, and less controversially, we might claim that B (assuming our original example where the pay-off of C was $n+1$ and the pay-off of B was n) has an opportunity cost for Ginger of $+1$.

Given the probabilistic nature of most opportunities, distinctions must be made among opportunities, their results, and contingency. Consider, in Table 4.2, an opportunity to push a button, the results of the opportunity, and the (non-epistemic) probabilistic nature of the opportunity and the result.

Table 4.2
Opportunities Table

	Opportunities that are certain	Contingent or uncertain opportunities
Results that are certain	100% chance of pushing a button and a 100% chance of winning $50 as the result	50% chance of pushing a button and a 100% chance of winning $50 as the result
Results that are uncertain or contingent	100% chance of pushing a button and 50% chance of winning $50 as the result	50% chance of pushing a button and a 50% chance of winning $50 as the result

This relatively simple table becomes more complex when we consider multiple contingent opportunities with multiple contingent results. Imagine the case where my opportunity of getting a job is contingent upon my learning about it and my continued existence, while my chance of actually getting the job is dependent on the number of applicants who are more qualified than I am, the employer offering the job to me, and my acceptance of the job. It is trivial to say that there are some opportunities that are contingent or uncertain—some opportunities have probabilities attached. Right now I have the opportunity to get a job at General Motors (assuming that they are hiring) but, given the economy and my skills, it is highly unlikely. Furthermore, it seems problematic to claim there are opportunities that are certain (independent of results). My opportunity to do or obtain anything is dependent on my existence and thus is contingent and uncertain.[46] For now, the possibility that some opportunities are certain and promise results that are certain will be left open.

In addressing opportunity costs it could be argued that the worth of an opportunity is a function of the probability and the value of the pay-off. The worth of an opportunity is a probabilistically weighted value of the various outcomes—this will include the probability that the action in question will produce the outcome, but also the probability that the action in question is available. If it is certain that the outcome of opportunity B is n, then the value or worth of opportunity B is the value of n (assuming that the opportunity is certain). If there is a .5 chance that a non-contingent opportunity B will yield n, then the value of B is half of the value of n. As a fall-back position we can claim that it is plausible to discount potential benefits if the opportunity or result in question is contingent. It may be sufficient to show that opportunities that have probabilities attached, to either the result or the opportunity itself, are worth less than non-contingent opportunities with results that are certain. There is a monotonic relationship between the probability of an opportunity (and its results) and the value of the opportunity. This is to say as the probability goes up so does the value and vice versa. In a world of uncertain opportunities (and uncertain results), opportunities are not worth their results, they are worth something less. Compensation for lost opportunities may cost less than it would otherwise appear.[47]

The upshot of this discussion is that opportunities can be understood as chances to do or obtain something beneficial and may be worth less than the results they promise. If so, compensation for lost opportunities may be easier than expected. Although the root idea of an opportunity has been examined and some (minimal) information about their worth has been provided, the question of how one would compensate another for lost opportunities must still be considered. Compensation for an individual's lost opportunities could take many forms, ranging from the augmentation of their remaining opportunities, to the creation of new opportunities, to providing other benefits. Moreover, compensation can take place at both the act level and the system level. Fred himself may compensate Ginger by augmenting her opportunities or the system of property relations that they both engage in may provide compensation. This latter form of compensation will be taken up in chapter 6 while the former will occupy us presently.

Consider again the exploited worker case, in which Ginger's opportunities to achieve a certain level of material well-being have been eliminated by Fred's appropriation of the entire island that they both inhabit. It is claimed that Ginger has been worsened but suppose that, instead of offering Ginger a wage that equals her independent income in the commons, Fred offers her a higher wage that accounts for her future material success (this might include allowing her to buy part of the island, etc.). Although Fred has eliminated many of Ginger's opportunities, he has created new opportunities for her or supplied her with other benefits. In such a case, it seems that Ginger is not worsened in any morally relevant sense and Fred's appropriation is thus justified.[48] Suffice it to say that act level compensation can and does occur.[49] But further clarification of this kind of compensation requires consideration of the final major problem surrounding the implementation of a proviso—the baseline problem.

The Baseline Problem

The starting point, which sets the context of the baseline, is the state of nature which is characterized as that initial state where no injustice has occurred. Moreover, in the state of nature the moral landscape has yet to be changed by formal property relations. Indeed, it would be odd to assume that individuals come into the world with complex property relations already intact with the universe—that individuals or groups have some "built in" Honoréan[50] rights to the universe or parts of the universe. Prima facie, the assumption that the world is devoid of such property relations seems much more plausible.[51] The moral landscape is barren of such relations until some process occurs. It is not assumed that the process for changing the moral landscape the Lockean would advocate is the only justified means to this end.[52]

We may challenge this view of the baseline. Why is it the case that the only two situations that are to be compared are the acquisitive case and the commons? Why not compare the case where Fred appropriated something (the acquisitive case) to the case where Fred had not appropriated but someone else had? Further still, why not compare the case where Fred has appropriated something to the case where Fred and Ginger had incorporated the object in a system of joint ownership?[53]

For now, assume a state of nature situation where no injustice has occurred (no violations of body rights) and where there are no material relations in terms of use, possession, or rights. Each individual in this state has a specific level of material well-being based on legitimate opportunities to increase her material standing. All anyone has in this initial state are opportunities to increase their material standing because it is assumed that there are no current material relations of any sort. Suppose Fred acquires an object and does not worsen his fellows—alas, all they had were contingent opportunities and Fred's taking adequately benefits them in other ways. After the acquisition Fred's level of material well-being has changed. Now, he has a material possession that he holds legitimately, as well as all of his previous opportunities.[54] Along comes Ginger who acquires some other object and considers if her exclusion of it will worsen Fred. But what two situations should Ginger compare? Should the acquisitive case (Ginger's acquisition) be compared to Fred's initial state (where he had not yet legitimately acquired anything) or to Fred's situation immediately before Ginger's taking? It seems clear that because an individual's level of material well-being changes the baseline must also change. If bettering and worsening are to be cashed out in terms of an individual's level of material well-being and this measure changes over time, then the baseline of comparison must also change. In the current case we compare Fred's level of material well-being when Ginger possesses and excludes some object to Fred's level of material well-being immediately before Ginger's acquisition.

Some have argued that individuals who cannot acquire objects from an unowned state have been worsened. No one today has the opportunity to acquire an acre of unowned land in Ohio and it might be claimed that they are worse-off than they would have been because of this fact.[55] This view is mistaken. The acquisition of land took place in a certain context of material well-being and opportunities. The baseline is how the individual is now, compared to how they would have been had they acquired land from an unowned state (or had the opportunity to acquire land from an unowned state). There can be no doubt that an individual's level of well-being is higher now than it would have been had they been able to acquire unowned land at the time of original acquisition. This view is summed nicely by David Schmidtz:

> Philosophers who write on the subject of original appropriation tend to speak as if people who arrive first, and thus do all the appropriating, are much luckier than those who came later. The truth is, first appropriators begin the process of resource creation while latecomers like ourselves get most of the benefits. Consider the Jamestown colony of 1607. Exactly what was it, we should ask, that made their situation so much better than ours? Of course, they never had to worry about being overcharged for car repairs. They were never awakened in the middle of the night by noisy refrigerators, or leaky faucets, or flushing toilets. They never had to agonize over the choice of long-distance telephone companies. Are those the things that make us wish we had gotten there first?[56]

All things considered, individuals are better-off now even though they can no longer acquire land (and many other goods) from an unowned state. In this, and in many ways, we stand on the shoulders of those who came before.

I have claimed that bettering and worsening should (in part?) be cashed out in terms of an individual's level of well-being, including opportunity costs, and that the baseline of comparison should be how you are now, after my acquisition, compared to how you were immediately before my acquisition. But consider the following counterexample to my account. What if a perverse inventor creates a machine that will save lives but decides to not allow anyone to use the machine. Those individuals who had, before the creation, no chance (opportunity) to survive now have a chance and are worsened because of the perverse inventor's refusal to let others use the machine.

But the baseline this case implies cannot be correct. On this view, to determine bettering and worsening we are to compare how individuals are before the creation of some value (in this case the life saving machine) to how they would be if they possessed or consumed that value. But we are all worsened in this respect by any value that is created and held exclusively. I am worsened by your exclusive possession of your car because I would be better-off if I exclusively controlled the car. Any individual, especially those who have faulty hearts, would be better-off if they held title to my heart compared to anyone else's holding the title. I am also worsened when you create a new philosophical theory and claim authorship—I would have been better-off (suppose it is a valuable theory) if I had authored the theory, so you have worsened me. Clearly this account of the baseline makes the notions of bettering and worsening too broad.[57]

The result of this lengthy discussion of material well-being, opportunity costs, and the baseline problem is the following proviso on original acquisition:[58]

> SP4: If an acquisition makes no one worse-off in terms of their level of material well-being (including opportunity costs) compared to their level of material well-being immediately before the acquisition, then the taking is permitted.

Test Cases

One way to test this new proviso (SP4) is to see how it handles the tough cases. Easy cases will be considered initially, and then more difficult cases will be examined. Consider, once again, Fred the small rock appropriator. In appropriating a small rock, he does not make his fellows worse-off in terms of their level of material well-being, given the abundance of small rocks. In this case, where scarcity is not an issue, SP4 yields the proper result. If someone objects Fred can say, and rightly so, "Get your own rock."[59]

Another test case is the only-water-hole-in-the-desert example. Imagine Fred trying to appropriate the only water hole in a desert, where many individuals are dependent upon the water for survival. In trying to obtain exclusive rights to the water, Fred makes his fellows worse-off, for without the water, all of their opportunities to acquire wealth along with their ability to maintain their current level of well-being are eliminated. In this case of extreme scarcity water is important material. Notice that we have a case of worsening regardless of the preferences of Fred's fellows. They may all actually prefer that Fred own the water and charge starvation prices for it. SP4 gives us the desired result in this case. The appropriation would be illegitimate unless compensation is paid.

It is also the case that SP4 would correctly adjudicate the exploited worker case where Fred appropriates everything and offers Ginger a wage that benefits her only slightly above what she could earn by herself in the commons.[60] Part of Ginger's well-being in the commons is her opportunities to achieve a higher level of material well-being at some later time. In appropriating the island, Fred effectively eliminates these opportunities and thus drives Ginger below what we have found to be a morally relevant base point. Fred's appropriations may still be legitimate, but only if he compensates Ginger for her lost opportunities to achieve a certain standard of living.

To take a famous example, consider the Robinson Crusoe case. Crusoe has a certain level of well-being and, supposing that he will never be rescued, his opportunities for material improvement are slim. Given there are no others around Crusoe appropriates the only fruit tree on the island. The reason he gives to justify his appropriation is that no one else has been worsened. Now suppose Friday washes ashore dying of scurvy and tries to eat from the fruit tree. Can Crusoe exclude Friday from this scarce resource? Part of Friday's opportunities to achieve any level of material well-being depend on his being able to freely use the fruit from the tree. That Crusoe did not know this does not matter.[61] But now things get tricky. What if Crusoe had saved the tree from dying and spent years laboring to nurture it back to health? In this case it seems that a labor or desert principle runs headlong into SP4.

Suppose that if Crusoe did not acquire and exclude the tree it would have died and Friday would have had no opportunities to use or acquire parts of the tree. In this case we look at Friday's level of material well-being the moment before Crusoe's acquisition which includes a dim future. The moment before Crusoe's acquisition Friday has no opportunities to use or acquire the tree because the tree's existence depends on Crusoe's acquisition. In this case SP4 would allow the appropriation of the tree by Crusoe.

Conclusion

I would like to conclude the chapter by summarizing a few important results. In conditions of abundance, the use of SP4 justifies individual acts of appropriation. This applies to relatively non-controversial cases like the appropriation of a grain of sand or Fred the small rock appropriator. Furthermore, in more controversial cases like Gauthier's Eve example, it is possible that land, as well as other relatively scarce goods, can be appropriated. In general, the theory represents Locke's intuition that so long as there is "enough and as good" an appropriation is of prejudice to no one and is therefore justified. This is a non-trivial result that, in part, solves Locke's original question—we have found a way for individuals to *unilaterally* generate rights to previously unowned objects.[62]

Notes

1. John Locke, *The Second Treatise of Government*, ed. T. Peardon (New York, Liberal Arts Press, 1952, Bobbs-Merrill Publishing, 1952), § 27.
2. Becker, *Property Rights: Philosophic Foundations* (London: Routledge & Kegan Paul 1977), 32.
3. There are several distinct strands to the Lockean argument. See Becker, *Property Rights*, 32-56.
4. A. John Simmons voices these problems in *The Lockean Theory of Rights* (Princeton, NJ: Princeton University Press, 1992), 267-69.
5. Jeremy Waldron, "Two Worries about Mixing One's Labor," *Philosophical Quarterly* (January 1983): 37, 40. David Hume, *Treatise of Human Nature*, 3.2.3.: "we cannot be said to join our labor to any thing except in a figurative sense."
6. Robert Nozick, *Anarchy, State, and Utopia* (New York: Basic Books, 1974), 175.
7. P. J. Proudhon, *What is Property?*, originally published in 1867, (New York: Howard Fertig, 1966), 61, and John Plamenatz, *Man and Society* (London: Longmans, Green, 1963), 1:247.
8. Geraint Perry, *John Locke* (London: Allen & Unwin, 1978), 52, and Waldron, "Two Worries," 42.
9. Nozick, *Anarchy*, 174, Thomas Maurtner, "Locke on Original Appropriation," *American Philosophical Quarterly* (July 1982): 261.
10. John Rawls, *A Theory of Justice* (Cambridge, MA: Harvard University Press, 1971), 104. Edwin Hettinger, "Justifying Intellectual Property," in *Intellectual Property: Moral, Legal, and International Dilemmas*, edited by A. Moore (Lanham, MD.: Rowman & Littlefield, 1997), chapter 2, 22, 26. Ruth Grant, *John Locke's Liberalism* (Chicago: University of Chicago Press, 1987), 112. I will return to this issue in chapter 7.
11. For example, Simmons in *The Lockean Theory of Rights* provides a complex analysis of Lockean property theory and attempts to answer many of these problems.
12. Nozick, *Anarchy*, 174-82.
13. John Locke, *The Second Treatise of Government*, II-27 (italics mine)
14. Nozick, *Anarchy*, 176
15. Nozick, *Anarchy*, 176. Nozick actually combines both ways to be worse-off (see NP2) into a stringent version of the proviso that he rejects as being too strong. One reason he gives for rejecting the stringent proviso is that the first way to be worse-off leads to the reverse domino problem.
16. Wendy Gordon presents a variation on this account of harm. ". . . the proviso treats only one kind of harm as relevant for property formation purposes: it protects the

propertyless from the depletion of the common." Gordon, "A Property Right in Self-Expression: Equality and Individualism in the Natural Law of Intellectual Property," *Yale Law Journal* 102 (1993): 1564. Surely this account of harm is overly simplistic. What if I deplete the commons yet open up other substantially valuable opportunities for you? Does lessening the commons by taking a grain of sand from an endless beach worsen or harm? What does depleting the commons mean in relation to physical goods or intellectual works?

17.   Nozick, *Anarchy,* 176.

18.   Nozick, *Anarchy,* 176.

19.   I should also note that even if these problems can be answered, satisfying NP2 would not, by itself, justify acquisition. NP2 is a necessary condition that must be joined with other requirements before an acquisition is justified.

20.   Another case similar to the exploited worker case is where Ginger, because she is temporarily sick, has limited capacities to use things. Fred appropriates everything and compensates Ginger for her 'sickly capacities' to use rather than her healthy capacities to use.

21.   There is a difference between mere possession and rights to exclude, use, and augment. One obvious difference is that when one has property rights one can exclude others from possessing or using an object even when the object is not in one's actual possession.

22.   David Gauthier, *Morals By Agreement* (Oxford: Oxford University Press, 1986), 279.

23.   It is important to note that, for Gauthier, the proviso does not have independent moral weight outside of his contractarian argument. For our purposes, we will treat Gauthier's proviso as if it has independent moral weight.

24.   See Don Hubin and Mark Lambeth, "Providing For Rights" in *Dialogue* (1986), for a more detailed discussion of the issues presented in this section.

25.   Gauthier, *Morals By Agreement*, 203. Crudely, subjective preference satisfaction theories hold that satisfying individual preferences or desires is intrinsically valuable. Jeremy Waldron also seems to endorse a subjective account of worsening citing the feelings of "distress" and "bitterness" as possible ways to be harmed. See Jeremy Waldron, "From Authors to Copiers: Individual Rights and Social Values in Intellectual Property" *Chicago-Kent Law Review* 68 (1993): 867.

26.   Gauthier, *Morals By Agreement*, 209.

27.   Gauthier, *Morals By Agreement*, 215.

28.   Gauthier, *Morals By Agreement*, 215.

29.   Gauthier, *Morals By Agreement*, 216 (italics mine).

30.   Gauthier's justification of property rights is actually a two-stage process. If Eve does not violate the proviso, then she obtains possession rights to an object. If taking Eve's object violates the proviso, then Eve has property rights to it.

31.   One could object to this case on the grounds that it depends on individuals taking an interest in one another's interests—this is to say that they have "tuistic" desires. Gauthier assumes that the proviso is intended to apply to interaction under the assumptions of individual utility maximization and mutual unconcern or disinterestedness. For problems with Gauthier's non-tuism assumption, see Don Hubin, "Non-Tuism," in *Canadian Journal of Philosophy* 21 (December 1991): 441-68.

32.   In part, these cases attempt to show the implausibility of maintaining the claim that the *sole* standard of intrinsic value—in fact, that which creates intrinsic value—is the satisfaction of desires and preferences. "It might be enough (*to eliminate the theory as a plausible contender*) to ask whether anyone finds it even possible to

think that goodness could be brought into being by the feeling of some one or other, no matter how vicious or stupid or ignorant he might be." D. Ross, "The Nature of Goodness" in *Readings in Ethical Theory*, edited by Sellers and Hospers (New York : Appleton —Century—Crofts, Inc. 1952) (italics mine).

33.   The objection usually voiced at this point is that the worry depends on an "odd" preference. If we rule out such preferences there is no problem. While this is a plausible strategy I have yet to come across any generally accepted procedure or rule that tells us which preferences count.

34.   Although P3 has not been closely examined it will have many of the same problems as P3'.

35.   Moreover, SP2 and P3' allow, as morally relevant worsenings, things that are not.

36.   Wendy Gordon, "A Property Right in Self-Expression: Equality and Individualism in the Natural Law of Intellectual Property," *Yale Law Journal* 102 (1993): 1545.

37.   The moral principles and claims that follow are part of a larger theory of value and deeper moral commitments. The view is Lockean in spirit and should be taken as an *assumption* in the argument that attempts to justify a system of private property relations based on a Pareto requirement. The explication and defense of a full-blown Lockean moral theory is left for another time.

38.   For similar views, see Rawls, *A Theory of Justice*, chapter VII; Aristotle, *Nicomachean Ethics*, bks. I and X; Kant, *The Fundamental Principles of The Metaphysics of Morals*; Sidgwick, *Methods of Ethics*; R. B. Perry, *General Theory of Value*; Loren Lomasky, *Persons, Rights, and the Moral Community* (Oxford: Oxford University Press, 1987).

39.   See Mill's notorious proof in *Utilitarianism*, chapter IV.

40.   For a defense of a view similar to the one I offer, see Warren Quin's *Morality and Actions*, especially chapter 11, "Rationality and the Human Good." See also, David Schmidtz, *Rational Choice and Moral Agency* (Princeton, NJ: Princeton University Press, 1995).

41.   A life of both intellectual and physical activity is necessary for human flourishing. Minimally the claim is that the individual who does not develop her intellectual capacities or engage in an active intellectual life cannot be said to flourish. Similarly, the individual who does not develop her physical capacities or engage in a robust life of physical activity (including material relations) cannot be said to flourish. Life projects that do not accommodate these general facts are irrational. Once again, a complete picture of what counts as a rational lifelong project will depend on the underlying moral theory and a refined theory of human nature.

42.   Lysander Spooner, *The Law of Intellectual Property* (Weston, MA: M & S Press, 1971), 10, 36 (Originally published in 1855).

43.   Gordon appears to fall prey to this worry. See Wendy Gordon in "A Property Right in Self-Expression: Equality and Individualism in the Natural Law of Intellectual Property," *Yale Law Journal* 102 (1993): 1564, 1574.

44.   Temporarily setting the baseline as Ginger's appropriation of some object compared to Fred's appropriation of it.

45.   See Heinz Kohler, *Scarcity And Freedom* (Lexington, MA: Heath and Company, 1977), or H. G. Heymann and Robert Bloom, *Opportunity Cost In Finance And Accounting* (New York: Quorum Books, 1990). For a more philosophical discussion closer to the views presented in this section, see Michael Levin, "Equality of Opportunity" in *The Philosophical Quarterly* (1981).

46.   Certainly we can cook up science fiction cases where taking some special pill guarantees both our existence and determines that a certain action will be performed.

But assuming that we are essentially contingent beings that have freewill, opportunities that are certain will be rare indeed.

47.   The assumption is that, "if it were the case that *A* then it might be that *B*." There are both epistemic and metaphysical issues attached to this "might conditional." A metaphysical assumption is that there are determinant probabilities that attach to the consequent. An epistemic consideration is how would we determine what the probabilities in question. When determining, epistemically, what some probability would be, it is proposed that we proceed as we normally do when assigning probabilities. Historical facts, previous analogous situations, physical laws, and the like, should be used in assigning the probability of the consequent of a "might conditional."

48.   For now, I will side-step issues like the loss of independence or self-government that may be caused by working for others.

49.   Once again, consider the case where Ginger is better-off, all things considered, if Fred appropriates everything compared to how she would have been had she appropriated everything (maybe Fred is a great manager of resources). Although Ginger has been worsened in some respects she has been compensated for her losses in other respects.

50.   Honoréan rights are: the right to manage, the right to transfer, the right to capital, absence of term, prohibition of harmful use, the right to possess, etc. See the relevant section of chapter 2.

51.   One plausible exception is body rights which are similar to, if not the same as, many of the rights that surround property.

52.   There may be many others such as consent theories, consequentialist theories, social contract theories, theories of convention, and so on.

53.   Wendy Gordon in "A Property Right in Self-Expression: Equality and Individualism in the Natural Law of Intellectual Property," *Yale Law Journal* 102 (1993): 1533-1609, seems to present a shifting baseline and account of harm. For example she writes, "A person who wants access is entitled to complain only if he is worse-off (in regard to the common) when he is denied access than he would have been if the item had never come into existence" (1563). Here it seems, to determine harm, we imagine a fellow in the commons and compare denied access to some object with the non-existence of it. Later we get, "having changed people's position, the inventor cannot then refuse them the tools they need for surviving under their new conditions" (1568). Now it seems we are to consider how someone is when they get to use some object or value compared to how they would be if they didn't get to use the object or value. Either one of these baselines and the account of harm adopted is awash with many of the problems that befall Nozick and Gauthier.

54.   Minus the opportunity to acquire the object he just acquired. But then again, his acquisition and exclusion of some object may create other opportunities as well.

55.   It should be clear that this is a problem with the baseline. Those who give this argument want to compare how they would be now, if they could acquire land from an unowned state, to how they actually are.

56.   David Schmidtz, "The Institution of Property," *Social Philosophy and Policy* 11 (1994): 45.

57.   For a similar, yet still mistaken, view of the baseline see Jeremy Waldron, "From Authors to Copiers: Individual Rights and Social Values in Intellectual Property," *Chicago-Kent Law Review* 68 (1993): 866.

58.   P4 permits the use, exclusion, and augmentation of an object. Although this does not give us a complete theory of property relations, it begins the process. It will be

argued that P4, whatever other forms of property relations it might allow, permits private property relations.

59.   This parallels the case of the person who claims she is worsened when you inhale because she has lost the opportunity to improve her situation by inhaling the very air you did.

60.   Notice that this is a fairly odd case where the results are certain and the opportunity is certain. It is more likely that had Fred not acquired everything Ginger would have only had a chance at future material success.

61.   For simplicity, I will imagine perfect knowledge or a "God's eye" view in these cases. In the real world with actual persons who have limited knowledge, we rely on micro and macro compensation or a principle of rectification. For a brief discussion of what a principle of rectification would look like, see Nozick, *Anarchy,* 151-53.

62.   Moreover, even in conditions of extreme scarcity restricted access to scarce goods might be required. If tragedy of the commons considerations are taken seriously, someone or some group must restrict access or else the resource will be destroyed. In this case, the only way to leave "enough and as good" is to exclude others from the scarce resource. See David Schmidtz, "When is Original Acquisition Required," in *The Monist* 73 (October 1990): 504-18.

5

Toward a Lockean Theory of
Intellectual Property

"Nor was this appropriation of any parcel of land by improving it any prejudice
to any other man, since there was still enough and as good left, and more than the
yet unprovided could use. So that, in effect, there was never the less left for others
because of his enclosure for himself; for he that leaves as much as another can
make use of does as good as take nothing at all."
—John Locke, *The Second Treatise of Government*[1]

Introduction

Most of us would recoil at the thought of shoplifting a ballpoint
pen from the campus bookstore and yet many do not hesitate to
copy software worth thousands of research dollars without paying
for it.[2] When challenged, replies like "I wouldn't have purchased
the software anyway" or "they still have their copy" are given to try
to quell the sinking feeling that something ethically wrong has occurred. Moreover, with the arrival of the information age, where digital formats make copying simple and virtually costless, this asym-
metry in attitudes is troubling to those who would defend Anglo-
American institutions of property protection.

One way of understanding these replies is that they suggest a real
difference between intellectual property and physical or tangible
property.[3] My use of your intellectual property does not interfere
with your use of it, whereas this is not the case for most tangible
goods. Justifying intellectual property in light of this feature raises
deep questions and has led many to abandon the romantic image of
"Lockean labor mixing" in favor of incentives-based, rule-utilitarian justifications. Labor-mixing theories of acquisition may work
well when the objects of property can be used and consumed by
only one person at a time, but they seem to lose force when the

103

objects of property can be used and consumed by many individuals concurrently.

In the following chapter a Lockean theory of intellectual property rights will be explained and defended. Building on the results of chapter 4, I will argue that individual acts of intellectual property appropriation can be justified in reference to Locke's proviso. If successful, the theory will support the intuition that something ethically wrong has occurred when computer software, music, or other intellectual works are pirated.

A Lockean Theory of Intellectual Property

As noted in chapter 3, Anglo-American systems of intellectual property are justified on rule-utilitarian grounds. Rights are granted to authors and inventors of intellectual property "to promote the progress of science and the useful arts."[4] Society seeks to maximize utility in the form of scientific and cultural progress by granting limited rights to authors and inventors as an incentive toward such progress. In general, patents, copyrights, and trade secrets are devices created by statute to prevent the diffusion and use of ideas before the author or inventor has recovered profit adequate to induce investment and creation of these ideas.

Many Lockeans, including myself, would like to provide a more solid foundation for intellectual property. Defenders of robust rights to property, be it tangible or intangible property, argue that something has gone awry with rule-utilitarian justifications. Rights, they claim, stand athwart considerations of utility-maximization or promoting the social good. As noted at the end of chapter 3, there is a kind of global inconsistency to utilitarian justifications of rights within the Anglo-American tradition. Why should my rights to physical property be somehow less subject to concerns of social utility than my rights to intellectual property? Within the Anglo-American tradition, "rights"—to physical property, life, the pursuit of happiness— are typically deontic in nature. Thus in generating rights to intellectual property on utilitarian grounds we are left with something decidedly less than what we typically mean when we say someone has a right.[5] In fact, it may be argued that what has been justified is not a right but something less, something dependent solely on considerations of the overall social good. Alas, if conditions change it may be the case that granting control to authors and inventors over what they produce diminishes overall social utility, and thus on utilitarian grounds society should eliminate systems of intellectual property.

Furthermore, over the past three decades rule-utilitarian moral theory, as well as utilitarian-based justifications for systems of intellectual property, have come under a sustained and seemingly decisive attack.[6] Suffice it to say that even if incentive-based, rule-utilitarian justifications remain viable, their mere viability does not exclude alternative justifications of intellectual property rights.

Before proceeding toward a Lockean theory of intellectual property, I would like to discuss two important differences between intellectual property and physical property. As noted in the opening, intellectual property is non-rivalrous in the sense that it can be possessed and used by many individuals concurrently. Unlike my car or computer, which can only be used by one person at a time, my recipe for spicy Chinese noodles can be used by many individuals simultaneously.

It may be objected that some intellectual works are rivalrous, for example the Mona Lisa or Michelangelo's David. What is rivalrous about these works is not the ideas that are embodied in the canvas or stone—it is the physical works themselves. We can all hang a copy of the Mona Lisa in our living rooms—we just can't have the original embodiment. Consider the following rivalry of goods table.

One way to clarify the non-rivalrous nature of intellectual property is by comparing it with the ownership of physical or tangible property. Physical property rights restrict what can be done with one's

Table 5.1
Rivalry of Goods[7]

	Rival	Non-Rival
	Ordinary Goods:	Copyable Goods: Sets of ideas:
Created	Cars, Computers, Guitars, etc.	Novels, Processes of Manufacture, Computer Programs, etc.
	Natural Resources:	
		Laws of Nature,
Discovered	Coal, Fish, Air, Water, Crude oil, Land, etc.	Mathematical Truths, etc.

property. For example, you cannot justifiably run your car through my house. Tangible property rights also limit intellectual property rights in that you cannot justifiably instantiate your intellectual property, without my consent, in my physical property—you can't build your new static electricity motor out of my nuts and bolts. As with tangible property rights, intellectual property rights restrict what individuals can do with their physical property. You cannot copy my intellectual property and instantiate it in your physical property. The way in which intellectual property is different than tangible property is that rights to intellectual property do not limit other intellectual property rights. My rights to control the set of ideas that comprise my new recipe for spicy Chinese noodles does not limit your rights to control your version of the same recipe. Assuming that we both have legitimate title, our rights are non-rivalrous in this respect.

Another difference between physical and intangible property concerns what is available for acquisition. While matter, owned or unowned, already exists, the same is not true of all intangible works. What is available for acquisition in terms of intangible property can be split into three domains. There is the domain of ideas yet to be discovered (new scientific laws, etc.), the domain of ideas yet to be created (the next *Lord of the Rings*, *Star Wars*, etc.), and the domain of intangible works that are privately owned. Since it is possible for individuals to independently invent or create the same intangible work and obtain rights, we must include currently owned intangible works as available for acquisition.[8] Only the set of ideas that are in the public domain or those ideas that are a part of the common culture are not available for acquisition and exclusion. I take this latter set to be akin to a public park.[9]

Original Acquisition

Following the themes started in chapter 4, we may begin by asking how property rights to unowned objects are generated. This is known as the problem of original acquisition and a common response is given by John Locke. "For this labor being the unquestionable property of the laborer, no man but he can have a right to what that is once joined to, at least where there is *enough and as good left for others*."[10] Moreover, Locke claims that so long as the proviso that enough and as good is left for others is satisfied, an acquisition is of "prejudice to no man."[11] The proviso is generally interpreted as a necessary condition for legitimate acquisition, but I would like to examine it as a sufficient condition.[12] If the appropriation of an unowned object leaves enough and as good for others, then the acquisition and exclusion is justified.

Before continuing, I would like to note that theories of collective ownership also face the problem of original acquisition. Opponents of private property generally champion this problem and claim that it provides a decisive case against individual accumulation of goods. It is rarely recognized that the problem of original acquisition is also a problem for collective ownership as well. Why should the group that arrives first be able to create duties of non-interference against all other groups simply because they arrived first? Certainly, arriving first is morally arbitrary. Why should the first comers, as a group, enjoy the privileged status of controlling the resources in a given geographic location? How can one group, all by itself, unilaterally change the moral landscape and create moral obligations binding countless other groups? Some have tried to answer this problem by noting that collective ownership means 'owned by everyone on earth'—not *group* ownership. But now we have a new group and a new arbitrary line. Why should Martians be excluded, or future generations, or evolved dolphins? Moreover, why does claiming that X is collectively owned, in whatever sense, count as justification for collective control—there is no argument here, just an assertion.[13]

To continue, suppose that mixing one's labor with an unowned object creates a prima facie claim against others not to interfere that can only be overridden by a comparable claim. The role of the proviso is to stipulate one possible set of conditions where the prima facie claim remains undefeated. This view is summed up nicely by Clark Wolf:

> On the most plausible interpretation of Locke's theory, labor is neither necessary nor sufficient for legitimate appropriation. Mixing labor with an object merely supports a presumptive claim to appropriate. The proviso functions to stipulate conditions in which this presumptive claim will be undefeated, or overriding, and will therefore impose duties of noninterference on others.[14]

Whether or not Wolf has interpreted Locke correctly, this view has strong intuitive appeal. Individuals in a pre-property state are at liberty to use and possess objects. Outside of life or death cases it is plausible to maintain that laboring on an object creates a weak presumptive possession and use claim against others. Minimal respect for individual sovereignty and autonomy would seem to support this claim. The proviso merely indicates the conditions under which presumptive claims created by labor, and perhaps possession, are not overridden by the competing claims of others. Another way of stating this position is that the proviso in addition to X, where X is labor or first occupancy or some other weak claim generating activity, provides a sufficient condition for original appropriation.

Justification for the view that labor or possession may generate prima facie claims against others could proceed along several lines. First, labor, intellectual effort, and creation are generally voluntary activities that can be unpleasant, exhilarating, and everything in-between. That we voluntarily do these things as sovereign moral agents may be enough to warrant non-interference claims against others.[15] A second, and possibly related justification, is based on desert. Sometimes individuals who voluntarily do or fail to do certain things deserve some outcome or other. Thus, students may deserve high honor grades and criminals may deserve punishment. When notions of desert are evoked claims and obligations are made against others—these non-absolute claims and obligations are generated by what individuals do or fail to do. Thus in fairly uncontroversial cases of desert, we are willing to acknowledge that weak claims are generated and if desert can properly attach to labor or creation, then claims may be generated in these cases as well.

Finally, a justification for the view that labor or possession may generate prima facie claims against others could be grounded in respect for individual autonomy and sovereignty. As sovereign and autonomous agents, especially within the liberal tradition, we are afforded the moral and legal space to order our lives as we see fit. As long as respect for others is maintained we are each free to set the course and direction of our own lives, to choose between various lifelong goals and projects, and to develop our capacities and talents accordingly. Simple respect for individuals would prohibit wresting from their hands an unowned object that they acquired or produced. I hasten to add that at this point we are trying to justify weak non-interference claims, not full-blown property rights. Other things being equal, when an individual labors to create an intangible work, then weak presumptive claims of non-interference have been generated on grounds of labor, desert, or autonomy.

As noted before, the role of the proviso is to stipulate one possible set of conditions where a prima facie claim to control remains undefeated. Suppose Fred appropriates a grain of sand from an endless beach and paints a lovely, albeit small, picture on the surface. Ginger, who has excellent eyesight, likes Fred's grain of sand and snatches it away from him. On this interpretation of Locke's theory, Ginger has violated Fred's weak presumptive claim to the grain of sand. We may ask, what legitimate reason could Ginger have for taking Fred's grain of sand rather than picking up her own grain of sand? If Ginger has no comparable claim, then Fred's prima facie claim remains undefeated. An undefeated prima facie claim can be understood as a right.[16]

A Pareto-Based Proviso

The underlying rationale of Locke's proviso is that if no one's situation is worsened, then no one can complain about another individual appropriating part of the commons. Put another way, an objection to appropriation, which is a unilateral changing of the moral landscape, would focus on the impact of the appropriation on others. But if this unilateral changing of the moral landscape makes no one worse-off, there is no room for rational criticism.

The proviso permits individuals to better themselves so long as no one is worsened (weak Pareto-superiority). The base level intuition of a Pareto improvement is what lies behind the notion of the proviso:

> One state of the world, S_1, is Pareto-superior to another, S_2, if and only if no one is worse-off in S_1 than in S_2, and at least one person is better-off in S_1 than in S_2. S_1 is *strongly* Pareto-superior to S_2 if everyone is better-off in S_1 than in S_2, and *weakly* Pareto-superior if at least one person is better-off and no one is worse-off. State S_1 is Pareto optimal if no state is Pareto superior to S_1: it is *strongly* Pareto optimal if no state is *weakly* Pareto superior to it, and *weakly* Pareto optimal if no state is *strongly* Pareto superior to it.[17]

If no one is harmed by an acquisition and one person is bettered, then the acquisition ought to be permitted. In fact, it is precisely because no one is harmed that it seems unreasonable to object to a Pareto-superior move. Thus, the proviso can be understood as a version of a "no harm, no foul" principle.

It is important to note that compensation is typically built into the proviso and the overall account of bettering and worsening.[18] Gauthier echoes this point in the following case:

In acquiring a plot of land, even the best land on the island, Eve may initiate the possibility of more diversified activities in the community as a whole, and more specialized activities for particular individuals with ever-increasing benefits to all.[19]

Eve's appropriation may actually benefit her fellows and the benefit may serve to cancel the worsening that occurs from restricted use. Moreover, compensation can occur at both the level of the act and at the level of the practice. This is to say that Eve herself may compensate or that the system in which specific property relations are determined may compensate.

This leads to a related point. Some have argued that there are serious doubts whether a Pareto-based proviso on acquisition can ever be satisfied in a world of scarcity. Given that resources are finite and that acquisitions will almost always exclude, your gain is my loss (or someone's loss). On this model, property relations are a zero-sum game.[20] If this were an accurate description, then no Pareto-superior moves can be made and no acquisition justified on Paretian grounds. But this model is mistaken. An acquisition by another may worsen your position in some respects but it may also better your position in other respects. Minimally, if the bettering and worsening cancel each other out, a Pareto-superior move may be made and an acquisition justified. Locke recognizes this possibility when he writes:

To which let me add, that he who appropriates land to himself by his labour, does not lessen, but increase the common stock of mankind; for the provisions serving to the support of human life, produced by one acre of enclosed and cultivated land, are ten times more than those which are yielded by an acre of land of equal richness lying waste in common.[21]

Furthermore, it is even more of a stretch to model *intellectual* property as zero-sum. Given that intellectual works are non-rivalrous—i.e., they can be used by many individuals concurrently and cannot be destroyed—my possession and use of an intellectual work does not exclude your possession and use of it. This is just to say that the original acquisition of intellectual or physical property does not necessitate a loss for others. In fact, if Locke is correct, such acquisitions benefit everyone.

Before continuing, I will briefly consider the plausibility of a Pareto-based proviso as a moral principle. First, to adopt a less-than-weak Pareto principle would permit individuals, in bettering themselves, to worsen others. Such provisos on acquisition are troubling because at worst they may open the door to predatory activity and at best they give anti-property theorists the ammunition to combat the weak presumptive claims that labor and possession may generate. Part of the intuitive force of a Pareto-based proviso is that it provides little or no grounds for rational complaint. Moreover, if we can justify intellectual property rights with a more stringent principle, a principle that is harder to satisfy, then we have done something more robust, and more difficult to attack, when we reach the desired result.

To require individuals, in bettering themselves, to better others is to require them to give others free rides. In the absence of social interaction, what reason can be given for forcing one person, if she is to benefit herself, to benefit others? If, absent social interaction, no benefit is required then why is such benefit required within society?[22] Moreover, those who are required to give free rides can rationally complain about being forced to do so, while those who are left (all things considered) unaffected have no room for rational complaint. The crucial distinction that underlies this position is between worsening someone's situation and failing to better it,[23] and I take this intuition to be central to a kind of deep moral individualism. This view is summed up nicely by A. Fressola: "Yet, what is distinctive about persons is not merely that they are agents, but more that they are rational planners—that they are capable of engaging in complex projects of long duration, acting in the present to secure consequences in the future, or ordering their diverse actions into programs of activity, and ultimately, into plans of life."[24] Moreover, the intuition that grounds a Pareto-based proviso fits well with the view that labor and possibly the mere possession of unowned objects creates a prima facie claim to those objects. Individuals are worthy of a deep moral respect and this fact grounds a liberty to use and possess unowned objects. Liberty rights to use and possess unowned objects, unmolested, can be understood as weak presumptive claims to objects.

I am well aware that what has been said so far does not constitute a conclusive argument. Rather, I have attempted to show that a Pareto-based proviso is a plausible moral principle. Minimally, those who agree that there is something deeply wrong with requiring some individuals, in bettering themselves, to better others (anything more than weak Pareto-superiority) should find no problem with a Pareto-based proviso on original acquisition. If you do not share my intuitions on this matter then take the plausibility of the proviso as an assumption.

Bettering, Worsening, and the Baseline Problem: Revisited

Assuming a just initial position[25] and that Pareto-superior moves are legitimate, there are two questions to consider when examining a Paretian-based proviso. What are the terms of being worsened? This is a question of scale, measurement, or value. An individual could be worsened in terms of subjective preference satisfaction, wealth, happiness, freedoms, opportunities, etc. Which of these count in determining bettering and worsening (or do they all)? Second, once the terms of being worsened have been resolved, which two situations are we going to compare to determine if someone has been worsened. Is the question one of how others are now, after my appropriation, compared to how they would have been were I absent, or if I had not appropriated, or some other state? This is known as the baseline problem.

In principle, the Lockean theory of intellectual property being developed is consistent with a wide range of value theories.[26] So long as the preferred value theory has the resources to determine bettering and worsening with reference to acquisitions, then Pareto-superior moves can be made and acquisitions justified on Lockean grounds. Continuing with the themes started in chapter 4, I will assume an Aristotelian eudaimonist account of value exhibited by the following theses:[27]

1.   Human well-being or flourishing is the sole standard of intrinsic value.

2.   Human persons are rational project pursuers, and well-being or flourishing is attained through the setting, pursuing, and completion of life goals and projects.

3.   The control of physical and intellectual objects is valuable. At a specific time each individual has a certain set of things she can freely use and other things she owns, but she also has certain opportunities to use and appropriate things. This complex set of opportunities along with what she can now freely use or has rights over constitutes her position materially—this set constitutes her level of material well-being.

While it is certainly the case that there is more to bettering and worsening than an individual's level of material well-being including opportunity costs, I will not pursue this matter further at present.[28]

Needless to say, a full-blown account of value will explicate all the ways in which individuals can be bettered and worsened with reference to acquisition. Moreover, as noted before, it is not crucial to the Lockean model being presented to defend some preferred theory of value against all comers. Whatever value theory that is ultimately correct, if it has the ability to determine bettering and worsening with reference to acquisitions, then Pareto-superior moves can be made and acquisitions justified on Lockean grounds.

The Baselind of Comparison

Lockeans as well as others who seek to ground rights to property in the proviso generally set the baseline of comparison as the state of nature. I have argued in chapter 4 that since an individual's level of well-being changes over time the baseline of comparison must also change. This is to affirm a dynamic, rather than static comparison point.

In general, the problem with static base points is that they fail to include morally relevant changes in well-being. The appropriate baseline for determining bettering and worsening with reference to acquisition is the acquisitive case compared to the moment before the acquisition. If Fred has produced some new intellectual work and is considering if his acquisition of it will worsen Ginger, the correct baseline would be how she is after the acquisition compared to how she was immediately before the taking. A proviso that combines this baseline with a eudaimonistic account of value would be:

> If an acquisition makes no one else worse-off terms of her level of well-being (including opportunity costs) compared to how she was immediately before the acquisition, then the taking is permitted.

If correct, this account justifies rights to intellectual property. When an individual creates an original intellectual work and fixes it in some fashion, then labor and possession creates a prima facie claim to the work. Moreover, if the proviso is satisfied the prima facie claim remains undefeated and rights are generated.

Suppose Ginger, who is living off of the commons, creates through a painstaking process a new gathering technique that allows her to live better with less work. The set of ideas that she has created can be understood as an intellectual work. Given that Ginger has labored to create this new gathering technique, it has been argued that she has a weak presumptive claim to the work. Moreover, it looks as if the proviso has been satisfied given that her fellows are left, all things considered, unaffected by her acquisition. This is to say that they are free to create, through their own efforts, a more efficient gathering system, or even one that is exactly the same as Ginger's.

So far I have been pursuing a kind of top-down strategy in explicating certain moral principles and then arguing that rights to intellectual works can be justified in reference to these principles. In the next section, I will pursue a bottom-up strategy by presenting certain cases and then examining how the proposed theory fits with these cases and our intuitions about them.

Overall, the structure of the argument that I have given is:

1.   If the acquisition of an intangible work satisfies a Paretian-based proviso, then the acquisition and exclusion are justified.

2.   Some acts of intangible property creation and possession satisfy a Paretian-based proviso.

3.   So, some intangible property rights are justified.

Support for the first premise can be summarized in three related points: (1a) *The Paretian Intuition*—if no one is harmed by an acquisition and one person is bettered, then the acquisition ought to be permitted. This "no harm no foul" principle leaves little room for rational complaint; (1b) A less-weak-Pareto principle would allow predation and a stronger-than-weak Pareto principle would allow parasitism; and (1c) A Pareto-based proviso is consistent with the view that individuals are worthy of a deep moral respect, that their lives and lifelong goals and projects are not justifiably sacrificed for incremental gains in social utility.

Support for the second premise can be summarized as follows: (2a) Intangible property is non-rivalrous—it is capable of being used and possessed by many individuals concurrently; (2b) The "same" intangible work may be created and owned by many different individuals concurrently (non-zero sum); (2c) The number of ideas, collections of ideas, or intangible works available for appropriation is practically infinite (this makes the acquisition of intangibles similar to Locke's water drinker example); (2d) Institutions or systems of intangible property may provide compensation for apparent worsenings that occur at the level of acts;[29] and (2e) Many creations and inventions are strongly Pareto-superior—meaning that everyone is bettered and no one is worsened.

More Test Cases

Suppose Fred, in a fit of culinary brilliance, scribbles down a new recipe for spicy Chinese noodles and then forgets the essential ingredients. Ginger, who loves spicy Chinese food, sees Fred's note and snatches it away from him. On this interpretation of Locke's theory the proviso has been satisfied and Ginger has violated Fred's right to control the collection of ideas that comprise the recipe. We may ask, what legitimate reason could Ginger have for taking Fred's recipe rather than creating her own? If Ginger has no comparable claim, then Fred's prima facie claim remains undefeated.

We can complicate this case by imagining that Fred has perfect memory and so Ginger's theft does not leave Fred deprived of that which he created. It could be argued that what is wrong with the first version of this case is that Fred lost something that he created and may not be able to recreate. Ginger still betters herself, without justification, at the expense of Fred. In the second version of the case Fred has not lost and Ginger has gained and so there is nothing wrong with her actions. But from a moral standpoint, the accuracy of Fred's memory is not relevant to his rights to control the recipe and so this case poses no threat to the proposed theory. That intellectual property rights are hard to protect has no bearing on the existence of the rights themselves. Similarly, that it is almost impossible to prevent a trespasser from walking on your land has no bearing on your rights to control, although such concerns will have relevance when determining legal issues. In creating the recipe and not worsening Ginger, compared to the baseline, Fred's presumptive claim is undefeated and thus creates a duty of non-interference on others. One salient feature of rights is that they protect the control of value and the value of control. As noted in chapter 2, a major difference between intellectual property and physical property is that the former, but not the latter, are rights to types. Having intellectual property rights yields control of the type and any concrete embodiments or tokens, assuming that no one else has independently created the same set of ideas.

Rather than creating a recipe, suppose Fred writes a computer program and Ginger simultaneously creates a program that is, in large part, a duplicate of Fred's. To complicate things further, imagine that each will produce and distribute their software with the hopes of capturing the market and that Fred has signed a distribution contract that will enable him to swamp the market and keep Ginger from selling her product. If opportunities to better oneself are included in the account of bettering and worsening, then it could be argued that Fred violates the proviso because in controlling and marketing the software he effectively eliminates Ginger's potential profits. The problem this case highlights is that what individuals do with their possessions can affect the opportunities of others in a negative way. If so, then worsening has occurred and no duties of noninterference have been created. In cases of competition it seems that the proviso may yield the wrong result.

This is just to say that the proviso is set too high or that it is overly stringent. In some cases where we think that rights to property should be justified, it turns out, on the theory being presented, that they are not. But surely this is no deep problem for the theory. In the worst light it has not been shown that the proviso is not sufficient but only that it is overly stringent. And given what is at stake (the means to survive, flourish, and pursue lifelong goals and projects) stringency may be a good thing. Nevertheless, the competition problem represents a type of objection that poses a significant threat to the theory being developed. If opportunities are valuable, then any single act of acquisition may extinguish one or a number of opportunities of one's fellows. Obviously this need not be the case every time, but if this worsening occurs on a regular basis then the proposed theory will leave unjustified a large set of acquisitions that we intuitively think should be justified.

Even so, it has been argued that in certain circumstances individual acts of original acquisition can be justified. Protection at this level could proceed along the lines of contracts and licensing agreements between specific individuals. But I think that when pushed, systems or institutions of intellectual property protection will have to be adopted, both to explicate what can be protected legally and to solve competition problems and the like. As was noted early in this chapter, compensation for worsening could proceed at two levels. In acquiring some object Ginger, herself, could better Fred's position or the system that they both operate within could provide compensation. This is just to say that it does not matter whether the individual compensates or the system compensates: the agent in question is not worsened. This higher level justification, one that solves the competition problem, will be taken up in the following chapter.

Conclusion

While the preceding discussion has been sketchy, I think that important steps have been taken toward a Lockean theory of intellectual property. If no one is worsened by an acquisition, then there seems to be little room for rational complaint. The individual who takes a good long drink from a river does as much as to take nothing at all and the same may said of those who acquire intellectual property.[30] Given allowances for independent creation and that the frontier of intellectual property is practically infinite, the case for Locke's water-drinker and the author or inventor are quite alike. What is objectionable with the theft and pirating of computer software, musical CDs, and other forms of digital information is that in most cases a right to the control of value or the value of control has been violated without justification. Although the force of this normative claim is easily clouded by rationalizations like, "but they still have their copy" or "I wouldn't have purchased the information anyway," it does not alter the fact that a kind of theft has occurred. Authors and inventors who better our lives by creating intellectual works have rights to control what they produce. We owe a creative debt to individuals like Aristotle, Joyce, Jefferson, Tolkien, Edison, and Jimi Hendrix.

Notes

1.   John Locke, *The Second Treatise of Government*, ed. T. Peardon (New York : Liberal Arts Press, 1952, Bobbs-Merrill Publishing, 1952), § 33.

2.   Adapted from a case in David Carey's *The Ethics of Software Ownership* (Pittsburgh University : Ph.D. Dissertation 1989, Pittsburgh). Two examples come from Lotus and Apple Computers. Lotus claims to lose approximately $160 million a year (over half of the program's potential sales) due to piracy and casual copying of 1-2-3. Apple Computer claims similar losses for MacPaint and MacWrite. See John Gurnsey, *Copyright Theft* (Aldershoot; Brookfield, VT, Gower, 1995), 111-121.

3.   Frank Easterbrook sees things differently. "Patents are not monopolies, and the tradeoff is not protection for disclosure. Patents give a right to exclude, just as the law of trespass does with real property. Intellectual property is intangible, but the right to exclude is no different in principle from General Motors' right to exclude Ford from using its assembly line, or an apple grower's right to its own crop." Frank Easterbrook, "Intellectual Property is Still Property," *Harvard Journal of Law and Public Policy* 13 (1990): 109.

4.   U.S. Constitution, § 8, para. 8.

5.   For exegetical reasons I will continue to talk of utilitarian justified "rights" even though what is being justified is, in a deep sense, decidedly different from traditional deontic conceptions of rights.

6.   See generally chapter 3.

7.   The table derives directly from Patrick Croskery, "The Intellectual Property Literature: A Structured Approach" in *Owning Scientific and Technical Information*, ed. Weil & Snapper (New Brunswick, NJ: Rutgers Press, 1989), 270

8.   Unlike copyrights and trade secrets, patents exclude other independent inventors from obtaining rights to a work already patented. The Lockean model of intangible property that I will sketch does not include such a rule.

9.   While I have claimed that the set of publicly owned ideas or collections of ideas cannot be acquired and held as private property, it could be argued that this need not be so. If an author or inventor *independently* reinvents the wheel and satisfies some rights generating process, then it may be argued that she has private property rights to her creation. The trouble is, given that the set of ideas that comprise "the wheel" is public property, each of us has current rights to use and possess those ideas. Thus the inventor in this case may indeed have moral rights to exclude others and to control her idea, but given that we all have similar rights to the very same collection of ideas, such control and exclusion are meaningless.

10.   John Locke, *The Second Treatise of Government*, edited by Thomas Peardon (Indianapolis, IN: Bobbs-Merrill Publishing, 1952), § 27 (italics mine).

11.   Locke, § 33, 34, 36, 39.

12.   Both Jeremy Waldron, "Enough and as Good Left for Others," *Philosophical Quarterly* (1979): 319-328, and Clark Wolf, "Contemporary Property Rights, Lockean Provisos, and the Interests of Future Generation," *Ethics* (July, 1995): 791-818, maintain that Locke thought of the proviso as a sufficient condition and not a necessary condition for legitimate acquisition.

13.   This concern was originally voiced by Robert Nozick, *Anarchy, State, and Utopia* (New York: Basic Books, 1974), 178.

14.   Clark Wolf, "Contemporary Property Rights, Lockean Provisos, and the Interests of Future Generations," *Ethics* (July 1995): 791-818.

15.   Even Marx never explicitly denies that laborers are entitled to the fruits of their labor—"Indeed, it is natural to think that his condemnation of capitalist exploitation depends on a conviction that laborers are entitled to the whole fruits of their labor." Lawrence Becker, *Property Rights: Philosophic Foundations* (London: Routledge & Kegan Paul, 1977), n2, 121. See also, Karl Marx, *Capital* (New York: International Publishers, 1967), vol. 1, part VIII, chapter xxvi.

16.   For a defense of this view of rights, see G. Rainbolt, "Rights as Normative Constraints," *Philosophy and Phenomenological Research* (1993): 93-111, and Joel Feinberg, *Freedom and Fulfillment: Philosophical Essays* (Princeton, NJ: Princeton University Press, 1986).

17.   Adapted from G. A. Cohen's "The Pareto Argument For Inequality," in *Social Philosophy & Policy* 12 (Winter 1995): 160. Unless indicated, I will use Pareto superiority to stand for *weak* Pareto superiority. The "Pareto" condition is named after Vilfredo Pareto (1848-1923) an Italian economist and sociologist.

18.   As noted in chapter 4, consider the case where Ginger is better-off, all things considered, if Fred appropriates everything than she would have been had she appropriated everything (maybe Fred is a great manager of resources). Although Ginger has been worsened in some respects she has been compensated for her losses in other respects.

19. Gauthier, *Morals By Agreement* (Oxford University Press, 1986), 280.
20. For a more precise analysis of the zero-sum model of property, see James Child's article, "The Moral Foundations of Intangible Property," in *Intellectual Property: Moral, Legal, and International Dilemmas*, edited by A. Moore (Lanham, MD: Rowman & Littlefield, 1997), chapter 4.
21. Locke, *Second Treatise of Government*, § 37.
22. I have in mind Nozick's Robinson Crusoe case in *Anarchy, State, And Utopia* (New York: Basic Books, 1974), 185.
23. The distinction between worsening someone's position and failing to better it is a hotly contested moral issue. See Gauthier, *Morals By Agreement*, 204; Shelly Kagan, *The Limits of Morality* (Oxford: Oxford University Press, 1989), chapter 3; John Harris, "The Marxist Conception of Violence," *Philosophy & Public Affairs* 3 (1973-74): 192-220; John Kleinig, "Good Samaritanism," *Philosophy & Public Affairs* 5 (1975-76): 382-407; and Eric Mack's two articles, "Bad Samaritanism and the Causation of Harm," *Philosophy & Public Affairs* 9 (1979-80): 230-59, and "Causing and Failing To Prevent Harm," *Southwestern Journal of Philosophy* 7 (1976): 83-90. This distinction is even further blurred by my account of opportunity costs—see chapter 4.
24. Anthony Fressola, "Liberty and Property," *American Philosophical Quarterly* (October 1981): 320.
25. One problem with a Pareto condition is that it says nothing about the initial position from which deviations may occur. If the initial position is unfair then our Pareto condition allows that those who are unjustly better-off remain better-off. This is why the problem of original acquisition is traditionally set in the state of nature or the commons. The state of nature supposedly captures a fair initial starting point for Pareto improvements.
26. It has been argued that subjective preference satisfaction theories fail to give an adequate account of bettering and worsening. See D. Hubin and M. Lambeth's "Providing For Rights," *Dialogue* (1989). See chapter 4.
27. Aside from being intuitive in its general outlines, the theory fits well with the moral individualism that grounds both a Pareto-based proviso and the view that liberty rights entail weak presumptive claims to objects.
28. If the analysis of the proviso and bettering and worsening in chapter 4 is at all successful, then much of the work has been done—any defensible account of bettering and worsening with reference to acquisition will include material well-being and opportunities as valuable. Note also the kinds of harms that cannot be defended as morally relevant.
29. Suppose that one way to achieve Pareto-superior results is by adopting an institution that promotes and maintains restricted access, or fencing, of intellectual works. This is to say that, given our best estimates, everyone is better-off living within an institution where fencing is permitted and protected as opposed to alternative institutions where fencing is prohibited. If such a case can be made, then the Paretian may have a way to justify specific acts of appropriation by appealing to the level of institutions. I will argue for this thesis in chapter 6.
30. Easterbrook notes, "Intellectual property is no less the fruit of one's labor than is physical property. True, you need the government to enforce your property rights by preventing strangers from using your ideas to make their own products, but you ordinarily need the government to enforce your rights in physical property against predators." Frank Easterbrook, "Intellectual Property is Still Property," *Harvard Journal of Law and Public Policy* 13 (1990): 113.

6

Justifying Acts, Systems, and Institutions

"Each individual's status as a moral end-in-himself with a life of his own to lead, requires that his person not be subjected to assault, invasion, or seizure. The status of persons as ends-in-themselves requires that the use, acquisition, stocking, transformation, incorporation, and deployment of those extra-personal objects in and through which human individuals create and advance their lives not be subject to assault, invasion, or disruption. Respect for the entitlements conferred by a justified practice of private property is respect for separate project pursuers as beings whose lives are necessarily engaged in and contoured to and by the extra-personal world."

—Eric Mack, "Self-Ownership and the Right of Property"[1]

Introduction

An alternative strategy for justifying rights to intellectual works is found if we move upward from the level of acts to the level of systems or institutions. On this view, rather than trying to justify each act we might try to justify a system of property protection. Specific acts are justified if they satisfy the entitlement conferring rules found within any justified system of property relations. David Schmidtz, following Rawls and others, offers the following analogy that explains this strategy in reference to the rules and actions of a game:

Note there is a distinction between justifying institutions that regulate appropriation and justifying particular acts of appropriation. . . . [w]e may think of original appropriation as a game and the particular acts of appropriation as moves within the game. . . . Particular moves within the game may have nothing to recommend them. Indeed, suppose we say that any act of appropriation will appear morally arbitrary when viewed in isolation. Even so, there may be morally compelling reasons to have an institutional framework in which claims to property are recognized on the basis of moves that would carry no moral weight in an institutional vacuum.[2]

The strategy is a familiar one and is similar to the account given by many rule utilitarians, where actions are justified by appealing to rules and rules are justified by appealing to the principle of utility.[3]

Suppose that one way to achieve Pareto-superior results is by adopting an institution that promotes and maintains restricted access, or fencing, of intellectual works. This is to say that, given our best estimates, everyone is better-off living within an institution where fencing is permitted and protected as opposed to alternative institutions where fencing is prohibited.[4] If such a case can be made, then the Paretian may have a way to justify specific acts of appropriation by appealing to the level of institutions.

In chapters 4 and 5, I have sought to justify rights to control intellectual works at the level of acts. If the acquisition and control of an intellectual work does not worsen one's fellows compared to the baseline situation, then the taking is permitted. If I am correct, some acquisitions satisfy this requirement and are therefore justified. This kind of strategy falls under the general heading of an "Act Theory of Entitlement." But as already noted, justification of rights to intellectual property may occur at different levels. I find it helpful to think of justification and compensation for worsening possibly occurring at three different levels. Justification can occur at the level of acts (e.g., Paretian theory—chapters 4-5), at the level of systems (e.g., copyright, patents, trade secrets), or at the level of institutions (e.g., private property, collective ownership, or usufructory relations).

Before considering the justification of intellectual property at the level of systems and institutions, a general examination of the strengths and weaknesses of act theories will be helpful. In light of certain limitations that act theories face, I will move on, in a second part, to examine a Paretian test on institutions of property relations. Finally, in a final section, the justification of systems of intellectual property will be considered.

Act Theories of Entitlement[5]

Act theories justify individual acts of appropriation rather than systems or institutions. As noted, the Paretian theory developed in chapters 4 and 5 is an example of an act theory of entitlement. If no one is worsened by the acquisition of some intellectual work, then presumptive use rights remain overriding, and in effect become minimal property rights. Another example of an act theory is exhibited by the liberty argument.[6] On this view individuals have liberty rights that are best understood as freedom from interference rights. Acquiring and using unowned objects and incorporating them into one's lifelong goals and projects is part of each individual's right to liberty. Seizure or interference with objects that have been acquired by others is a violation of their rights to liberty. This position is summed up nicely by Antony Fressola:

> The claim of a right to liberty is embedded within a conception of morality that accords central importance to respecting persons as persons. Yet, what is distinctive about persons is not merely that they are agents, but more that they are rational planners—that they are capable of engaging in complex projects of long duration, acting in the present to secure consequences in the future, or ordering their diverse actions into programs of activity, and ultimately, into plans of life. The right to liberty, insofar as it gives expression to a respect for persons, must be a right to carry through on such of these projects and programs of action as persons can without infringing the similar right of their fellows.[7]

While Fressola puts the point in a general way, the argument can be interpreted to justify individual acts of acquisition. If an individual incorporates an unowned object into her lifelong goals and projects, then a non-interference claim against others arises. Interfering with such an object, without consent, would be a violation of the owner's liberty rights.[8]

An interesting feature of act theories of entitlement is that they justify rights independent of systems, conventions, or legal structures. Eric Mack echoes this point succinctly:

> What Act theories can provide us with are certain particularly vivid instances of property rights—instances which have vivacity because these entitlements stand on their own. They need not draw their moral force from their place within any larger normative system.[9]

Justified entitlement conferring acts are, in a sense, self-sufficient. All one has to do to verify a particular entitlement is to consider the conditions and history that led to the acquisition. Thus many act theories are historical, in that justification is determined by the history of a particular holding.[10]

Even though act theories can provide us with salient examples of justified acquisition, or so I have argued, they face a number of objections. First, it is unclear, even if rights to control are generated, that rights to transfer are included. Upon satisfying some entitlement conferring procedure it may be true that something close to property rights have been justified, but why think that transfer rights have also been included, or for that matter, anything close to full ownership rights?[11] Maybe all that is justified are rights to use, possess, augment, and consume.

Mack, on behalf of unnamed act theorists, answers this charge by claiming that there is no actual transfer of rights when Ginger gives Fred her property. Ginger merely abdicates ownership of an object in such a way that only Fred can acquire it. The object is left un-owned and Fred, if he wants to acquire it, must satisfy some act entitlement generating process. Absent social interaction and systems of property protection, this response suggests a kind of strategy that may be adequate.[12] Surely Ginger can renounce her property claim to a justly acquired object. Moreover, it seems that she would be doing nothing illicit if she were to conspire with Fred so that he is the only individual in a position to justifiably acquire her former property.

Another reply to this problem, attempted by many act theorists, has to do with the contracts and binding agreements. If Fred can consume, augment, and possess some object, X, and others must not interfere with Fred's control, we may ask what has changed when Fred transfers control of X to Ginger. Putting aside competition problems and the like, it would seem that, with respect to everyone else, X has ceased to play a role in their lives. Surely Fred and Ginger have the right to make binding agreements and in this case their contract leaves others as they were before. There are no new obligations on the moral landscape—except between Fred and Ginger. We can separate a general right to make contracts from the rights to control some item. On this view rights to use, augment, and consume, in addition to the right to make agreements, would yield a right to transfer. Suppose we each have a general right to make contracts and when a certain level of control is obtained specific agreements may be entered into. Thus a right to transfer is not a part of my initial entitlement, it arises from my entitlement along with a general right to make contracts.

Finally, while I am unsure about the force of these replies, I do think that the aforementioned problem is fairly anemic. Act theorists, generally, are not in the game of justifying full ownership rights to physical or intellectual objects. Such justifications would come, if they come at all, at higher levels. What I have tried to establish is that in certain cases individuals have long-term moral claims to that which they create—minimal property claims. I have not argued that creation and satisfying the proviso yields the set of full property rights found in mature legal systems. Nevertheless, this theory does not merely generate long-term use claims to objects. How would such claims be any different than our current claims to use unowned and unpossessed objects? On my view, labor and creation generate weak presumptive claims to use and possess an intellectual work. The proviso tells us when these use and possession claims become exclusive.

A second objection commonly given is that only a small number of current holdings live up to the self-sufficing standard exhibited by act theories. Most of us, in acquiring property, did not satisfy some act entitlement conferring procedure. Once again Mack echoes this point:

> The validity of these entitlements is not conditional upon each link in their history being a self-sufficient exemplar of entitlement generation or transfer. Rather, their legitimacy rests on their being the entitlements of peaceful and honest individuals to the possession they have respectively acquired in accordance with their society's generally recognized and justifiable rules for the rightful acquisition of the types of objects in question.[13]

This criticism focuses on the historical nature of many act theories of entitlement. It is generally the case that individuals acquire property rights via a transfer from previous owners. Ultimately, all current rights to property rest on the justified acquisition of formerly unowned objects. The problem is that it is almost impossible to trace the history of any particular object back to a justified original acquisition. Imagine trying to trace the ownership of a plot of land back to its original acquisition in England or in any European country. Moreover, according to most act theories, given the wars, invasions, and crusades, not to mention royal favors, privileges, illicit deals, and the like, it is probably a good bet that most lands and other physical goods were not acquired justly. And if current rights must rest on a history of just transfers and just acquisition, then most current holdings are unjustified. This objection to act theories amounts to nothing more than the claim that most of our current holdings do not conform to rights conferring processes at the level of acts. Many, including Mack, have argued that this is a telling and deep problem for many act theories of entitlement.

Even so, it seems that this kind of objection has little force. Again, it should be noted that act theorists are typically not in the game of trying to justify every current holding (or even most current holdings). Holdings that do not conform to some act theory are either justified on other grounds or they are unjustified. That most current holdings do not conform to some justified entitlement conferring procedure at the level of acts is of little significance to the act theorist. A salient feature of act theories is that property rights can be generated in a way that is largely independent of conventions and legal structures. If correct, act theories justify acquisitions that stand against claims that private property rights can *never* be justified.[14] This seems like a small victory but I think that it is an important one. Sometimes individuals can unilaterally change the moral landscape.

Moreover and more importantly, the way individual acts are justified may restrict the kinds of institutions and systems that may be adopted. If act theories justify rights to property in certain cases, then these moral claims should be considered in the formulation of systems and institutions of property protection. In the end, the act theorist may have to bite the bullet on this one (given the historical uncertainty of most acquisitions), but the bullet has at least been softened.

Finally, it is not clear that this kind of objection directly applies to intellectual property. Where the history of some physical object may be difficult to trace this need not be the case for most intellectual works. Many intellectual works are created, in a sense, *ex nihilio* (from nothing) and so there is, generally, fewer problems in tracing the history of an intellectual work. All we need to determine is originality and this is a question for the courts. I am not claiming that intellectual works are created in a vacuum and are completely independent from what came earlier. The point is that the intellectual work in question did not exist before and this does not preclude it from being spawned from other ideas or collections of ideas. Assuming a creation model of intellectual works, as opposed to a discovery model, when a new idea is born it is not merely a rearrangement of old ideas—something new exists.[15] In one sense this is not the case for tangible goods. When I carve a stick into a walking staff no new matter has been created, all that occurs is a rearrangement of matter. Thus the history of the stick may be very important in determining justified entitlement.

As was noted in chapter 5, a major difference between physical and intellectual property is the characterization of their respective pools of appropriatable items. While all physical property, owned or unowned, already exists the same is not true of intellectual property. The obvious exception is ideas that are *discovered* rather than *created*. But given that two or more individuals can discover or create the same ideas or collection of ideas what is available for appropriation is still practically boundless. Assuming a creation model, the set of unowned intellectual works is both practically infinite and non-actual. In determining what can be legitimately acquired, we must include the set of privately owned intellectual works along with the practically infinite set of non-actual ideas or collections of ideas because it is possible for the same set of ideas to be owned concurrently by many individuals. I find the following analogy to be helpful when considering the set of appropriatable intellectual items.

Imagine that, rather than living on a sphere, we inhabited a plane-world that was, for all practical purposes, boundless. On this world there is always a frontier or another mountain range to push beyond. An interesting feature of this world is that physical objects are multiply instantiated in the sense that there are a practically infinite number of exact duplicates of almost every physical item. Imagine also, that access to unclaimed items is fairly easy. If Fred wants to acquire a plot of land similar to Ginger's plot, all he has to do is travel a few miles beyond the frontier and stake his claim. My suggestion is that the intellectual commons closely approximates the commons found in this plane-world example. Ginger's taking and excluding some intellectual work does not, by itself, worsen Fred because he can still independently create the same intellectual work and obtain rights—Ginger's having X and benefiting from it does not exclude Fred's having X and benefiting from it. Such is generally the case with objects in our plane-world example. Except for spatial location, Ginger's ownership of some object does not exclude Fred's ownership of a very similar object, albeit in a different location. My goal in presenting this plane-world example is to show the non zero-sum nature of intellectual works on a creation model.

If this characterization of appropriatable intellectual property is correct and assuming the possibility of concurrent ownership, the historical problems largely fall away. Ginger's heretofore unthought collection of ideas has no history to be traced and so long as she appropriated the intellectual work in a just manner there is little room for criticism.

Kant's Critique of Act Theories[16]

In *The Metaphysical Elements of Justice,* Kant develops a general objection to act theories of entitlement. Kant distinguished between "empirical" and "external" possession that correspond to mere *use* or *possession* rights and *property rights* respectively. Possession rights ("empirical possession" for Kant) are rights to use and control an object, but only when it is in one's possession—one has an internal right to exclusively use what one possesses. Property rights ("external possession" for Kant) are rights to complete control even when the object in not in one's possession. A general feature of many act theories is that through the extension of some internal right, like self-ownership rights or labor rights, agents can unilaterally generate private property rights. Kant's general critique is that these internal rights will never suffice to generate anything more than use and possession rights. Mack summarizes Kant's argument in the following way:

1.   Appeals to an "internal right" (like a self-ownership right) can at most support entitlements to mere use and possession.

2.   At least some entitlements are to external possessions—indeed, something's being "externally mine" is paradigmatic of entitlement.

3.   Hence, doctrines that appeal only to internal rights can never be adequate theories of entitlement.[17]

Self-ownership rights may be extended to include the liberty to possess physical objects, but it is unclear how this internal right can be extended to include property rights. Kant writes:

if I am the holder of a thing (that is, physically connected to it), then anyone who touches it without my consent (for example, wrests an apple from my hand) affects and diminishes that which is internally mine (my freedom). Consequently, the maxim of his action stands in direct contradiction to the axiom of justice [rights]. Thus, the proposition concerning empirical possession does not extend beyond the right of the person with respect to himself.[18]

Kant concludes that if property rights to physical objects are to be sustained we must appeal to something other than an internal right. Mack concurs with Kant and if they are correct, then act theories of entitlement are inadequate.

Hopefully, it is clear that this kind of objection simply begs the question against many act theories of acquisition. The liberty argument and the Paretian-based theory both attempt to show how internal rights can be extended, unilaterally, to generate something close to, if not the same as, private property rights. If the Paretian theory developed in chapters 4 and 5 is correct, then weak presumptive claims to possession are transformed into property claims. Moreover, even if Kant's objection has any force, it does not show that there can be no entitlements, however minimal, generated by act theories. If the objection is merely the claim that act theories have trouble justifying the full ownership rights found in modern societies, then, given the replies that the act theorist has made to earlier problems, Kant's objection seems fairly weak.

One final objection typically leveled at act theories of entitlement is that they cannot stand reflective scrutiny. One proponent of this argument, Jeremy Waldron, claims that act theories fail because they entail unilateral impositions of moral obligations—and upon reflection, he argues, we will find such "moral burdens" "radically unfamiliar" and "repugnant."[19] How, it may be asked, can the unilateral actions of one individual create obligations and duties of non-interference on the whole of humanity?

While this kind of objection has been given mileage by Waldron and others, I think that the act theorist has the resources to marshal an adequate reply. Consider, for a moment, the "moral burdens" unilaterally generated upon the creation of a new and unique philosophical theory. Upon completion and dissemination an obligation has been created not to plagiarize the work or misrepresent the views of the author. To take an example from Gaus and Lomasky, consider the obligation to give people what they deserve.[20] In this case, the individual does something, or fails to do something, etc., and her actions create desert-based obligations and duties on others. These cases indicate that, while the unilateral actions of one individual may create "moral burdens" on the rest of us, the burdens are not "radically unfamiliar" or "repugnant."

Act theories of entitlement are important because, if correct, they provide salient examples of justified unilateral changes in the moral landscape. Independent of social institutions, conventions, or legal systems, individuals can justifiably appropriate intellectual works or physical goods. Moreover, if legal systems are to account for moral rights and act theories provide cases where such rights are generated, then the systems themselves will have to accommodate, in some form, act theories of entitlement. Nevertheless there are clear limits to the moral force of act theories. As noted earlier, act theories are hard pressed to justify full ownership rights found in modern societies. And if there is no further justification of entitlements, beyond the self-sufficient examples provided by act theories, then many current holdings are morally unjustified. These limitations push us to go beyond act theories to the justification of systems and institutions of property protection.

Justifying Institutions

It has been argued that in determining what it means to be better-off and worse-off, an "all things considered" notion of well-being should be used, which includes both compensation at the level of the act (micro level) and at the level of the institution (macro level). When an individual creates an intellectual work she may, herself, bring about greater opportunities and wealth for her fellows that serves to compensate them for lost opportunities. But, as institutions of property relations arise, the institutions themselves may confer benefits that serve to cancel out apparent worsenings. Institutions of property relations may arise that augment everyone's wealth while initiating new opportunities to increase well-being. An example of macro-compensation is the possibility of diversified activities that institutions of property relations provide for everyone. If compensation at the level of institutions can and does occur, then the question becomes what justifies the institution.

Rather than trying to justify every particular appropriation by appealing to a Pareto-based version of the proviso, we might try to justify an institution. Consider the following macro proviso (MP) on institutions of property relations:

MP: If an institution of property relations does not worsen any individual in terms of her level of well-being (including opportunity costs), then the institution is permitted.

Bettering and worsening are, as before, cashed out in terms of an individual's level of well-being with opportunity costs. At some point in a culture's advancement a legal system will be developed to, in part, uphold and defend an institution of property relations.[21] By adopting a specific institution of property relations an individual may suffer instances of worsenings that are compensated by the benefits and increased opportunities (to that individual) provided by the institution as a whole. This is to say that where micro-compensation fails macro-compensation may succeed. The context of the baseline is the chosen institution (or the institution arrived at by convention) compared to the state of nature situation where there is no institution of property relations. Since the comparison situation (the state of nature situation) includes opportunity costs, we must consider how individuals may have been under alternative institutions of property relations.

Problems with assigning probabilities to opportunities in the macro case are more acute than was exhibited at the level of acts. The question is, what are the chances that some individual would have been better-off under some *justified* alternative system of property relations? The word "justified" in here is important because we do not want to compare institutions that are unjustified with other institutions to determine if these latter institutions are justified. There is no need to argue that the institution of private property is Pareto-superior to unjustified institutions of property relations. In any case the Paretian test, as I have explicated it, is a test of sufficiency and this leaves open the possibility of alternative justifications.[22]

Imagine Ginger's opportunities and level of well-being under a system of property relations where use is based on need compared to her actual situation where she is middle class and living in Ohio.[23] In assigning probabilities to Ginger's chances for well-being under some justified alternative system of property relations we use our best empirical information about the alternative institution, its average level of material well-being, how it handles tragedy of the commons problems (see below), and the like. If the probabilities cannot be determined because of lack of information, then until such information arises and worsening is determined, the institution is permitted.[24] In cases of uncertainty, the shadow of the proviso will hang over both rights to particular items and the institution itself.

Suppose there is some alternative institution of property relations, Z, that yields Ginger $n+1$ benefit where the system she finds herself engaged in, R, only nets her n benefit. R would then seemingly violate MP (a macro proviso). If $n+1$ is certain for Ginger, meaning that if Z is adopted she *will* obtain $n+1$, then R is illegitimate unless compensation is paid. But as we have seen, it is more likely the case that Ginger only has a chance to obtain $n+1$—she has an opportunity to achieve a certain level of material well-being under an alternative institution of property relations—alas, the world is a risky place. If opportunities are worth less than the results they promise, then compensation will be some percentage of the $+1$ benefit Z produces over R for Ginger.

This is a welcome result. The institution of property relations that produces the highest level of well-being and opportunities for each individual will satisfy MP. Suppose some system of property relations, Z, provides more opportunities and material well-being than any competing system. Moreover, suppose R manages, what we might generally call, tragedy of the commons problems as well as or better than other institutions. Tragedy of the commons problems are problems of incentive, pollution, and efficiency. In this case R will provide benefits and opportunities over and above its competitors and will most likely satisfy MP. Individual acquisitions may worsen one's fellows so long as the institution provides compensation in the form of opportunities and benefits.[25]

This, in a way, solves the competition problem and similar problems, mentioned in chapter 5. The competition problem arises in cases where two or more individuals are in competition to market a product and the first to access the market with a new product worsens the position of others. The problem is that while such activity may not pass the Paretian test, it seems to be justifiable nonetheless. One answer to this problem is to reiterate the fact that the Paretian test is a test of sufficiency. This is just to say that by itself the test may not pick out every justifiable acquisition. A separate strategy for answering the competition problem is to note that the opportunities that Ginger loses when Fred markets his software are dependent on the institution of property relations that they both operate within. It would be illicit for Ginger to complain about lost opportunities that were themselves dependent on an institution of private property.

We are now in a position to examine a seemingly serious objection raised by G. A. Cohen in "Self-Ownership, World-Ownership, and Equality" concerning the baseline. Cohen argues, "When assessing A's appropriation we should consider not only what would have happened had B appropriated, but also what would have happened had A and B cooperated under a socialist economic constitution."[26] B may be better-off in a socialistic system of property relations than in a system of private property. And since we are building in opportunity costs this alternative system would be reflected in B's baseline. So A's appropriation would be unjustified even though he has bettered her situation in relation to a baseline grounded in the commons. Moreover Cohen claims:

And since a defensibly strong Lockean proviso on the formulation and retention of economic systems will rule that no one should be worse off in the given economic system than he would have been under some unignorable alternative, it most certainly follows that not only capitalism but every economic system will fail to satisfy a defensibly strong Lockean proviso, and that one must therefore abandon the Lockean way of testing the legitimacy of economic systems.[27]

If Cohen is correct, any proviso which includes opportunity costs will be set too high to justify property rights—any system of appropriation will make someone worse-off.

Cohen's general attack on the context of the baseline will be examined first. His conclusion, "it almost certainly follows that not only capitalism but every economic system will fail to satisfy a defensibly strong Lockean proviso, and that one must therefore abandon the Lockean way of testing economic systems,"[28] is mere speculation. Moreover, our discussion of the Lockean proviso has centered around what justifies individual acts of appropriation and systems of property relations and not what legitimates economic systems. Cohen writes as if there is a deep connection between a system of private property and capitalism in the sense that if private property relations obtain then capitalism necessarily follows. This is clearly false. An institution of private property is compatible with many economic arrangements that would not be considered capitalistic. We can easily imagine cases where individuals privately own tangible and intellectual items but where no capitalistic economic arrangement is in place. Cohen seems to forget that a salient feature of private property is that individuals can do what they want with their property and this includes giving it to the collective.[29] That B is better-off in some other economic arrangement is not necessarily an indictment against private property, although it may be an indictment against an economic system.

In challenging the context or baseline of the proviso, Cohen might have argued that we must compare alternative institutions of property relations (not economic arrangements). Maybe B would be better-off under a system of property where need determined use rights and important needs were specified by committees. Only when such a theory is worked out can it be compared to a institution of private property, along with tragedy of the commons considerations, which include incentive and efficiency arguments. And even if such an alternative institution of property relations yields an individual better prospects, it cannot be concluded that she has been worsened, so long as compensation is allowed.

Institutions of private property are generally beneficial because the internalization of costs discourages value-decreasing behavior. If Fred forgets to put oil in his car he will pay the costs of his forgetfulness. If Ginger does not market her new motor that harvests static electricity from the atmosphere and other inventors produce rival inventions she will pay the costs of her inactivity—her invention will likely decrease in economic value. Moreover, by internalizing benefits:

> property rights encourage the search for, the discovery of, and the performance of "social" efficient activities. Private property rights greatly increase people's incentives to engage in cost-efficient conservation, exploration, extraction, invention, entrepreneurial alertness, and the development of personal and extra-personal resources suitable for all these activities. . . . These rights engender a vast increase in human-made items, the value and usefulness of which tend, on the whole, more and more to exceed the value and usefulness of the natural materials employed in their production.[30]

If this is true, the upshot of this discussion is that the Paretian has the resources to argue for specific institutions of property relations. We have good reason to conclude that the institution of private property can be justified on Paretian grounds. Put another way, it is likely, especially in light of tragedy of the commons problems and the like, that the institution of private property yields individuals better prospects than any competing institution of property relations.[31] A different way to put this point is represented in the following figure.

Figure 6.1
Pareto Superiority and Private Property Relations

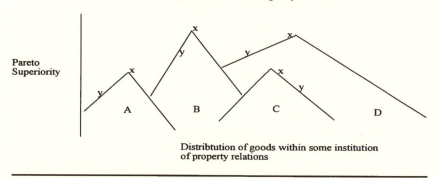

Pareto
Superiority

Distribtution of goods within some institution
of property relations

A, B, C, D = Pareto non-comparable peaks
x = Private Property Relations
y = Common Ownership Relations or
      Usufructory Relations

For any distribution of goods within some institution of property relations there is a corresponding distribution of goods within an institution of private property that is Parteo-superior. To put this in weak Pareto-superior terms, given some distribution of goods within an institution of common ownership or usufructory relations (for example, peak A, y), no one is worsened and one person is bettered if we were to move from either of these institutions to an institution of private property (x). In strong Pareto-superior terms, everyone would be bettered and no one worsened if we were to move from common ownership or usufructory ownership to an institution of private property relations. I am not claiming that a situation where Ginger *owns* everything is Parteo-superior to the situation where Fred gets to *use* everything—these distributions within different institutions would be Pareto non-comparable. The point is, keeping the distribution of control fixed, institutions of private property are Pareto-superior when compared to rival institutions. This is just to say that the institution where Ginger *owns* everything is Pareto-superior to the institution where she gets to *use* everything.

The general strategy has been to argue that institutions of private property are strongly Pareto-superior when compared to their competitors.[1] If this conclusion is probable, and since *strong* Pareto-superiority greatly overdetermines and entails *weak* Pareto-superiority, we have good reason to think that the weaker test has been satisfied. Moreover, I am not arguing that the value-protecting and enhancing effects of private property relations maximizes social utility and should therefore be adopted. This would be to give a consequentialist argument and I have explicitly rejected such justifications. The point here is that the institution of private property is more likely to better everyone when compared to its rivals and this satisfies the Paretian test.

Justifying Systems[33]

Assuming that all this is true it might be asked what has become of the justification of systems of intellectual property protection, like copyright and patents? The preceding analysis has been concerned with property relations and not systems of intellectual property. An institution of property relations is more general than the systems of property protection found within the institution. For example, copyright protection is a *system* of intellectual property protection found within the Anglo-American *institution* of private property. One could also imagine, within a Marxian institution of collective ownership, there being systems of use protection for intellectual property. As noted in the opening section, I find it helpful to think of justification possibly occurring at three distinct levels. Justification, and compensation for apparent worsenings, can occur at the level of acts, at the level of systems, or at the level of institutions.

Consider the following diagram:

Figure 6.2
Levels of Justification

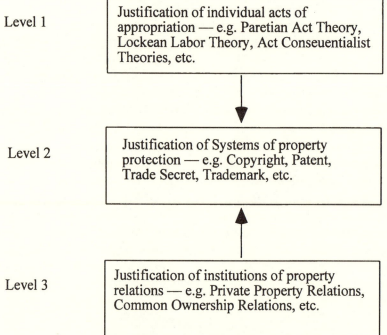

Level 1 — Justification of individual acts of appropriation — e.g. Paretian Act Theory, Lockean Labor Theory, Act Conseuentialist Theories, etc.

Level 2 — Justification of Systems of property protection — e.g. Copyright, Patent, Trade Secret, Trademark, etc.

Level 3 — Justification of institutions of property relations — e.g. Private Property Relations, Common Ownership Relations, etc.

In giving a justification for mid-level systems of intellectual property protection, I will adopt the following strategy. Chapters 4 and 5, if correct, justify individuals unilaterally changing the moral landscape by creating property rights. If the second part of this chapter is correct, then the institution of private property has been justified on Paretian grounds. These two levels of justification will, in turn, set the boundaries of systems of intellectual property protection. This is just to say that if a system is to be justified it must be compatible with the property claims generated at the level of acts and consistent with the overall institution of property relations.[34]

Before indicating how a Paretian might justify a system of rules that protect intellectual property, a characterization of these mid-level systems is necessary. Each system of intellectual property protection is comprised of a number of rules. Minimally, to be a system of property protection the collection of rules should include the following five features:[35]

1.   specify entitlement conferring procedures or processes;

2.   be functional;

3.   be comprehensive;

4.   specify a domain of protection; and,

5.   be justifiable.

The specification of entitlement conferring procedures or processes is an essential feature of systems of intellectual or physical property. If a system is to protect ownership and justify ownership, there must be some set of rules or criteria that determine when an object has been acquired correctly. Each entitlement conferring procedure will consist of a number of requirements or rules that pick out certain types of actions as being entitlement conferring and other types of actions as being non-entitling. Outside of providing criteria for how unowned objects can be acquired, a system will include rules about transfer, gift giving, and the like.

A system is functional when its rules are readily knowable to those within the institution and authorize identifiable and predictable property claims. Included in a functionality component are specifications of the range and limits of ownership rights.

To be comprehensive, the rules of the system should be dynamic. This is to say that the rules should be expandable to include new forms of property that fall within the general scope of the system as defined below. It has been argued that Anglo-American rule-utilitarian based systems of intellectual property are not comprehensive—in general the rules are not expandable to include the protection of intellectual works placed online.

Included in systems of property protection is a characterization of the domain of protection. Different systems will protect different kinds of objects or entities. This feature is exhibited by the separation of physical property, copyright, patent, trade secret, and trademark protection. Given that entitlement conferring rules will likely be suited to the acquisition of specific kinds of property, it is advantageous to separate domains or subject matter.

Finally, to be justifiable, a system must be consistent with the property claims generated at the level of acts. If copyrights, patents, and trade secrets are to account for moral rights, and act theories provide cases where such rights are generated, then the systems themselves will have to be consistent with rights generated at the act level. Beyond this requirement, the system will have to be ratified via some process or social contract. This is just to say that systems that are consistent with claims generated at the level of acts are not necessarily justified.

My characterization of Paretian theory is deontic in nature and this would seem to require that systems of intellectual property protection be deontic as well. There can be no sacrifice of any individual to obtain an incremental increase of utility for the whole of society. As noted at the end of chapter 3, this feature alone would call into question rule-utilitarian justifications of Anglo-American intellectual property systems. Finally, if I am correct about the nature of intellectual property, then a large number of original acquisitions will satisfy the Paretian test at the level of acts. Hence, systems of intellectual property protection, if they are to be morally justified, will have to accommodate the property claims generated at the level of acts.

Suppose that to be *fully* justifiable a system of intellectual property must specify entitlement conferring procedures, indicate a domain of protection, and be functional, comprehensive, and justifiable. Within these constraints, it is very difficult to give a Pareto-based argument for one set of rules opposed to another. Complex sets of rules that will likely make up systems of intellectual property seem resistant to Pareto-based justifications. In fact, it is likely that each slightly different set of rules would be Pareto non-comparable. This is to say that there is no set that leaves no one worse-off when compared to another set. It is possible, though, for a Paretian to give an argument in support of adopting some systems that protect the intellectual efforts of authors and inventors rather than having a policy of no protection.

An Intellectual Property Tragedy

It could be argued that there can be no tragedy of the commons when considering intellectual property. Given that intellectual property cannot be destroyed[26] and can be concurrently used by many individuals, there can be no ruin of the commons. Upon closer examination I think that there can be a tragedy of the commons with respect to intellectual property. To begin, we may ask "What is the tragedy?" Well generally, it is the destruction of some land or other object and the cause of the destruction is scarcity and common access. But the tragedy cannot be the destruction of land or some physical object because, as we all well know, matter is neither created nor destroyed. The tragedy is the loss of value, potential value, or opportunities. Where there was once a green field capable of supporting life for years to come there is now a plot of mud, a barren wasteland, or a polluted stream. If access is not restricted to valuable resources, the tragedy will keep occurring. A prime example is the Tongan coral reefs that were being destroyed by unsavory fishing practices.[27] It seems that the best way to catch the most fish along the reef was to poor bleach into the water bringing the fish to the surface and choking the reef.

The tragedy in such cases is not only the loss of current value but of future value. Unless access is restricted in such a way that promotes the preservation or augmentation of value, a tragedy will likely result. Now suppose that intellectual works were not protected—that if they "got out" any one could profit from them. In such cases individuals and companies would seek to protect their intellectual efforts by keeping them secret. Secrecy was the predominant form of protection used by guilds in the Middle Ages. The result can be described as a tragedy or a loss of potential value. If authors and inventors can be assured that their intellectual efforts will be protected, then the information can be disseminated and licenses granted so that others may build upon the information and create new intellectual works. The tragedy of a "no protection rule" is secrecy, restricted markets, and lost opportunities.[28] This view is echoed by Roger Meiners and Robert Staaf:

> The same story has been told about patents. If inventions lost their exclusivity and became part of the commons, then in the short run there would be over-grazing. The inventor could not exclude others, and products that embody previously patentable

ideas would now yield a lower rate of return. There would be lower returns to the activity of inventing, so that innovative minds would become less innovative. In the case of open ranges, common rights destroy what nature endows, and in the long run keeps the land barren because no one will invest to make the land fertile. Similarly, common rights would make the intellectual field of innovations less productive relative to a private property right system.[6]

If true, the Paretian has provided the outlines of an argument for protecting the intellectual efforts of authors and inventors as opposed to no protection. The strategy has been, once again, to support the claim that protection of intellectual property is strongly Pareto-superior when compared to no protection. Hence, weak Pareto-superiority is likely. Again, this is not to argue that private property relations with respect to intellectual property are justified on consequentialist grounds. Here I am simply illustrating how private property relations are Pareto-superior to a "no-ownership" view. While this result does not yield a specific set of rules, it does link nicely with the Paretian justification at other levels. Ultimately, the exact set of rules that make up copyright, patent, or trade secret protection will have to be justified on other grounds because of the Pareto non-comparability mentioned earlier. One obvious candidate for justifying mid-level systems of intellectual property protection is by contracts or engaging in the democratic method. Largely, I will leave such justifications, within the Paretian-based constraints already in place, for another time.

The Liberty Objection to Intellectual Property Rights

Tom Palmer and Jan Narveson have argued that intellectual property rights are morally objectionable because they interfere with individual liberty. These rights restrict an entire range of actions ". . . unlimited by place or time, involving legitimately owned property (VCRs, tape recorders, typewriters, the human voice, and more) by all but those privileged to receive monopoly grants from the state."[40] In response to the charge that all rights restrict individual liberty Narveson writes:

This is to talk as though the 'restrictions' involved in ownership were nothing but that. But that's absurd! The essence of my having an Apply Macintosh is that I *have* one, at my disposal when I wish, which latter of course requires that you not be able to use it any time you like; it's *not* that *you can't have one unless I say so*.[41]

When an individual owns a physical item her rights exclude others from interfering with her control of it. But intellectual property rights sweep across the entire domain of human action, restricting individual liberty even in the privacy of one's own home. Palmer continues:

> My ownership claim over my computer restricts your access to that computer, but it is not a blanket restriction on your liberty to acquire a similar computer, or an abacus, or to count on your fingers or use a pencil and paper. In contrast, to claim a property rights over a process is to claim a blanket right to control the actions of others. For example, if a property rights to control the use of the abacus were to be granted to someone, it would mean precisely that others could not make an abacus unless they had the permission of the owner of that right. It would be a restriction on the liberty of everyone who wanted to make an abacus with their own labor out of wood that they legitimately owned.[9]

Palmer concludes that intellectual property rights are morally objectionable and that patent and copyrights institutions should be dismantled. It is interesting to note, however, that Palmer (and presumably Narveson) advocates market-based and contractual rather than legal-based solutions for protecting or fencing intellectual works. In chapter 7 I argue that binding contracts presuppose justified prior entitlements—thus to replace Anglo-American copyright and patent institutions with a contract and market-based model presupposes that authors and inventors have justified entitlements to what they fence. But this is getting ahead of ourselves.

In response to Palmer and Narveson's view that intellectual property rights are objectionable because they limit individual liberty, I have two main criticisms. First, the problem they mention seems inapplicable to the Lockean theory being developed or to the rule-utilitarian model discussed in chapters 2 and 3. Current Anglo-American institutions of intellectual property have built-in provisions that limit the rights of authors and inventors.[10] These limitations, for example "fair use" and "first sale," allow individuals to use a patented or copyrighted work for personal use, non-profit, or educational purposes.[11] Under current law it is permissible that I make back-up copies of my computer games or copy a chapter of a book from the library.

Moreover, assuming that restricting individual liberty is a bad consequence of intellectual property rights, the rule-utilitarian could merely incorporate more restrictions on ownership rights. Maybe what is needed to maximize overall social utility is a provision that allows for personal non-profit use of any protected intellectual work. Thus, the rule-utilitarian merely incorporates the bad consequences of restricting human liberty into his overall maximization scheme.

It is also the case that the Lockean model could accommodate personal use provisions. These provisions could also be built into the contract between the owners of intellectual works and those who purchase the information—but again, we are getting ahead of ourselves.

The second criticism of Palmer and Narveson's view is that rights of all sorts restrict what individuals can do with their bodies and property. Palmer and Narveson act as if restricting individual liberty is a special feature of intellectual property rights and not of other rights. But this is clearly false. My right to a car prohibits all of humanity from swinging a bat and damaging my car. Other people's life rights prohibit you from drinking martinis and playing with a nuclear bomb in your basement. Most rights restrict liberty and prohibit what others can do with their property.[12] Even in the privacy of your own home you cannot punch me in the face or destroy my property or engage in risky activities that threaten one's neighbors. Thus, if Palmer and Narveson's argument works against intellectual property rights it would seem that it works against all rights, including life rights and tangible property rights.

Conclusion

In closing I would like to mention three differences between the Paretian approach offered and the rule-utilitarian approach that was rejected in chapter 3. First, a minor difference is that the Paretian theory aims at justifying rights to property while rule-utilitarians and act-utilitarians typically seek to establish claims about the value enhancing characteristics of certain actions or classes of actions. This leads directly to a second difference. In many cases the rule-utilitarian and the act-utilitarian are concerned with maximizing expected utility, while the Paretian is merely worried about not harming. Whether or not an act, system, or institution, maximizes total or average utility, is beside the point for the Paretian. There is no requirement to maximize social utility. There are no required sacrifices, even in principle, of one person's life or goals for the greater good. For the Paretian there is something deeply wrong with a moral theory that *requires* some individuals to sacrifice themselves when there are alternative Pareto-superior actions available. This last point drives home a third difference between utilitarians and Paretians. Paretian theory, at least as I have explicated it, is deontic in nature. Individuals are worthy of a deep moral respect that stands athwart utility maximization arguments or policies. The Paretian test, or so I have argued, respects the integrity and dignity of human beings and human life.

Notes

1. Eric Mack, "Self-Ownership and the Right of Property," *The Monist* 73 (October 1990): 519-43.
2. David Schmidtz, "The Institution of Property," *Social Philosophy & Policy* 11 (Summer 1994): 49. See also J. Rawls, "Two Concepts of Rules," *Philosophical Review* 64 (1955): 3-32, reprinted in *Theories of Ethics*, ed. Phillippa Foot (London: Oxford University Press, 1967), 144-70 (all page citations refer to the reprint). If I am correct in chapters 4 and 5, some individual acts of acquisition will not appear morally arbitrary when viewed in isolation.
3. See R. G. Frey, "Introduction: Utilitarianism and Persons" in *Utility and Rights*, edited by R. G. Frey (Minneapolis: University of Minnesota Press, 1984), 3-19; J. J. C. Smart's "Extreme and Restricted Utilitarianism, in *Theories of Ethics*, edited by Philippa Foot (Oxford: Oxford University Press, 1967); David Lyons, *Forms and Limits of Utilitarianism* (Oxford: Clarendon Press, 1965); and Smart & Williams, *Utilitarianism: For And Against* (London: Cambridge University Press, 1973).
4. Such an institution would be *strongly* Pareto-superior in comparison to its rivals.
5. My presentation in the first section of this chapter is deeply indebted to Eric Mack's treatment of Act and Practice Theories in "Self-Ownership and the Right of Property," in *The Monist* 73 (October 1990): 524-32.
6. Still another example of an act theory of entitlement is Locke's labor theory of acquisition. If an individual labors on an unowned object and satisfies certain other requirements, then the act or taking is justified. See Locke's, *The Second Treatise of Government*, chapter V.
7. A. Fressola, "Liberty And Property," *American Philosophical Quarterly* (October 1981): 320.
8. Act consequentialist theories are also given as justification for particular acquisitions. Crudely, on this view we ought to perform the action that leads to the best consequences. In some cases, acquiring and excluding others from some object yields the best results, and so it follows that we ought to acquire in these cases.
9. Eric Mack, "Self-Ownership and the Right of Property," 529.
10. Note that not all act theories of entitlement are historical. Act consequentialists theories are future oriented in the sense that holdings are justified only if they lead to, or are expected to lead to, the best results.
11. This problem is raised in Mack, "Self-Ownership and the Right of Property," 526. For a description and analysis of full ownership, see chapter 2; A. M. Honoré, "Ownership" in *Oxford essays in Jurisprudence*, edited by A. G. Guest (Oxford: Clarendon Press, 1961), 107-47; and Lawrence Becker, *Property Rights, Philosophic Foundations* (London: Routledge & Kegan Paul 1977), 19.
12. It is less clear how this reply or strategy would handle gift giving, for gifts seem to be transfers of titles that do not require anything, accept acceptance, of the receiver.
13. Eric Mack, "Self-Ownership and the Right of Property," 529-30.

14. See K. Marx, *Capital* (New York: International Publishers, 1967) vols. 1 and 2, and P. J. Proudhon, *What is Property,* translated by Tucker (New York: Howard Fertig, 1966), first published in English in 1890.
15. As noted in an earlier chapter a discovery model of intellectual works assumes that all ideas already exist and must be discovered (sometimes referred to as a Platonic model) whereas a creation model assumes that some ideas are discovered and some are created. An example of an idea that was discovered would be f=ma, while the song *La Villa Strangato* by Rush would be an example of a work that was created.
16. My analysis of Kant's argument is, once again, deeply indebted to Eric Mack's presentation in "Self-Ownership and the Right of Property," 530-32.
17. Adapted from Mack, "Self-Ownership and the Right of Property," 530.
18. Kant, *The Metaphysical Elements of Justice* (New York: Bobbs-Merrill, 1965), 57 (250).
19. Jeremy Waldron, *The Right To Private Property* (Oxford: Oxford University Press, 1988), 264-70. Alan Gibbard voices a similar complaint in "Natural Property Rights," *Readings in Social and Political Philosophy*, edited by Robert M. Stewart (Oxford: Clarendon Press, 1986), 217-44. For a parallel discussion of this problem and available replies, see A. John Simmons, "Original-Acquisition Justification of Property," *Social Philosophy & Policy* 11 (Summer 1994): 63-84, and Gaus and Lomasky, "Are Property Rights Problematic?" *The Monist* 73 (October 1990): 492-93.
20. Gaus and Lomasky, "Are Property Rights Problematic?" 492.
21. I take a virtue of this theory to be that the institution adopted will be chosen on empirical grounds. The institution that provides the most opportunities and benefits for each will likely satisfy MP in terms of compensation — in providing spiraling opportunities and benefits an institution will compensate those individuals who had the opportunity to be better-off in an alternative institution. Note: we are not justifying distributions of property within a system, we are justifying the institution or relations themselves.
22. In conditions of extreme scarcity the Paretian theory under consideration will not sanction any acquisitions because someone will always be worsened. In such conditions, the Paretian theory will have to be supplemented so that justified acquisitions are possible.
23. It may be the case that Ginger would not have existed if another institution of property relations had been in place at the time of her birth. Maybe her parents would have never met if an alternative institution had developed. For now, assume that Ginger would have existed in this alternative institution of property relations.
24. Some would ague that this should not be the default position—we should assume that acquisitions always worsen and the evidence must show otherwise for us to deviate from this position. I think that this view is dubious given the value-enhancing effects that restricted access offers—the question becomes what kind of restricted access should we adopt? Below I will argue that the institution of private property is strongly Pareto-superior when compared to its rivals. Thus the question of the correct default position is largely moot.
25. I should note that it is not as if the institution *owes* an individual compensation. The compensation that occurs at this level is an epiphenomenon or by product of numerous individuals acting in certain ways. It would be rather odd to maintain that a way of behaving or relating to objects—an institution of property relations—could *owe* compensation.
26. G. A. Cohen, "Self-Ownership, World-Ownership, and Equality," in *Justice and Equality Here and Now,* edited by F. S. Lucash (Ithaca, NY: Cornell University Press, 1989), 132.

27. Cohen, "Self-Ownership, World-Ownership, and Equality," 133.
28. Cohen, "Self-Ownership, World-Ownership, and Equality," 133.
29. Within a general institution of private property individuals are free to be communists, socialists, communitarians, or capitalists with their property. There is no moral reason forbidding individuals from voluntarily arranging a commune where use is based on need or arranging a social institution where property relations are ordered to help the least well-off be better-off. So it is possible for individuals to voluntarily move from a system of private property to some other system of property relations. All that is forbidden is a kind of coercion—individuals cannot be forced into these arrangements. Within a system of private property individuals can do what they want with their property, but this is not the case for many alternative systems of property relations.
30. Eric Mack, "The Self-Ownership Proviso: A New and Improved Lockean Proviso," *Social Philosophy & Policy* 12 (Winter 1995): 207-8.
31. Harold Demsetz in "Toward a Theory of Property Rights," *American Economic Review* 47 (1967): 347-59, argues that an institution of property rights is the answer to the negative externalities that befall the commons. For general discussions, outside of Demsetz, extolling the virtues of private ownership over various rival institutions see, Garrett Harden, "The Tragedy of the Commons," *Science* 162 (1968): 1243-48; and Anderson and Hill, "The Evolution of Property Rights: A Study of the American West," *Journal Of Law And Economics* 18 (1975): 163-79.
32. As noted in in chapter 5, one state of the world, S_1, is Pareto-superior to another, S_2, if and only if no one is worse-off in S_1 than in S_2, and at least one person is better-off in S_1 than in S_2. S_1 is *strongly* Pareto-superior to S_2 if everyone is better-off in S_1 than in S_2, and *weakly* Pareto-superior if at least one person is better-off and no one is worse-off.
33. In examining the justification of systems of intellectual property protection I work within natural law legal theory,—i.e., I assume that the task of legal structures is to reflect and augment moral rights, obligations, duties, and the like.
34. Needless to say, this strategy will call for radical revisions in modern Anglo-American systems of intellectual property protection. In chapter 7, I will examine various revisions in Anglo-American systems of intellectual property.
35. Adapted from Mack. Mack also includes a coherence requirement that seems inappropriate for systems of intellectual property. "To be coherent, the specification of entitlement-conferring actions must be such that non-compossible entitlements do not arise, so that compliance with the resulting entitlements will always be possible." (535) Since it is possible for compossible entitlements to occur within systems of intellectual property, this feature is omitted.
36. While intellectual works cannot be destroyed they may be lost or forgotten—consider the number of Greek or Mayan intellectual works that were lost.
37. The example comes from D. Schmidtz, "When is Original Acquisition Required," in *The Monist* 73 (October 1990): 513.
38. Not all secrecy is a bad thing. Surely, keeping sensitive personal information to oneself is justified. My position here is that having an option to disclose or not is generally a good policy. Certain kinds of information will be disclosed so that licenses may be granted and profits maximized, while other kinds of information will be held as secrets. For more about secrecy and the control of sensitive personal information see chapters 8-11.
39. Roger Miners and Robert Staaf, "Patents, Copyrights, and Trademarks: Property or Monopoly," in *Harvard Journal of Law and Public Policy* 13 (Summer 1990): 919.
40. Tom Palmer, "Are Patents and Copyrights Morally Justified?" in *Harvard Journal of Law and Public Policy* 13 (Summer 1990): 830.

146   Intellectual Property and Information Control

41.   Jan Narveson, *The Libertarian Ideal* (1988), 77.
42.   Tom Palmer, "Are Patents and Copyrights Morally Justified?" 831.
43.   See, for example, 17 U.S.C. § 107 and District Judge Leval's opinion in *New Era Publications International v. Henery Holt and Co.*, 695 F.Supp 1493 S.D.N.Y. 1988 (fair use); and 17 U.S.C. § 304 (limited duration); 17 U.S.C. § 109(a) (first sale).
44.   *See* 17 U.S.C. § 107 and District Judge Leval's opinion in *New Era Publications International v. Henery Holt and Co.*, 695 F.Supp 1493 S.D.N.Y. 1988.
45.   For example, see U.S. CONST. amend. IV; Restatement of the Law of Property, Chapter 1, The American Law Institute (1936); W. Hohfeld, *Fundamental Legal Concepts As Applied In Judicial Reasoning* (1919).

7

A New Look at Copyrights, Patents, and Trade Secrets

"Market-mediated innovation is definitely the way to go, and my bottom line on the intellectual property front is let us not screw it up. The agonizing thing is, I cannot tell whether that means do nothing or do something radical."
—Mitchell D. Kapor, chairman, ON Technology, Inc.[1]

Introduction

Suppose the Lockean theory of intellectual property developed in the last three chapters is largely correct and that rule-utilitarian models for justifying rights to intellectual works have been undermined. Once the rule-utilitarian underpinnings are stripped away we are in a position to reexamine intellectual property institutions with an eye toward incorporating Lockean principles. Continuing with the themes started in chapter 2, I will present an alternative model of intellectual property and provide a taxonomy of ownership rights.[2]

Explaining and defending a new Lockean model of intellectual property will require a review of the dominant rules found within Anglo-American institutions. The immediate questions that leap to mind are: What does the Paretian have to say about the actual practices and institutions of Anglo-American copyright, patent, and trade secret law? What of the fair use and first sale rules, the idea/expression distinction, and the limits on ownership rights?[3]

John Stuart Mill once said, "it is sometimes both possible and useful to point out the way, though without being oneself prepared to adventure far into it."[4] In this chapter, I will try to do better than merely point the way. I will argue that we ought to narrow the scope of the idea/expression distinction, consider the possibility of perpetual rights for certain types of intellectual property, and abandon the fair use limitation as well as the first sale rule.

In place of fair use and first sale, I will defend a contract-based system that will, in many cases, parallel the effects of these rules and limit government incursions into the realm of property creation.[5] The proposed Uniform Commercial Code (UCC) Article 2B, now known as UCITA, is intended to provide a contract-based framework for transactions that fall within copyright and other information industries. "To date, there is no statute or body of law which is able to effectively handle the unique and cutting edge issues that have risen . . . relating to the intangible asset of information and the rights associated with its use."[6] One of the complaints against Article 2B is that it seems to provide a contractual way for rights holders to circumvent or bypass the free use zones created by first sale and fair use. Article 2B fits well with the model of intellectual and intangible property defended in this volume. As Locke noted many times, the primary purpose for creating and maintaining a commonwealth is the protection of individual property. Sadly, with respect to intellectual property, governments have gone far beyond this line.[7]

Economic Rights, Creator's Rights, Contractual-Based Rights, and Intellectual Property

There are a number of different kinds of rights that may surround the ownership of intellectual property. There are economic rights, creator's rights, and rights generated from valid contracts or agreements. Each of these different categories of rights mark out different domains of protection for the owner of intellectual property. I will assume that economic rights and creator's rights are generated, and justified, at the level of acts, systems, and institutions. Suppose, for instance, that the democratic process, or some such process, yields justified entitlement-conferring rules so long as these institutions are consistent with the Lockean theory of intellectual property developed in chapters 4 through 6. Obviously, there is a plethora of systems of intellectual property that do not conflict with the theory that I have presented. Nonetheless, there are certain features that will be ruled out and a general sketch along Lockean lines will be helpful in deciding how to amend Anglo-American systems of intellectual property protection.

Economic Rights

Owning an intellectual work confers certain economic rights on the property holder.[8]   While these rights differ depending on the domain of what is protected, they center on the control of physical expressions or embodiments of intellectual works. Our economic life takes place in the realm of physical objects, and so economic rights to intellectual works confer control over concrete expressions. Almost to the exclusion of all other rights, Anglo-American systems of intellectual property have been concerned with the economic rights of authors and inventors.[9] Non-economic rights are not granted because they afford no further incentive for the production of intellectual works. Upon rejecting rule-utilitarian models, new room has been found for what many think are canonical cases of intellectual property violations.

The economic rights that are conferred on a copyright holder are the rights to reproduce, adapt and distribute copies, and to control public displays or performances of the work.[10] Patent holders have the economic rights of production, use, sale, and transfer.[11] Similar rights protect trademarks and mere ideas.[12] In any case, these rights allow the control of physical embodiments of intellectual works.

Many authors maintain that there are no further rights to intellectual works than economic rights.[13] They argue that granting non-economic rights to authors and inventors will allow for the control of mere ideas and restrict the intellectual life and thought processes of everyone. Radical adherents to this view conjure up images of the "thought police" who monitor everyone's thoughts and punish infringers. As we shall see, this view is clearly mistaken, for there are, upon analysis, relatively few creator's rights and, furthermore, these rights do not call for the "thought police" or restrict the thoughts of anyone.

Creator's Rights

Leaving aside economic rights, authors and creators have rights to control abstract ideas.[14] Take, for example, the non-economic rights that surround the creation of new theories of science, history, literary criticism, philosophy, and the like. Einstein's control of his Theory of Relativity is more than just a right to be given due credit as the original author of the theory. He also has the right to create and publish in any form desired, the right to prevent any deformation, mutilation or other modification of the expression, and a right against misappropriation or plagiarism.[15] This latter right is understood by many within the Western academic tradition to be moral bedrock. There is something deeply wrong with copying the ideas of someone else and claiming that they are your own or knowingly misrepresenting a theory or argument. Before turning to the notion of creator's rights found on the European continent I will briefly consider the relationship between these rights and plagiarism.

In one sense, plagiarism seems to be a simple example of fraud and not directly relevant to intellectual property violations. Those who plagiarize take credit for something that they did not create. In an effort to pass themselves off as being more intelligent, witty, or engaging, and deserving of more respect, money, or a better grade, plagiarizers maintain a false appearance. On this view, what makes plagiarism morally objectionable is not that someone's intellectual property has been violated, but that the plagiarizer is maintaining a lie to obtain some benefit for himself.

Nevertheless, those who plagiarize may violate another's rights to control an intellectual work. This is obvious in cases where the individual who plagiarizes sells what he has copied—a case where economic rights are violated. The question is what non-economic rights, if any, are violated when plagiarism occurs? Surely we can imagine cases where plagiarism damages the reputation of the creator through the mutilation of some intellectual work.

Even so, there seems to be no necessary connection between plagiarism and the violation of intellectual property rights, for we can also imagine cases where plagiarism occurs and no property rights are violated. For example, suppose a student copies something from the public domain that was created by an author who remained anonymous. Given that there are no economic rights in this case and that there is no author to damage there can be no intellectual property violations. This case of plagiarism appears to be nothing more than a simple case of misrepresentation or fraud.

Within the French system of intellectual property there are four personal rights that are retained by the author even after she has transferred her economic rights.[16] These rights are: the right of attribution (due credit as the author); the right to disclosure (to publish in any form desired); the right of integrity (similar to rights against deformation, etc.); and the right of retraction.[17] In a 1902 French court case focusing on whether the ex-wife of an artist had the right to share in the economic rights of her husband, the court ruled that she did. At the same time the court made it clear that this decision did not "detract from the right of the author, inherent in his personality, of later modifying his creation, or even suppressing it."[18]

Josef Kohler, a prominent defender of creator's rights, summarizes the view nicely:

> The writer can not only demand that no strange work be presented as his, but that his own work not be presented in a changed form. The author can make this demand even when he has given up his copyright. This demand is not so much an exercise of dominion over my work, as it is of dominion over my being, over my personality which thus gives me the right to demand that no one shall share in my personality and have me say things which I have not said.[19]

Thus, misrepresenting what an author says or mutilating a work of art and allowing those who view it to think that it is *entirely* the original author's creation is to (potentially) damage the personality of the creator. It should also be noted that these rights have been extended to include resale royalty rights which grant monetary compensation to creators when their work is resold for substantial profits.[20] This matter may be best left to contractual arrangements between the owner of the intellectual work and the buyer of the concrete expression (see contractual rights below).

The primary thrust of these non-economic rights is to protect the integrity of the author or inventor from slanderous attacks and public ridicule. Also protected is the creator's right to control initial disclosure which can be understood as an extension of her rights to control the initial disclosure of her own thoughts. Protecting these rights do not call for the "thought police" or alarming invasions of individual privacy. Once an author or inventor voices her idea, the cat is out of the bag, so-to-speak.[21] In such cases the idea has entered the public domain of thought and language, but it does not follow that the author or inventor has automatically renounced all economic and non-economic claims to the intellectual work.[22] Even though the ideas have entered the public domain there are certain restrictions on what can be done with them. For example, an individual may not claim that the ideas of another are his own, nor may he knowingly alter or distort these ideas and then attribute them to the original author.

Similar examples are easily found with other forms of intellectual property.[23] Imagine that someone mutilated and subsequently released a new song by Pearl Jam so that both personal and economic damage fell upon the band members. Or suppose someone alters and distorts a painting by Hugh Syme damaging his reputation as well as his ability to procure new painting contracts. All of these examples show how it is possible that the ideas that make up expressions can be widely circulated and not invalidate property claims by the author.

Moreover, it should be noted that it is up to the author or inventor to disclose her intellectual work or to keep it a secret. This view is summed nicely by Lynn Sharp Pain and Lysander Spooner:

> If a person has any right with respect to her ideas, surely it is the right to control their initial disclosure. A person may decide to keep her ideas to herself, to disclose them to a select few, or to publish them widely. Whether those ideas are best described as views and opinions, plans and intentions, facts and knowledge, or fantasies and inventions is immaterial. While it might be socially useful for a person to be generous with her ideas there is no general obligation to do so.[24]

> Nothing is, by its own essence and nature, more perfectly susceptible of exclusive appropriation, than thought. It originates in the mind of a single individual. It can leave his mind only in obedience to his will. It dies with him, if he so elect.[25]

This view fits well with the Lockean theory presented in earlier chapters. Individuals are worthy of a deep moral respect and have a kind of absolute sovereignty over their thoughts, feelings, hopes, wishes, and intellectual creations. I take this to be akin to presumptive claims of non-interference against others with respect to the initial disclosure of the contents of one's own mind. Whatever else is true about controlling ideas or intellectual works, if we have absolute sovereignty over anything, surely it is over our own thoughts.[26]

Contractual-Based Rights and Intellectual Property

Contracts and agreements may also generate rights that allow for the control of intellectual works. If I own some intellectual work and the physical expression of it and you would like to purchase it, then we can negotiate the terms of sale. Our agreement might include a prohibition of renting the expression to your friends or even giving it away as a gift. The terms of the contract would be up to us, and if the agreement is made under fair conditions it would be enforceable in a court of law.

To be sure, contracts concerning what can be done with an intellectual work or a physical expression depend on prior entitlements. If Ginger does not own some intellectual work or the physical embodiment of it, then any contract she makes concerning the future use of these items is suspect. This is just to say that with respect to intellectual works or physical objects, justified entitlements are prior to the binding agreements that range over the goods in question.

An example of contracts grounding the control of intellectual works is exhibited by Anglo-American trade secret. Employees of many companies are sworn to secrecy and sign contracts that require that they not divulge company secrets even upon termination of employment.[27] Coupled with a privacy right to control one's own thoughts and maybe creator's rights, contractual obligations concerning what can be done with physical expressions, as well as the ideas themselves, may arise.

Physical Property Rights

Rights to control physical goods can be distinguished from intellectual property rights or (IP) economic rights, creator's rights, and agreement-based rights. For example, suppose Fred owns a computer program as intellectual property, does not own any physical expression of the program, and is negotiating the sale of his (IP) economic rights to Ginger.[28] After the sale, Ginger has obtained economic control of Fred's computer program and makes a limited agreement with Crusoe, who owns vast numbers of blank computer disks, to produce and distribute 10,000 copies of the program. Finally, suppose Friday purchases a copy of the computer program at the local software outlet.

The rights relationships in this case are quite complex. Fred retains creator's rights to the computer program but has contracted and sold the economic rights to Ginger. Ginger, in turn, has granted Crusoe limited control over the economic rights which allow him to embody the intellectual work in his physical property—the blank computer disks. Friday, in buying a copy of the computer program, has certain rights to do what he pleases with his copy. He does not, however, obtain any economic rights or creator's rights unless specified in the prior contracts of Fred and Ginger, Ginger and Crusoe, and Crusoe and Friday. Fred may even make it part of his deal with Ginger that Friday not be given any economic rights.

Ideas and Expressions, First Sale, Fair Use, and Multiple Patent Rights

With this taxonomy of rights in place, I would like to reexamine a number of dominant rules found within Anglo-American institutions of intellectual property. As we shall see, many of these rules are difficult to justify on Lockean grounds, and a few must be abandoned—arguments that may work well for the rule-utilitarian cannot be embraced by the Lockean.

Ideas and Expressions

A salient feature of Anglo-American institutions of intellectual property is that expressions, and not ideas, are protected.[29] It is an old truism in copyright and patent law that you cannot protect an idea but only your expression or the physical embodiment of it. Ideas, like facts, are in the public domain and cannot and should not be exclusively controlled by anyone. Defenders of this position typically conjure up images of the "thought police" and argue along rule-utilitarian lines claiming that protecting mere ideas would diminish social utility. Not only would such protection be logistically impossible but it would also require invasions of privacy that most would find distasteful.[30]

As was noted earlier, Einstein's Theory of Relativity, as expressed in various articles is not protected under copyright law. The individual who copies abstract theories and expresses them in her own words may be guilty of plagiarism, but she cannot be held liable for copyright infringement. The distinction between the protection of fixed expressions and abstract ideas has led to the "merger doctrine":

> The rule is that if a certain order of words is the only reasonable way, or one of only a few reasonable ways, of putting an idea to use, that precise order of words will be protected narrowly or not at all.[31]

If there is no way to separate idea from expression, then a copyright cannot be obtained. Suppose that I create a new recipe for spicy Chinese noodles and there is only one way, or a limited number of ways, to express the idea. If this were the case, then I could not obtain copyright protection, because the idea and the expression have been merged. Granting me a copyright to the recipe would amount to granting a right to control the abstract ideas that make up the recipe.[32]

Consistent with the theory developed in the last few chapters, a theory that will at best put constraints on the kinds of rules that may be used to restrict domains of protection, the question becomes what are we willing to protect within Anglo-American intellectual property institutions? As I have already noted, the Paretian theory developed in chapters 4-6 will not and cannot provide a set of rules that mark out some particular domain of intellectual property protection—one set of rules will most likely be Pareto non-comparable when compared to another. The best the Paretian and Lockean can do is to determine which rules cannot be defended. Simply put, our system of intellectual property must be consistent with the rights generated at the level of acts, an institution of private property relations, and grounded or constrained by deontic considerations that underlies these moral claims.

Trade secret protection represents a domain that allows for the ownership of ideas—it is not as if the notion of "idea ownership" is actually foreign to us.[33] That copyright and patent systems adhere to some version of the idea/expression distinction may be simply a matter of what we are, as a society, willing to protect within these domains. Those who wish to defend property claims to ideas may have to do so within the institution of trade secret or by the common law tradition sometimes called "the law of ideas."[34] When Buchwald sued Paramount Pictures and won he was asserting rights to control a set of ideas no matter what their particular expression.[35] Moreover, rights that protect style, reputation, and the like may be protected within the domain of creator's rights.

Thus, the idea/expression distinction should be abandoned as a kind of across-the-board rule regarding intellectual property. Such policies have been undermined to the extent that their rule-utilitarian justifications have been undermined and they are not consistent with the Lockean theory presented in earlier chapters. On my view it does not matter whether or not some idea can be expressed in a limited number of ways—if no one is worsened by the taking then it should be permitted.

Music, literature, poetry, sculpture, live performances, and the like, are examples of ideas (loosely construed) and expressions that are merged. It is not the notes that Hendrix plays or words that he sings but the way *he* plays those notes and sings those words. Similarly, there is more to Hemingway's *The Sun Also Rises* than the mere words on the page. Part of the work, maybe even the most important part, is Hemingway's style, and style is more general and seemingly prior to expression. Creator's rights may provide the appropriate forum to discuss violations or copying of style—to copy or imitate style is a kind of plagiarism that may damage reputation as well.

It might be argued that allowing creator's rights will lead to an alarming expansion of protection for those intellectual works where idea and expression are merged. In general we may ask, are there any new rights generated for the intellectual property holder when the ideas and their expressions cannot be separated? First, even if there is an expansion of rights in these cases, I do not see this as a problem. But, even more to the point I would deny there is any expansion of rights at all. These authors and inventors have economic and non-economic rights that are protected in certain ways—it seems that once we recognize non-economic rights the expansion has already occurred. For example, suppose that I have rights to control the set of ideas that make up my new recipe for spicy Chinese noodles. What new right would I have if this recipe were written down—I would still have rights to control the ideas, as trade secrets maybe, as well as rights to control the tangible expression.

If the idea/expression distinction and the merger doctrine are necessary for a workable system of copyright protection, then there would be a compelling case for keeping these rules. So long as there are other, maybe overlapping, domains of protection that protect justified property claims to ideas, I see no reason to abandon this feature of copyright law. Thus copyrighted protection may still allow for freedom of thought and expression although creator's rights, for example, may limit what can be done with a particular expression after dissemination.

The First Sale Rule: A Moratorium on Libraries?

Within Anglo-American copyright institutions once an author sells an expression or physical embodiment of her intellectual work she loses control over its further distribution.[36] The owner of the copy can do whatever she wants with the expression except violate the economic rights of the intellectual property holder. Owners of expressions can give them away, sell and rent them, or destroy them. The exceptions to this "first sale" doctrine are musical recordings and videos where owners retain the right to derive income through rental agreements.[37] The underlying assumption of the first sale rule is that we can distinguish between the owner of an intellectual work and the owner of the physical embodiment of that intellectual work. As noted in chapter 3, the rights of intellectual property holders are limited after the first sale because of utilitarian concerns. Granting authors and inventors control of expressions beyond the first sale would diminish overall social utility giving away too much with minimal gains in incentives. This is just to say that there would be no overbalancing loss in the production of intellectual works by not allowing authors and inventors control over expressions after the first sale. Moreover, granting such control may hinder the operation of libraries and other general information stores.[38]

Given my rejection of rule-utilitarianism in general and of the specific rule-utilitarian argument that justifies the first sale rule, we may ask the question of how the first sale rule may fair within the model under consideration. What does the Lockean have to say about this rule and public information storehouses like libraries? My view is that once intellectual property rights have been determined, at the level of acts, systems, or institutions, the issues surrounding the first sale rule largely dissipate and become a matter of contracts.[39]

Public information storehouses, like libraries and data banks, would not be protected under the auspices of promoting education and social utility. These warehouses of information could be filled with intellectual works that are already in the public domain (more on this later), but they could not include currently owned intellectual property unless specified by the owner. For example, imagine that Ginger has satisfied a rights-generating process at the level of acts and systems for her new theory of literary criticism and suppose that she publishes the theory herself. On my view, she has intellectual property rights to her work and, in this case, owns the physical embodiment of her intellectual work as well. The distribution and subsequent control of the expression, outside of her copyrights and creator's rights, is a matter of manipulating a physical object—and is therefore not directly a part of protecting her intellectual property. We can separate economic rights, creator's rights, physical property rights, and rights generated by valid contracts. So, if Ginger wants copies of her book to find their way into libraries, then it is up to her. For example, when she sells a copy of her book to Fred she may explicitly agree that he may sell the book to any person or institution, including information storehouses like libraries. She may also, however, make it an explicit part of the agreement that Fred not sell the book to anyone.

Currently owned intellectual works and their physical expressions may be included in a public information storehouse only if the relevant agreement has been made. As a matter of legal expediency we may adopt a first sale rule unless a contract has specified otherwise. But, whatever the default position is, contracts may serve to restrict what can be done with the physical embodiments of intellectual works. This policy would allow artists to sell their art with the provision that they get a share of the profits should the work become trendy. It would also allow authors and inventors to build into contractual arrangements provisions that allow them to retain some control of an intellectual work well after the first sale. It should be noted, however, that such provisions will drive down the value of owning the expression.[40]

Once rights are established it will be up to the holders of those rights to determine subsequent limitations on use and sale. For example, I may build into a sale agreement that my land never be developed or that in fifty years it be given to the city. If these requirements are binding it is because I hold legitimate title to the land in the first place. Similarly with intellectual works. Moreover, once creator's rights are recognized there will be even more control afforded to authors and inventors after the first sale. A painter may prohibit modification of some work, including restoration. Movies may be sold with the provision that they not be altered from the original black and white. Reputations may be protected by prohibiting alterations in presentations or additions to some intellectual work.

The position that I have been sketching may cause great alarm for some. Libraries will be gutted and education curtailed—the commons of thought and speech will become impoverished.[41] I think that such predictions are clearly false, but even if they were not, I would still advocate contracts as a basis for controlling embodiments of intellectual works. The charge seems to be that we must override individual rights to intellectual works with respect to the first sale rule because of the loss of social utility if we did not. But this has all too often been the calling card of oppression and is the first step down a very slippery slope. Loren Lomasky puts the point nicely:

Even when arguments for overriding rights are couched in the most high-minded terms, laced with references to the general welfare of the need for mutual sacrifice in a just cause, one may suspect that the rhetoric is meant to veil the quest for power or personal advancement. History is a textbook for cynics. Having read from it, we may be prompted to insist on undeviating respect for rights, no matter how beckoning the inducements to the contrary, because we have no confidence in people's ability to discriminate accurately and dispassionately between incursions that will maximize public good and those that will debase it. If we are to err either on the side of too much flexibility or excess rigidity, better—far better!—the latter.[42]

I am not here arguing that rights should be upheld even though the heavens may fall. A more moderate deontic position leaves open the possibility, in certain cases, for rights to be trumped when the consequences are dire. It would not, however, allow rights to be overridden for mere incremental increases in overall social utility. Consequentialists who claim that defenses of robust rights are "radical" or "extreme" have misplaced these terms in most cases. For we may ask, is there any room within consequentialist moral theory for rights that stand independent of all but the most dire of consequences?

While the elimination of the first sale rule may cause some decrease in the overall amount of available and useful information, I do not think that information storehouses will dry up. My reasons for thinking this are primarily market-based. First, much of the information found in libraries and the like is non-commercial information. For example, new theories explaining the fall of the Roman Empire, philosophical views, and books on literary criticism, have little or no market value. The creators of these kinds of works would have little incentive to restrict the distribution of their ideas. And given that, in many cases, careers, tenure, and reputation are at stake, these authors would actually desire the widest distribution of their ideas and theories as possible. In these cases, libraries would serve the career and long-term economic interests of authors and inventors.

Moreover, other economically viable information may be distributed in the hopes of fostering profits through licensing agreements and to preempt independent creation.[43] In discussing the strategy of information distribution and licensing agreements with a number of executives in the computer field, I have found this to be the case.[44] While I don't know if this is a general strategy, it seems likely to be the case, especially in light of the market advantages it offers.[45]

Finally, libraries and other information storehouses are already filled with works that are available for use. These works are not available for appropriation and make up a vast block of knowledge that anyone can access and build upon. Thus, given market forces, licensing strategies, and the like, it is arguably the case that information warehouses will not become impoverished.

Fair Use[46]

In many cases where issues of infringement arise two principles of rule-utilitarian based copyright law clash. One principle, typically understood as the foundation for protection, is the need to protect the economic rights of the author so that incentives to produce are maintained. The second principle is found in the desire to disseminate information as widely as possible so that progress is optimized. As was noted in earlier chapters, these interests create a basic tension within the Anglo-American tradition. Maximal long-term progress that is generated by the widespread dissemination of information is only obtained by restricting the information flow temporarily. But, this need not entail absolute control of the intellectual work or its physical expressions. This view has led to a number of restrictions on the holders of intellectual property. One restriction on copyright is known as "fair use."

The fair use rule has been a recent source of much debate within the academic community since publishers brought suit against copying done by CopyEase and Zips. Judge Leval sums up the dominate view about fair use in his 1988 opinion in *New Era Publication International v. Henry Holt and Company*:

> Although the law zealously protects the commercial interests of the artist from unscrupulous opportunistic interlopers, it recognizes that not all copying of artistic invention is necessarily undesirable piracy. Certain forms of copying of artistic creation are indispensable to education, journalism, history, criticism, humor and other informative endeavors; the statute therefore allows latitude in appropriate circumstance for copying of protected artistic expression and exempts such copying from a finding of infringement. The doctrine of *fair use* identifies this category of permissible copying. It offers a means of balancing the interests of the copyright holder against the public interest in dissemination of information.[47]

The notion of "fair use" made its debut in American law in *Folsom v. Marsh* (9 F.Cas. 342 (C.C.D. Mass. 1841)) but was only recently codified in section 107 of the 1976 Copyright Act. It is typically argued that:

> Notwithstanding the provisions of section 106 (limitations due to subject matter, etc.), the fair use of a copyrighted work, including such use by reproduction in copies of

phonorecords or by any other means specified by that section, for purposes such as criticism, comment, news reporting, teaching (including multiple copies for classroom use), scholarship, or research, is not an infringement of copyright. In determining whether the use made of a work in any particular case is a fair use the factors to be considered include:

1.   the purpose and character of the use, including whether such use is of a commercial nature is for nonprofit educational purposes;

2.   the nature of the copyrighted work;

3.   the amount and substantiality of the portion used in relation to the copyrighted work as a whole; and,

4.   the effect of the use upon the potential market for or value of the copyrighted work.[48]

The justification that is typically given for the fair use rule is that these limitations on the rights of authors do not cause a significant decrease in the incentive structure of the institution. Moreover, if these limitations do cause a loss in incentives and a corresponding loss in the production of intellectual works, these losses are overbalanced by the overall social good that obtains through fair use.

To be sure, the preceding argument leaves the Lockean cold and assuming that rule-utilitarian justifications have failed, we may ask what the Lockean has to say about fair use. I will argue that fair use should be contractual between the buyers and sellers of intellectual property and that there should be no mandatory government legislated policy of fair use.

Before continuing though, I would like to address a mistake that may be made concerning my version of Locke's proviso related to fair use. It could be argued that since the fair use of a work generally requires that the situation of the owner not be worsened economically the proviso actually justifies the fair use rule. How could the copyright holder have any complaint? No harm, so no foul. But violating a right, already established, does not need to worsen to be wrong. Consider Hubin's Dr. Demento case.[49] Dr. Demento, a demented scientist, has developed a rejuvenation pill that allows him to use the bodies of unsuspecting individuals while they are asleep. The pill, once administered, causes the victim's body to rejuvenate as it normally would from sleep. Demento uses his victim's bodies in demented ways but they are not worsened. Each morning they arise as if they had slept soundly for eight hours. The peeping Tom does not need to economically worsen his victim to have violated a right to privacy. You need not have harmed me to have trespassed. Moreover, it could be argued that a loss of control *is* a relevant kind of worsening or harm, especially if we view intellectual property rights as affording a kind of control to authors and inventors.[50]

To continue, fair use should be contractual between the buyers and sellers of intellectual property. On this view, it is up to the owner an of intellectual work whether or not she wants to allow her property to be used, without compensation, in various ways. As before, suppose Ginger creates a new theory of critical assessment in literature and publishes her views in a book. If she wants her theory to be cited and widely critiqued she may allow the aforementioned uses of her work. She may also give up rights to her work entirely. But if she wants to maintain strict control there is nothing to prevent her. She could refuse any direct copying of her theory or as part of the sale contract require that the ideas in her work not be discussed with anyone. Absent such limitations her fellows could discuss her work or express her ideas in their own words and give her credit. Once her theory has entered the public domain of language and thought, Ginger has lost absolute control of the ideas that make up her theory in the following sense. She cannot control the thought processes of others when they think about her ideas. What she can control, however, are expressions of her ideas—she can exclude any unauthorized embodiments of her work.

At this point detractors will claim that such a policy will hinder research, education, literature, and cause a general decrease in social progress. This charge parallels the objection to abandoning the first sale rule, and my reply to that objection applies *mutatis mutandis* to this kind of objection. If a loss of social progress is the price that must be paid for upholding rights then so be it. More to the point, however, there are market-based reasons for why authors and inventors would, in large part, continue current practices.

Furthermore, the practice of maintaining free use zones, such as fair use, first sale, and the European personal use exemption, cannot be maintained in digital environments like the World Wide Web.[51] There can be no trade-off between access and protection in these environments. If I have access to your work, then there is nothing to stop me from downloading the work and distributing encrypted copies to my friends. Copying the intellectual efforts of others used to be time consuming and produced inferior products. This is why the pirating of print media, however alarming, remained relatively infrequent—imagine copying an entire book. With the digitization of print media, as well as many other kinds of intellectual works, copying has become virtually costless and incredibly easy. The problem is that when works are placed online, protection will require that those who browse the work pay first[52]—there can be no free use of protected materials online, because such use would imperil protection. With the proliferation of encryption programs and applications that allow for anonymous digital transfers, no copyrighted worked placed online will be completely protectable.[53] Nevertheless, certain technological advances in digital environments will afford some protection, but not if free use provisions are maintained.[54]

Eliminating Exclusive Patent Rights

Current practice within the Anglo-American tradition excludes someone who independently invents an already patented intellectual work from ownership. The general rule is that the first person to reduce a new invention to practice will obtain a patent monopoly that excludes all others from using the patented work. This kind of exclusive monopoly is only allowed for processes of manufacture, compositions of matter, and the like—it holds only for the subject matter of patents. Trade secrets and copyrights do not exclude others from *independently* creating or inventing a preexisting work and obtaining title to their expression or secret. The justification typically given for granting exclusive monopoly rights to patents is rule-utilitarian in nature. This rule ensures that valuable ideas will be reduced to practice quickly, so that patents can be obtained and market shares increased or maintained. The rule also limits conflicting patent and infringement claims and requires disclosure so that information can be widely disseminated.

The Paretian and Lockean theory under consideration, cannot make use of such justifications. Crudely, intellectual property rights arise when others are not worsened by such acquisitions. But surely those who have independently created a patented process are worsened by being excluded from obtaining intellectual property rights. This point was originally voiced by Robert Nozick:

> The theme of someone worsening another's situation by depriving him of something he otherwise would possess may also illuminate the example of patents. An inventor's

patent does not deprive others of an object which would not exist if not for the inventor. Yet patents would have this effect on others who independently invent the object. Therefore, these independent inventors, upon whom the burden of proving independent discovery may rest, should not be excluded from utilizing their own invention as they wish (including selling it to others).[55]

Imagine the case where company X is a mere two weeks behind company Y in producing the machine that physically embodies the idea or ideas that make up an intellectual work. To simplify matters, suppose that X and Y will not be in competition—maybe X owns certain other patents that Y cannot invent around and vice versa, leaving both in separate markets. If Y obtains exclusive patent rights to this machine, then X is surely worsened. Moreover, why allow multiple copyright and trade secret rights but prohibit multiple patent rights—the arguments grounding this provision for patents would seemingly work for copyrights and trade secrets as well.

This just could be a cost of doing business, however. A defense of exclusive patent rights might appeal to the notion that these rights, and subsequent apparent worsenings, are built into the institution private property and capitalism. In essence, this was my answer to the competition problem—apparent worsenings at the level of acts are overcome at the institutional level. Those who lose out are not worsened because the lost opportunities in question are dependent on a system that allows for this exclusivity. But clearly such exclusivity would run afoul of the rights that may be generated at the level of acts. Moreover, it is not as if this provision is somehow a necessary part of the institution of private property itself.[56]

It may be argued that multiple patent rights should not be granted because of a problem similar to the following concern voiced by William Leggett:

Two authors, without concert or intercommunication, may describe the same incidents, in language so nearly identical that the two books, for all purposes of sale, shall be the same. Yet one writer may make a free gift of his production to the public, may throw it open in common; and then what becomes of the other's right of property?[57]

If we allow multiple individuals to patent the same intellectual work, then problems may arise when one of these property holders decides to give her invention to humankind or when the rights lapse. What becomes of X's property right to some intellectual work when Y decides to allow free use of the invention?

Aside from noting that this problem would fall on copyright institutions as well, in this case, non-owners are free to make copies and produce artifacts based on Y's intellectual work—but not X's.[58] While the practice of giving up one's intellectual property rights and allowing anyone to use the intellectual work would be rare, given market forces, such things may occur. Suppose that an author independently rewrites *Like Water For Chocolate* and gives his expression to all of humankind. What then becomes of Laura Esquivel's rights to her work? On my view Esquivel would retain rights to control any embodiment of her work. She could not, however, control copies of the new independently created version. This may mean that Esquivel would lose out in economic terms—assuming that everyone who wanted a copy would obtain a free one—but it does not invalidate any of her intellectual property rights. And the same is true of patent rights. In the aforementioned case, company X would retain control over any instantiations of their intellectual work, but this would not include controlling every instantiation—e.g., it would not include rights to control the embodiments of Y's intellectual work.

Limits on Ownership Rights: The Shadow of the Proviso

Within the Anglo-American tradition intellectual property rights have a built-in sunset that is justified on the following grounds.[59] Rights are granted as incentive for the production of intellectual works and this production in turn allows for the widespread dissemination of information. This is just to say that there is a kind of trade-off between short-term protection and long-term access to information. If intellectual property rights did not lapse after a certain amount of time, if there were no built-in sunset on these rights, then access to information could be indefinitely restricted. Such a system would not be as good as a system where incentives were maintained and access to information was also maximized. These concerns have led to the current practice of limiting patent rights to twenty years and copyrights to the lifetime of the author plus seventy years.[60]

As with the justification for the free use zones of "first sale" and "fair use," the Lockean theory that I have presented cannot make use of this trade-off position between protection and access. On my view, rights are not justified because they provide for incentives that in turn lead to widespread dissemination of information and corresponding gains in social utility (although such considerations may have a place when considering the *Pareto superiority* of institutions of private property compared to rival arrangements). We may ask, what does the Lockean have to say about this issue—should intellectual property rights be perpetual and, if not, what would justify limiting these rights?

Robert Nozick suggests that intellectual property rights be limited because allowing perpetual or lengthy rights will worsen others:

> Furthermore, a known invention drastically lessens the chances of actual independent invention. For persons who know of an invention usually will not try to reinvent it, and the notion of independent discovery here would be murky at best. Yet we may assume that in the absence of the original invention, sometime later someone else would have come up with it. This suggests placing a time limit on patents, as a rough rule of thumb to approximate how long it would have taken, in the absence of knowledge of the invention, for independent discovery.[61]

This argument for limiting rights to intellectual works has to do with what I shall call the shadow of the proviso. The proviso sanctions takings so long as others are not worsened. If opportunities are valuable, and I think that they are, then as time passes the probability that some other inventor has been worsened with respect to a certain intellectual work grows. Suppose that had Fred not invented X Ginger would have, and upon hearing of Fred's creation she pursues other goals. Given the difficulty in reinventing X and proving independent creation Ginger merely abandons her project and refocuses her energy elsewhere. We can also imagine numerous other individuals who would have invented X had they not heard of it. Now it might be the case that these individuals have been bettered by being engaged in this system—maybe they are worsened at the level of acts but compensated overall, by being part of a system that affords better opportunities and welfare. In essence, this was my answer to the competition problem. But some of these individuals may be worsened nonetheless, and limitations on the rights of authors and inventors may serve to cancel out such worsenings.

To be sure, there will be line drawing problems and any fixed sunset will seem arbitrary. Nozick claims that we should use a rough rule to approximate the life of rights to control intellectual works. Nonetheless, there seems to be no straightforward argument for placing the time limit on patent rights at twenty years as opposed to twenty-five, or fifty years as opposed to lifetime plus seventy years for copyrights. Maybe such rules can be justified at the level of systems via the democratic process or some such process.

Another, quite different, problem is the assumption that had X not been invented it would have been invented sometime later by someone else. This may be true for some intellectual creations but it is most likely not always true. Some creations are so ingenious and unique that had their original inventor not created them they may have never existed. Take, for example, J. R. R Tolkien's famous trilogy *The Lord of the Rings*. Is it really plausible to maintain that had Tolkien not created this expression that someone else would have sometime later? Is it even plausible to maintain that someone else would have come up with something substantially similar? I think not. It may be actually worse than this, especially in the realm of fine arts. Is it plausible to maintain that had Picasso not painted or Bach not created that someone else sometime later would have created similar expressions? Lysander Spooner puts the point nicely. "Who can say, or believe, that if Alexander, and Caesar, and Napoléon had not played the parts they did in human affairs, there was another Alexander, another Caesar, another Napoléon, standing ready to step into their places, and do their work? Who can believe that the works of Raphael and Angelo could have been performed by other hands then theirs? Who can *affirm* that anyone but Franklin would ever have drawn the lightnings from the clouds? Yet who can say that what is true of Alexander, and Caesar, and Napoléon, and Raphael, and Angelo, and Franklin, is not equally true of Arkwright, and Watt, and Fulton, and Morse? Surely no one."[62]

Many of these cases concern intellectual works that fall under the creation model of intellectual property, but there are also discoveries and maybe Nozick's view can find purchase in this latter model. Had Newton not discovered the calculus or Crick and Watson the human gene, someone else would have and these others would be worsened by allowing the original discoverers perpetual rights. While some discoveries may be unique and in a sense difficult to find, it is likely that someone sometime later would indeed discover them. Examples of multiple independent discoveries are too numerous to mention. It would follow that the shadow of the proviso hangs over these discoveries and provides a basis for limiting discoverer's rights.[63]

While I find Nozick's suggestion for limiting intellectual property rights with respect to discoveries convincing, I do not think a similar case can be made for intellectual works that are created. Moreover, I do not find the prospect of perpetual rights for created intellectual works alarming. Suppose, that so long as authors and inventors and their heirs defend property claims that these rights are perpetual, similar to property rights in tangible objects.[64] Right now I own a Fender Stratocaster and my property rights are perpetual in a sense. If I so choose, I can bequeath this guitar to my heirs, and they can bequeath it to theirs. If this were to happen the Strat would perpetually be the property of my family. While eminent domain laws have been established to allow for the justified taking of physical property essential for social utility, these laws are limited in scope and application. First, eminent domain is exercised on a case by case basis—hardly what is proposed in setting time limits on almost every kind of intangible property right. Second, eminent domain seizures require just and fair compensation. Note the basic reverence for private property rights here. Overriding property rights is the exception, not the rule. Takings are permitted only when there is a compelling public interest and when just compensation is offered. This raises the bar fairly high and puts the burden of justification where it should be.[65]

Trade secrets can be held perpetually and since this form of intellectual property can encompass the domain of patents and copyrights it is at least possible that any kind of intellectual property can thus held. Many do not find trade secret control alarming and most do not find perpetual physical property rights alarming. Given this, why is the prospect of perpetual copyrights and patents over created intellectual works troubling?

It should be noted that in many fields of industry the value of some created intellectual works drops rapidly upon dissemination. Obviously, the original programs created for the first computers are almost worthless today and it would be odd for the owners of such property to defend their property claims indefinitely. This would leave economically worthless intellectual works in the public domain. Spooner put the point the following way:

> Few inventions are very long lived. By this I mean that few inventions are in practical use a very long time, before they are superseded by other inventions, that accomplish the same purposes better. A very large portion of inventions live but a few years, say five, ten, or twenty years. I doubt if one invention in five (of sufficient importance to be patented) lives fifty years. And I think it doubtful if five in a hundred live a hundred years.
>
> Under a system of perpetuity in intellectual property, inventions would be still shorter lived than at present; because, owing to the activity given to men's inventive faculties, one invention would be earlier superseded by another.[66]

One problem with this view is that perpetual rights to some intellectual works will allow their owners to control entire industries. Suppose that some company creates an intellectual work that provides the basic building blocks for a new industry. Other companies that wish to compete will have to obtain licensing agreements to be able to build upon prior intellectual works. This may allow the owner of such property to monopolize the entire industry. But given that I have rejected exclusive patent monopolies in the case of independent creation, it will always be possible for others to invent around or reinvent existing intellectual works. This is just to say that within a Lockean model of intellectual property such monopolies will be rare.[67]

A final worry that I would like to consider has to do with the notion of "independent" discovery and invention after dissemination. As already noted by Nozick, after an invention is produced and information about it widely disseminated the notion of "independent" discovery becomes murky indeed. In fact, maybe simply knowing that something is possible will undermine claims of independent creation.

This is a difficult issue—one that I confess to be uncertain about. If independent discovery or creation is necessary for justified entitlements, then the amount of available information about some intellectual work becomes important. The Lockean model that I have presented does not require disclosure. Thus, widespread dissemination of information about some particular intellectual work might be understood as an attempt to undermine the possibility of independent invention. My hope is that in such cases the burden of proof would fall on the established rights holders. In other cases the default position may fall, as it currently does, on those seeking rights to already protected works.

The Social Nature of Intellectual Works

Before concluding, I would like to present one final argument for limiting the rights of authors and inventors that builds upon a problem related to the aforementioned worry about "independent" discovery or creation. On this view property rights are justifiably limited because of the inherent social nature of intellectual works. Individuals are raised in societies that endow them with knowledge which these individuals then use to create intellectual works of all kinds.

On this view the building blocks of intellectual works—knowledge—is a social product. Individuals should not have exclusive and perpetual ownership of the works that they create because these works are built upon the shared knowledge of society. Allowing perpetual rights to intellectual works would be similar to granting ownership to the individual who placed the last brick in a public works dam. The dam is a social product, built up by the efforts of hundreds, and knowledge, upon which all intellectual works are built, is built up in a similar fashion.

Similarly, the benefits of market interaction are social products. Why should the individual who discovers crude oil in their backyard obtain the full market value of their find? And why should the inventor who produces the next technology breakthrough be allowed to harvest full market value when such value is actually created through the interactions of individuals within a society? Simply put, the value produced by markets and the building blocks of intellectual works are social products. This would undermine any claims to clear title:

> Locke himself uses examples that point to the social nature of production (*The Second Treatise of Government*, II 43). But if the skills, tools, or invention that are used in laboring are not simply the product of the individual's effort, but are instead the product of a culture or a society, should not the group have some claim on what individual laborers produce? For the labor that the individual invests includes the prior labor of many others.[68]

A mild form of this argument may yield a justification for limiting the ownership rights of authors and inventors—alas, these individuals do not deserve the full value of what they produce given what they produce is, in part, a social product. Maybe rules that limit intellectual property rights can be justified as offering a trade-off position between individual effort and social inputs. A more radical form of this argument may lead to the elimination of intellectual property rights. If individuals are, in a deep way, social products and market value and knowledge are as well, then the creator-centered paradigm that grounds Anglo-American systems of intellectual property would be undermined.

This argument, in either version, is severely limited for several reasons. First, I doubt that the notion of "society" employed in this view is clear enough to carry the weight that the argument demands. In some vague sense, I know what it means to say that Lincoln was a member of American *society* or that Aristotle's political views were influenced by ancient Greek *society*. Nevertheless, I think that the notion of "society" is conceptually imprecise—one that it would be dubious to attach ownership or obligation claims to. Those who would defend this view would have clarify the notions of "society" and "social product" before the argument could be fully analyzed.

But suppose for the sake of argument that supporters of this view come up with a concise notion of "society" and "social product." We may ask further, why think that societies can be *owed* something or that they can *own* or *deserve* something?[69] Surely, it does not follow from the claim that X is a social product that society owns X. Likewise, it does not follow from the claim that X is produced by Ginger, that Ginger owns X. It is true that interactions between individuals may produce increased market values or add to the common stock of knowledge. What I deny is that these by-products of inter-action, market value and shared information, are in some sense owned by society or that society is owed for their use. Why assume this without argument? It is one thing to claim that information and knowl-edge is a social product—something built-up by thousands of indi-vidual contributions—but quite another to claim that this knowledge is owned by society or that individuals who use this information owe society something in return.[70]

Suppose that Fred and Ginger, along with numerous others, inter-act and benefit me in the following way. Their interaction produces knowledge, that is then freely shared, and allows me to create some new value, V. Upon creation of V, Fred and Ginger demand that they are owed something for their part. But what is the argument from third party benefits to demands of compensation for these benefits? Why think that there are "strings" attached to freely shared informa-tion? And if such an argument can be made, then why don't burdens create reverse demands. Suppose that the interaction of Fred and Ginger produces false information that is freely shared. Suppose further that I waste ten years trying to produce some value based, in part, on this false information. Would Fred and Ginger, would soci-ety, owe me compensation? The position that "strings" are attached in this case runs parallel to Nozick's benefit "foisting" example. In Nozick's case a benefit is foisted on someone and then payment is demanded. This seems an accurate account of what is going on in this case as well:

One cannot, whatever one's purposes, just act so as to give people benefits and then demand (or seize) payment. Nor can a group of persons do this. If you may not charge and collect for benefits you bestow without prior agreement, you certainly may not do so for benefits whose bestowal costs you nothing, and most certainly people need not repay you for costless-to-provide benefits which yet *others* provided them. So the fact that we partially are "social products" in that we benefit from current patterns and forms created by the multitudinous actions of a long string of long-forgotten people, forms which include institutions, ways of doing things, and language, does not create in us a general free floating debt which the current society can collect and use as it will.[71]

I would argue that this is also true of market value. Given our crude oil example, the market value of the oil is the synergistic effect of individuals freely interacting. Moreover, there is no question of desert here—if the acquisition does not worsen, then "no harm, no foul." Surely the individual who discovers the oil does not deserve full market value any more than the lottery winner deserves her winnings. Imagine we set up a pure lottery where the payout was merely the entire sum of all the tickets purchased. Upon determining a winner, suppose someone argued that the sum of money was a social product and that society was entitled to a cut of the profit. An adequate reply would be something like "but this was not part of the rules of the game, and if it was, it should have been stated before the investment was made."

On my view common knowledge, market value, and the like, are the synergistic effects of individuals freely interacting. If a thousand of us *freely* give our new and original ideas to all of humankind it would be illicit for us to demand compensation, after the fact, from individuals who have used our ideas to create things of value. It would even be more questionable for individuals ten generations later to demand compensation for the current use of, the now very old, ideas that we freely gave. Lysander Spooner puts the point succinctly:

> *What* rights society have, in ideas, which they did not produce, and have never purchased, it would probably be very difficult to define; and equally difficult to explain *how* society became possessed of those rights. It certainly requires something more than assertion, to prove that by simply coming to a knowledge of certain ideas—the products of individual labor—society acquires any valid title to them, or, consequently, any *rights* in them.[72]

But once again, suppose for the sake of argument that the defender of this view can justify societal ownership of general pools of knowledge and information. Have we not already paid for the use of this collective wisdom when we pay for education and the like? When a parent pays, through fees or taxation, for a child's education it would seem that the information—part of society's common pool of knowledge—has been fairly purchased. And this extends through all levels of education and even to individuals who no longer attend school.

In summary my position against the social nature of intellectual works argument is, (1) the notion of "society" is not clear enough to carry the weight that some theorists would like, (2) there is no good reason to think that society owns freely shared information or that society should be compensated for the use of such knowledge, and (3) even if society had some claim on certain pools of knowledge, individuals have fairly purchased such information through education fees and the like.

As I have already noted, I do not think that the rights generated by the Lockean model under consideration are absolute. Sometimes it is appropriate to allow bad consequences to override individual rights. It may be the case that term limits are necessary for any workable system of protection and given that we stand on the shoulders of those who came before—and that "independent" discovery or creation may be near impossible in an information age—term limits may be justifiable for some types of intellectual property. In any case, I think that it is important to note that such arguments will not have the same force for trade secrets, the law of ideas, and creator's rights.

Conclusion

As with any new theory that calls for changes in complex legal systems, there is much to be worked out. Nevertheless, first steps must be taken down new roads, and echoing Mitchell Kapor in the quote that opens this chapter, "my bottom line on the intellectual property front is let us not screw it up." Our current views about intellectual property are changing as information and intellectual works are placed online. The old cannons of rule-utilitarian based copyright and patent law are rusting as much from within as from without. The bit streams that inhabit the World Wide Web are not fixed expressions and there is no easy method for ensuring both protection and access. In most cases, if I have access to your stream of bits, then there can be no protection.

In this chapter, I have sought to provide a sketch of what a Lockean model of intellectual property would look like. There is no room in this account for the free use zones of first sale or fair use, and limits on the rights of created, rather than discovered, intellectual property. While these changes may sound radical, I have argued that upon adopting a Lockean model we have good reason to believe that actual practices will not change much. What will have changed, however, is our underlying theoretical commitment to protecting the rights of authors and inventors.

Notes

1.   Quoted in Robert P. Benko, *Protecting Intellectual Property Rights* (Washington, DC: American Enterprise Institute for Public Policy Research, 1987).
2.   I am assuming that the generic model sketched at the end of chapter 2 is a good starting point—"utilitarian-free" copyright, patent, and trade secret, mark out recognizable domains of protection.
3.   See below or the relevant sections of chapter 2 for more information about these provisions.
4.   J. S. Mill, *The Logic of the Moral Sciences* (La Salle, Ill: Open Court Classics, 1987), 21.
5.   ". . . you can create most of the interesting features of intellectual property by contract. For example, a manufacturer may refuse to sell its widget but lease it on terms that prevent its duplication or sale." Frank Easterbrook, "Intellectual Property is Still Property," *Harvard Journal of Law and Public Policy* 13 (1990): 113.
6.   Amy M. Harris, "The Proposed UCC Article 2B," *Intellectual Property Update* (1998): 5. Some version of Article 2B is expected to be adopted by July of 1999 and then presented to each state for consideration. See also, Robert L. Oakley, "UCC Article 2B: Some Preliminary Comments on a New Issue for the Library Community." Presented at the Annual Meeting of the Association of Research Libraries, October 16, 1997. See also *Aronson v. Quick Point Pencil Corp.*, 440 U.S. 257 (1979)—a case where contracts for the use of intellectual works were enforced even though the relevant patent application had been denied.
7.   Consider, for example, the franchises, royal favors, and monopolies, that have been granted to individuals and companies to line the pockets of those in power. Bruce Bugbee discuses numerous examples of state created illicit monopolies in *The Genesis of American Patent and Copyright Law* (Washington, DC: Public Affairs Press, 1967), 1-56.
8.   Unless indicated I will use the phrase "economic rights" to refer only to intellectual property—obviously there are economic rights with respect to physical property, but these rights are not our concern.
9.   In 1988 the United States became the seventy-eighth nation to join the Berne Copyright Convention. Along with the economic rights previously mentioned, the Berne Convention grants authors rights of paternity and integrity. In recent years, to reflect statutes found in the Berne Convention Treaty, the United States has moved to expand copyright protection to include creator's rights. *See* 17 U.S.C. § 106(a)(1990). These rights are non-economic, however, and in many cases run against rule-utilitarian justifications.
10.   See 17 U.S.C. § 106 and the relevant sections of chapter 2.
11.   See 35 U.S.C.A. § 154 (1984 and Supp., 1989) and the relevant sections of chapter 2.
12.   See 15 U.S.C.A. § 1057(b), 1060, 1065, 1072 and the relevant sections of chapter 2.

13. For example, see Ayn Rand, "Copyrights and Patents," in *Capitalism: The Unknown Ideal* (New York: New American Library, 1966), 130-34.
14. The well-known German classical liberal Wilhelm von Humboldt also championed the non-economic rights of authors and inventors. Humboldt argued that the full development of individual potential, capacities, and talents requires the protection of both economic property rights and creator's rights. See W. von Humboldt, *The Limits of State Action*, translated by J. Coulthard (1969).
15. The colorization of movies provides an interesting case with respect to creator's rights. Would coloring old black and white movies and rebroadcasting them constitute deformation or mutilation? Many European systems give authors such control. An even better example comes from the case of Alan Douglas and the Jimi Hendrix estate. At one time, Douglas remastered a number of Hendrix songs adding new bass and drums, a second guitar, and backup singers. Needless to say, the Hendrix faithful were outraged that these altered songs were advertised as Hendrix *originals*.
16. My exposition in the next few paragraphs draws directly from Tom Palmer's analysis. See Tom G. Palmer, "Are Patents and Copyrights Morally Justified? The Philosophy of Property Rights and Ideal Objects," in the *Harvard Journal of Law and Public Policy*, 13 (1990): 817-65 (specifically 841-43).
17. C. civ. art. 543, Code Pénal [C.pén.] arts. 425-429 ("Law of March 11, 1957 on literary and artistic property"); *see also* Loi du 11 mars 1957 sur la propriété littéraire et artistique, 1957 Journal Officiel de la République Française [J.O.] 2723, 1957 Recueil Dalloz Législation [D.L.] 102 (for amendments and cases interpreting the statute); and Damich, *The Right of Personality: A Common-Law Basis for the Protection of the Moral Right of Authors*, 23 *Georgia Law Review* 2-25 (1988). See also Damich, "The Right of Personality: A Common-Law Basis for the Protection of the Moral Right of Authors," *Georgia Law Review* 23 (1988): 2-25.
18. *Cinquin v. Lecocq, Req. Sirey,* 1900.2121, note Saleilles (1902)(cited in S. Stromholm, *I Le Droit Moral De L'Auteur* (1966), 285.
19. J. Kohler, *Urheberrecht An Schriftwerken Und Verlagsrecht* (1907), 15 (quoted in Damich, "The Right of Personality: A Common-Law Basis for the Protection of the Moral Right of Authors," *Georgia Law Review* 23 (1988): 29.
20. See Markey, "Let Artists Have a Fair Share of Their Profits," *New York Times*, December 20, 1987, sec. 3, at 2, col. 2.
21. Thus when the Scientologist preaches to us telling us how we ought to live she is throwing ideas out into the commons of thought and discussion. Minimally, if no expressions are copied a critique of these ideas is perfectly appropriate. *Maxtone-Gram v. Burtchaell*, 803 F.d2 1253 (2d Cir.), *cert. denied*, U.S. 1059 (1987).
22. Would this would be akin to arguing that by allowing others to see your car you have thereby renounced all claims to it?
23. Imagine that a Jimi Hendrix song is found, but one that he explicitly wanted to remain unreleased. Suppose that someone digitally sampled the song and altered it by moving every fifth guitar note down a half step. Imagine further that the song is released and it is so bad that ardent Hendrix fans lose their lust for more music, t-shirts, and videos, and the Hendrix estate collapses in economic ruin. To be sure, a number of economic rights have been violated in this case, but the question that I want to push is "Have any non-economic or creator's rights been violated?" It seems that the answer is yes. Hendrix's personality, integrity, and perceived musical ability, have been undermined through the manipulation of one of his creations. That he is

no longer alive to care about such concerns is beside the point. Rather than economic ruin, suppose that the song brought massive profits—would the conclusion be any different? Would it be any different if the song in question was 2,000 years old?

24.   Lynn Sharp Pain, "Trade Secrets and the Justification of Property: A Comment On Hettinger," in *Intellectual Property: Moral, Legal, and International Dilemmas*, edited by A. Moore (Lanham, MD: Rowman & Littlefield, 1997), chapter 3, 39.

25.   Lysander Spooner, *The Law of Intellectual Property:* or An Essay on the Right of Authors and Inventors to a Perpetual Property in Their Ideas, in *The Collected Works of Lysander Spooner*, edited by C. Shively (1971).

26.   This view leads to another problem with rule-utilitarian intellectual property, for suppose that social progress would be maximized by *requiring* the disclosure of all economically viable thoughts and plans (suppose these kinds of thoughts could be determined by the "thought police"). In principle, the rule-utilitarian has no recourse here. If such a policy would maximize social utility, then it should be adopted. It should be clear that the Lockean theory that I have presented does not fall prey to this kind of objection—there is no maximization requirement.

27.   This is a contentious issue, because in some cases secrecy requirements may limit the job opportunities of ex-employees. See Lynn Sharp Paine "Trade Secrets and the Justification of Intellectual Property: A Comment on Hettinger," and John Burges, "Unlocking Corporate Shackles," in *Washington Business* (December 11, 1989), 1. See chapter 9 for a more detailed discussion of this issue.

28.   An interesting feature of creator's rights is that they seem to be non-transferable. Although an author may renounce her theory she will always be identified as the original author. Intellectual works can thus become unwelcome tar babies that authors can never be rid of.

29.   17 U.S.C. sec. 102(b) (1988).

30.   Landes and Posner, two authors sympathetic to a cost/benefit or utilitarian model of intellectual property, seem to reject the idea/expression distinction. Writing about the "look and feel" virtual desktop issue: "[We] hope the debate will be resolved not by the semantics of the words 'idea' and 'expression' but by the economics of the problem and, specifically, by comparing the deadweight costs of allowing a firm to appropriate what has become an industry standard with the disincentive effects on originators is such appropriations is forbidden." William Landes & Richard Posner, "An Economic Analysis of Copyright Law," *The Journal of Legal Studies* 18 (1989): 325.

31.   William S. Strong, *The Copyright Book: A Practical Guide*, 3rd ed. (Cambridge, MA: The MIT Press, 1990), 12. See also, *Morrissey v. Proctor & Gamble Co.*, 379 F.2d 675 (1st Cir. 1967).

32.   This is why recipes cannot be copyrighted and are generally held as trade secrets.

33.   ". . . recognizing that the right to exclude others from using your idea is no more a monopoly than is the right to exclude others from using your barn." Frank Easterbrook, "Intellectual Property is Still Property," *Harvard Journal of Law and Public Policy* 13 (1990): 113.

34.   See the relevant sections of chapter 2.

35.   *Buchwald v. Paramount Pictures*, 13 U.S.P.Q. 2d 1497 (Cal. Super. Ct. 1990)

36.   *See* 17 U.S.C. § 109(a).

37.   17 U.S.C. § 910. The exceptions were enacted after intense lobbying by the relevant industries.

38.   If authors can decide to whom their work can be sold, then some authors will surely trade-off the public recognition that comes with the easy access of libraries for

profits and economic advantage.

39. There is also the following problem. "The first sale rule does not translate easily to the online environment, where most versions of the work are in an intangible format, whether stored, transmitted, or viewed on-screen. Until the work is printed onto paper (or perhaps saved to a floppy disk), there is no corporeal version of the work under traditional copyright notions. The online environment makes it tempting to view copyright law a relic of the past or the first sale doctrine as a simple inconvenience." Marci A. Hamilton "The TRIPS Agreement: Imperialistic, Outdated, and Overprotective," in *Intellectual Property: Moral, Legal, and International Dilemmas*, edited by A. Moore (Lanham, MD: Rowman & Littlefield, 1997), chapter 9. Obviously, a model that lacked a first sale rule would not have this worry—although it may have others.

40. Suppose, for example, that in selling my book on Chinese cooking I insisted that purchasers agree to a number of provisions that restricted what could be done with the book. Suppose I required that you not let others read the book or that it must never leave your possession. Surely these provisions would drive down the value, and sales, of the book.

41. When hearing these sentiments I sometimes get the feeling that turf is being protected rather than lofty ideals being voiced.

42. Loren Lomasky, *Persons, Rights, and the Moral Community* (New York: Oxford University Press, 1987), 18. "A century that has witnessed the Holocaust and the Gulag is not one which can aptly be characterized as paying too much heed to basic rights."

43. On my view there would be no exclusive rights to patents. If someone else independently invented one of IBM's patents, for example, then they can obtain rights to their ideas in the same way that IBM did. Such disclosure strategies, however, may ground a case for limiting the duration of copyrights and patents.

44. Interview with Morgan Jackson and Duane Smith, Vice President, Chief Operating Officer, Vision Quest 2000 Inc. See also, Sidney Winter, "Patents in Complex Contexts: Incentives and Effectiveness," in *Owing Scientific and Technical Information*, ed Weil and Snapper (New Brunswick, NJ: Rutgers University Press, 1989).

45. Moreover, if a company or an individual wants to keep information out of the public domain and information storehouses like libraries, then they can keep the idea or ideas as a trade secret. As was noted before, this seems a perfectly sensible notion, for if we have absolute dominion over anything it is our own thoughts—the corollary in the business domain are trade secrets. Surely no one who voices the concern we are considering would advocate that individuals should disclose their thoughts or companies their secrets so that libraries can be filled with lots of information.

46. For more about fair use see: *Sony Corporation of America v. Universal City Studios, Inc.,* 464 U.S. 417, 104 S.Ct. 774, 78 L.Ed.2d 574 (1984); *Pacific and Southern Co., Inc. v. Duncan,* 744 F2d 1490, *cert denied* 471 U.S. 1004, 105 S.Ct. 1867, 85 L.Ed.2d 161 (1985); *Time Incorporated v. Benard Geis Associates,* 293 F. Supp. 130 (U.S.D.C.N.Y. 1968); *Iowa State University Research Foundation, Inc. v. American Broadcasting Companies, Inc.* 621 F.2d 57 (United States Court of Appeals, Second Circuit, 1980); *Harper & Row Publishers, Inc. v. Nation Enterprises,* 471 U.S. 539, 105 S.Ct. 2218, 85 L.Ed.2d 588 (Supreme Court of the United States, 1985); *Salinger v. Random House, Inc.,* 811 F.2d 90, cert denied 484 U.S. 890, 108 S.Ct. 213, 98 L.Ed.2d 177 (1987); *Fisher v. Dees,* 749 F.2d 432 (United States Court of Appeals, Ninth Circuit, 1986).

47. From District Judges Leval's opinion in *New Era Publication International v. Henery Holt and Company,* 695 F.Supp. 1493 (S.D.N.Y. 1988).

48. Copyright Act, § 107 (1976).
49. Taken from Don Hubin and Mark Lambeth, "Providing For Rights," in *Dialogue* (1986).
50. Issues of privacy, access to personal domains, and information control independent of harm are taken up in chapters 8-10.
51. Most European countries recognize an exemption that allows individuals to use copyrighted works for personal use.
52. They would also have to agree not to make copies of the work (outside of backup copies) and not to decompile the work and delete the digital markers that signify their individual copy.
53. The encryption debate will be discussed in the final chapter.
54. A common worry within the academic community is how to protect original works that have been placed online. Most professors that I have talked to about this are hesitant to place manuscripts or other original works on an unprotected Web page—many won't even take the chance of placing original works on secure sites. In these environments, forced free access, will most likely lead to self-imposed censorship.
55. Robert Nozick, *Anarchy, State, And Utopia* (New York: Basic Books, 1974), 182.
56. Second inventors are not the only ones worsened by exclusive patent rights. There may be others who would have come up with the idea but pursue other endeavors rather than trying to reinvent something. As I will argue in the next section, this will be a compelling reason to limit patent rights in some cases.
57. W. Leggett, *Democratick Editorials: Essays In Jacksonian Political Economy* 397-98 (edited by L. White, 1984) quoted in T. Palmer's "Are Patents and Copyrights Morally Justified? The Philosophy of Property Rights in Ideal Objects," in *Harvard Journal Of Law & Public Policy* 13 (Summer 1990): 830.
58. Lysander Spooner responds to this problem in the following way. ". . . the fact that two men produce the same invention, is a very good reason why the invention should belong to both; but it is no reason at all why both should be deprived of it. . . The consequence is, that they must either use and sell the invention in competition with each other, or unite their rights, and share the invention between them." Spooner, 68.
59. The limit is required by the Constitution. "The Congress shall have the Power . . . To promote the Progress of Science and useful Arts, by securing *for limited Times* to Authors and Inventors the exclusive Right to their respective Writings and Discoveries." Article I, Section 8 (italics mine).
60. For a more detailed analysis of the limits placed or rights to control intellectual works, see chapter 2.
61. Nozick, *Anarchy*, 182.
62. Spooner, *The Law of Intellectual Property*, 67.
63. It is arguably the case that only part of the domain of patent protection covers discovered intellectual works. For example, mapping the human genome is surely a discovery of something that is already there. Conversely, inventing a gene therapy process that eliminates diabetes is a creation that is most likely not written into the fabric of the universe.
64. One rule of Anglo-American copyright and patent institutions is that property claims must be defended if they are to not lapse into the public domain. For example, this is why Paramount Inc. actively defends claims to its *Star Trek* logos. A Lockean could defend such a rule on the grounds that undefended property has been abandoned.
65. In chapter 8 I will discuss the often used "the benefits of the free flow of information" argument that is typically given at this point. Moreover, if Spooner is correct

(see below) there will be (1) no incentive to fence intellectual works after a short period due to the diminution in their value, and (2) no lessening of free thought and discussion given the market forces pulling toward dissemination.

66. Spooner, *The Law of Intellectual Property*, 159.

67. Frank Easterbrook puts the point the following way: "That a patent covers an 'entire' idea or product no more implies monopoly than the fact that USX Corporation owns the 'entire' South Works in Chicago. Frequently, indeed almost always, different patented goods and processes compete with each other and with unpatented good and processes. Before crying 'monopoly' in either case, we must determine what substitutes a customer could obtain and whether the seller could raise prices by curtailing output." Frank Easterbrook, "Intellectual Property is Still Property," *Harvard Journal of Law and Public Policy* 13 (1990): 109.

68. A. John Simmons *The Lockean Theory of Rights* (Princeton, NJ: Princeton University Press, 1992), 269. Ruth Grant in *John Locke's Liberalism* (Chicago: University of Chicago Press, 1987), Ian Shapiro in "Resources, Capacities, and Ownership: The Workmanship Ideal and Distributive Justice" *Political Theory* (February 1991), as well as others have argued along these lines. For earlier more general defenses of this sentiment see Karl Marx and Friedrich Engels, *The Communist Manifesto* and P. J. Proudhon, *What is Property? An Inquiry into the Principles of Right and of Government*, trans. by D. Kelly and B. Smith (New York: Cambridge University Press, 1994).

69. Does notions of *ownership*, *owing*, or *deserving* even make sense when attached to the concept of society? If so and if different societies can *own* knowledge, do they not have the problem of original acquisition? See Nozick, *Anarchy*, 178.

70. Lysander Spooner argued that one's culture or society plays almost no role in the production of ideas. "Nothing is, by its own essence and nature, more perfectly susceptible of exclusive appropriation, that a thought. It originates in the mind of a single individual. It can leave his mind only in obedience to his will. It dies with him, if he so elect." Spooner, The Law of Intellectual Property," 58.

71. Nozick, *Anarchy*, 95.

72. Spooner, *The Law of Intellectual Property*, 103.

8

Intangible Property: Privacy, Power, and Information Control[1]

"Imagine a place where trespassers leave no footprints, where goods can be stolen an infinite number of times and yet remain in the possession of their original owners, where businesses you never heard of can own the history of your personal affairs, where only children feel fully at home, where the physics is psychology, and where everyone is as virtual as the shadows in Plato's cave."
— John Perry Barlow, "Coming Into the Country"[2]

Introduction

It is an obvious truism that the proliferation of computer networks and the digitization of everything not obstinately physical[3] is radically changing the human experience. As more individuals obtain access to computer networks such as the Internet or the World Wide Web—the official word for this is to become "wired"—digital-based environments and information have come to play a central role in our everyday lives. Our money is stored and transmitted digitally, we listen to CDs where the music is recorded and played digitally, there are now digital cell-phones, cable television, and musical instruments. And all of this lies outside of the bit streams of 1s and 0s that make up computer networks, software programs, and operating systems. Many claim that the future holds information that cascades, not just through a PC, but across all forms of communication devices—headlines that flash across your watch, or a traffic map popping up on a cellular phone. It means content that will not hesitate to find you—whether you have clicked on something or not.[4] The integration, by digital technology, of what used to be disparate forms of communication is radically changing how we work and play.

At the center of this communication revolution is the control of information—who has it, how can it be gathered, can databases be owned, should information be "pulled" by users as a request or "pushed" to users who have shown interest? These concerns have obvious import into the areas of privacy and power. We each leave "digital footprints" that can be tracked by data mining companies and used to create purchasing profiles, medical summaries, political agendas, and the like. Moreover, this information is then sold to direct marketing companies—who will then call, write, or in the future, e-mail us—government agencies, private investigators, or to anyone for any reason. There used to be domains of a person's life that were totally inaccessible. A person's home and bedroom, notebook and hard drive, were all sanctuaries against the prying eyes and ears of others. It is alarming that digital technology is sweeping these domains away. Deborah Johnson accurately captures this sentiment:

> We have the technological capacity for the kind of massive, continuous surveillance of individuals that was envisioned in such frightening early twentieth-century science fiction works as George Orwell's *1984* and Zamyatin's *We*. The only difference between what is now possible and what was envisioned then are that much of the surveillance of individuals that is now done is by private institutions (marketing firms, insurance companies, credit agencies), and much of the surveillance now is via electronic records instead of by direct human observation or through cameras.[5]

The power of having such information should be obvious. Companies will be able to (and are able to) directly contact individuals who have shown interest in their products, or similar products, or their rival's products. And there are even more insidious uses for such information. Imagine a child custody case where one of the parents claims that the other is an unfit custodian for the children because the accused parent frequently views pornographic videos. Think of how governments could use such information to control populations or political opponents, or how insurance companies could use such information. In controlling information, especially sensitive personal information, the stakes could not be higher.

In this chapter, and in light of the Lockean model of intellectual property developed in earlier chapters, I will examine a number of these important applied issues. The Lockean theory that I have defended justifies rights to control intellectual works, that is, works that fall under the domain of copyright, patent, and trade secret. Intellectual property, however, falls under the umbrella of intangible property—both are rights to types not tokens. What will be examined in this chapter are kinds of intangible property that are not properly called intellectual property. First, to set the stage, a brief overview of the Lockean theory will be given. The remainder of the chapter will consist of applying this theory to the everyday problems of information privacy and control.

Overview of the Lockean Model

In the broadest terms, my goal in this work has been to justify rights to intellectual property. According to rule-utilitarians, who offer incentive-based arguments, rights should be granted to authors and inventors of intellectual property because granting such control provides incentives necessary for social progress. Society ought to maximize social utility, and therefore, temporary rights to intellectual works should be granted. This argument is typically given as the primary justification for Anglo-American copyright, patent, and trade secret institutions. Nevertheless, I think the argument is flawed.

First, a negative argument has been given that undermines rule-utilitarian justifications for intellectual property. I argued that by their own lights, rule-utilitarian arguments fail to justify rights to intellectual works. At worst they may actually give good reasons for eliminating institutions of intellectual property protection, and at best would call for radical revisions of these institutions. Not being able to justify current Anglo-American institutions of intellectual property is only a problem for those who think that rule-utilitarian justifications do justify these institutions—failing to justify current practices is not a general criticism.

In addition to the internal critique, an external critique of rule-utilitarian moral theory was offered. I argued that rule-utilitarianism faces a number of serious objections that may lead to its rejection as a plausible moral theory. If these arguments are correct, a justification for intellectual property will have to be found elsewhere and corresponding revisions in Anglo-American institutions will have to be implemented.

My positive argument began with an account of Locke's proviso that justified acquisitions of unowned objects must leave enough and as good for others. One way to interpret Locke's requirement is that it ensures that the position of others is not worsened. This can be understood as a version of weak Pareto-superiority. If the possession and exclusion of an intellectual work makes no one worse-off, then the acquisition ought to be permitted. In clarifying the issues that surround a Pareto-based proviso on acquisition, I defended an account of bettering and worsening and offered a solution to the baseline problem.

I have argued that rights to intellectual works can be justified at both the level of acts and at the level of institutions. At both levels my argument turns on two features of intellectual property. First, intellectual works are non-rivalrous, meaning that they can be created, possessed, owned, and consumed by many individuals concurrently. Second, including allowances for independent creation, I argued that the frontier of intellectual property is practically infinite. "Nobody could think himself injured by the drinking of another man, though he took a good draught, who had a whole river of the same water left him to quench his thirst . . ."[6] If correct about these features of intellectual property, the case for Locke's water-drinker and the author or inventor are quite alike.

In light of the argument at the level of acts, systems, and institutions, it was argued that a number of prominent features of Anglo-American copyright and patent law should be abandoned or restricted. I argued that the idea/expression distinction should be limited in scope, while the fair use limitation and the first sale rule should be eliminated. In their place a contract-based system was defended that, in many cases, parallels the effects of these rules and limits government incursions into the realm of property creation.

Intangible Property Rights and Privacy

If correct, the Lockean theory that I have presented may be expanded to justify rights to control information of all sorts. Lists of customers, purchasing summaries, medical records, criminal records, and the like are all kinds of information that can be owned and controlled.[7] Suppose that I do a little data-mining and discover that individuals who purchase cowboy boots prefer to shop by mail order catalogue or that those with diabetes live healthier lives if they have pets. Information like this can be extremely valuable. Moreover, my controlling or owing this information may satisfy the Paretian test.

Although a case may be made for granting intangible property rights to individuals in certain instances this does not mean that owners can do anything they want with their property.[8] To take a simple example, my property right in a Louisville slugger does not allow me swing it at your knees, nor can I throw it at your car. Property rights are generally limited by the rights of others. More specifically, there is a prohibition of harm with respect to property rights.[9] This means that you can do what you want with your property short of unjustly harming others. Furthermore, this restriction—call it the harm restriction—fits well with the Lockean model under consideration. The proviso, a no harm no foul rule, allows individuals to acquire unowned goods. The harm restriction limits harmful uses of those goods.

A second constraint has to do with privacy and information control. Privacy may be understood as that state where others do not have access to you or to information about you. I hasten to note that there are degrees of privacy. There are our own private thoughts that are never disclosed to anyone, as well as information we share with loved ones. Furthermore, there is information that we share with mere acquaintances and the general public. These privacy relations with others can be pictured "in terms of a series of 'zones' or 'regions' . . . leading to a 'core self.'"[10] Thus, secrets shared with a loved one can still be considered private, even though they have been disclosed.

In an important article dealing with privacy, morality, and the law, William Parent offers the following definition for privacy:

> *Privacy is the condition of not having undocumented personal knowledge about one possessed by others.* A person's privacy is diminished exactly to the degree that others possess this kind of knowledge about him. Documented information is information that is found in the public record or is publicly available (e.g. information found in newspapers, court proceedings, and other official documents open to public inspection).[11]

The problem with this definition is that it leaves the notion of privacy dependent upon what a society or culture takes as documentation and what information is available via the public record. Parent acts as if undocumented information is private while documented information is not, and this is the end of the matter. But surely the secret shared between lovers is private in one sense and not in another. To take another case, consider someone walking in a public park. There is almost no limit to the kinds of information that can be acquired from this public display. One's image, height, weight, eye color, approximate age, and general physical abilities are all readily available. Moreover, biological matter will also be left in the public domain—strands of hair and the like may be left behind. Since this matter, and the information contained within, is publicly available it would seem that all of one's genetic profile is not private information.

Furthermore, what is publicly available information is dependent upon technology. Telescopes, listening devices, heat imaging sensors, and the like, open up what most would consider private domains for public consumption. What we are worried about is what should be considered a "private affair"—something that is no one else's business. Parent's conception of privacy is not sensitive to these concerns.

A right to privacy can be understood as a right to maintain a certain level of control over the inner spheres of personal information. It is a right to limit public access to the "core self"—personal information that one never discloses—and to information that one discloses only to family and friends. For example, suppose that I wear a glove because I am ashamed of a scar on my hand. If you were to snatch the glove away you would not only be violating my right to property—alas the glove is mine to control—you would also violate my right to privacy; a right to restrict access to information about the scar on my hand. Similarly, if you were to focus your x-ray camera on my hand, take a picture of the scar through the glove, and then publish the photograph widely, you would violate a right to privacy.

Legal scholar William Prosser separated privacy cases into four distinct but related torts:

Intrusion: Intruding (physically or otherwise) upon the solitude of another in a highly offensive manner. For example, a woman sick in the hospital with a rare disease refuses a reporter's request for a photograph and interview. The reporter photographs her anyway, over her objection.

Private facts: Publicizing highly offensive private information about someone which is not of legitimate concern to the public. For example, photographs of an undistinguished and wholly private hardware merchant carrying on an adulterous affair in a hotel room are published in a magazine.

False light: Publicizing a highly offensive and false impression of another. For example, a taxi driver's photograph is used to illustrate a newspaper article on cabdrivers who cheat the public when the driver in the photo is not, in fact, a cheat.

Appropriation: Using another's name or likeness for some advantage without the other's consent. For example, a photograph of a famous actress is used without her consent to advertise a product.[12]

What binds these seemingly disparate cases under the heading "privacy invasions" is that they each concern personal information control. And while there may be other morally objectionable facets to these cases, for example the taxi driver case may also be objectionable on grounds of defamation, there is arguably privacy interests at stake as well.

Having said something about what a right to privacy is we may ask how such rights are justified. A promising line of argument combines notions of autonomy and respect for persons. A central and guiding principle of Western liberal democracies is that individuals, within certain limits, may set and pursue their own life goals and projects. Rights to privacy erect a moral boundary that allows individuals the moral space to order their lives as they see fit. Clinton Rossiter writes:

> Privacy is a special kind of independence, which can be understood as an attempt to secure autonomy in at least a few personal and spiritual concerns, if necessary in defiance of all the pressures of the modern society. . . It seeks to erect an unbreachable wall of dignity and reserve against the entire world. The free man is the private man, the man who still keeps some of his thoughts and judgments entirely to himself, who feels no over-riding compulsion to share everything of value with others, not even those he loves and trusts.[13]

Privacy protects us from the prying eyes and ears of governments, corporations, and neighbors. Within the walls of privacy we may experiment with new ways of living that may not be accepted by the majority. Privacy, autonomy, and sovereignty, it would seem come bundled together.

A second but related line of argument rests on the claim that privacy rights stand as a bulwark against governmental oppression and totalitarian regimes. If individuals have rights to control personal information and to limit access to themselves, within certain constraints, then the kinds of oppression that we have witnesses in the twentieth century would be near impossible. Put another way, if oppressive regimes are to consolidate and maintain power, then privacy rights (broadly defined) must be eliminated or severely restricted. If correct, privacy rights would be a core value that limited the forces of oppression.[14]

Arguably any plausible account of human well-being or flourishing will have as a component a strong right to privacy. Controlling who has access to ourselves is an essential part of being a happy and free person. This may be why "peeping Toms" and rapists are held up as moral monsters—they cross a boundary that should never be crossed without consent.

Surely each of us has the right to control our own thoughts, hopes, feelings, and plans, as well as a right to restrict access to information about our lives, family, and friends. I would argue that what grounds these sentiments is a right to privacy—a right to maintain a certain level of control over personal information.[15] While complete control of all our personal information is a pipe dream for many of us, simply because the information is already out there and most likely cannot or will not be destroyed, this does not detract from the view of personal information ownership. Through our daily activities we each create and leave digital footprints that others may follow and exploit—and that we do these things does not obviously sanction the gathering and subsequent disclosure of such information by others.

Whatever kind of information we are considering there is a gathering point that individuals have control over. For example, in purchasing a new car and filling out the car loan application, no one would deny we each have the right to demand that such information not be sold to other companies. I would argue that this is true for any disclosed personal information whether it be patient questionnaire information, video rental records, voting information, or credit applications. In agreeing with this view, one first has to agree that individuals have the right to control their own personal information— i.e., binding agreements about controlling information presuppose that one of the parties has the right to control this information.

Minimally, in gathering information about someone, weak presumptive claims have been generated. Moreover, if the proviso is satisfied then the presumptive claims remain undefeated. As I have already indicated, however, I do not think that gathering information about someone is analogous to creating or discovering unowned works—it is plausible to maintain that there are "strings" attached to sensitive personal information.

To continue, as a direct consequence of the proliferation of computer environments, information gathering points will become the battleground over the control of personal information. Individuals who wish to maintain control over this kind of information will insist on confidential disclosure agreements before yielding any personal information. The American Express Card case is a nice example of how individuals can control information gathering and subsequent sale. In May 1992 American Express, under pressure from various sources, agreed to allow cardholders to opt out of the credit company's policy of gathering and selling the purchasing habits of its members. For the young and the yet unborn, information gathering points will be very important. Those who wish to maintain privacy will have to be very careful with personal information. For the rest of us, who already are on at least 100 mailing lists and fifteen databases, these points are important as well.[16] Old and outdated information is relatively worthless and so as time passes we can, in a sense, distance ourselves from old personal data.

Aside from controlling information gathering points there is at least one other way in which individuals can protect themselves from invasions of privacy due to digital monitoring.[17] It may be possible to detach one's physical self from one's virtual self through the use of encryption. The founders of the Electronic Frontier Foundation, John Perry Barlow and John Gilmore, advocate this method. The idea is to encrypt all information that links data about you to your name, address, or social security number—i.e., leave no unencrypted links between your physical self and your electronic identity. Individuals would then just become a number that is identified with data in the form of e-mail letters, purchasing habits, voting records, credit reports, medical records, and the like. "From the standpoint of credit assurance, there is no difference between the information that John Perry Barlow always pays his bills on time or that Account #345 8849 23433 (to whomever that may belong) is equally punctilious."[18] And better still, different kinds of personal information could be encrypted with different codes with the result of better protection. I may wish that my doctor has access to my physical self and my medical records—suppose the tests that he just ran on me show a need for surgery—but there is no need that he know my voting record or that I prefer to watch "spaghetti" westerns to Friday night situation comedies.

While there may be a number of problems with maintaining an encrypted identity over long periods of time, it should be clear how technology can work on behalf of individuals maintaining control over their own personal information. The growth of computer technology may have played a damning role in laying open personal information for public consumption, but it can also provide the answer. Through the use of encryption technology, coupled with the control of information gathering points, individuals will be able to secure personal information and privacy. The problem is that encryption programs are seen as national security threats—an issue that is taken up in the final chapter.

Test Cases: Controlling Your Image

Having said all of this, I would like to test the Lockean model of intangible property with a very tricky case dealing with personal information control:

> A woman is kidnapped, taken to an apartment, stripped, and terrorized. The police— and the media—surround the apartment. The police eventually overcome the kidnapper and rush the woman, who clutches a dish towel in a futile attempt to conceal her nudity, to safety. A photograph of her escape is published in the next day's newspaper. She sued for invasion of privacy and eventually lost the case. (*Cape Publications, Inc. v. Bridges,* Florida 1982)[19]

According to the theory that I have sketched, the photographer may indeed have a property right to the photograph he took—if his mere acquisition does not worsen—but this does not mean that he can do anything with the photograph. His rights to control the picture are limited by the harm and privacy restrictions. So even if publishing the photograph did not harm the women involved, it would still be an illicit violation of privacy.

Now, it is clear that my view runs counter to prevailing attitudes about the First Amendment. I would place more restrictions on speech or expression than is currently found in the law. Not only can we not yell "fire" in a crowded theater—this would violate the harm restriction—we cannot publish sensitive personal information without permission. This is not to say that the harm restriction and the privacy restriction are exceptionless—those who live their lives in the public realm may have to endure a more limited sphere of privacy. Moreover, certain harms may be permitted in order to protect a community from criminals and the like—for example, consider laws that require public notification when a child predator is relocated to a new community. Politicians and entertainers, in a sense, sanction a more limited sphere of privacy by choosing a certain career path and a similar point can be made with respect to criminals. While the sphere of privacy protection may be more limited in these cases, there are still boundaries that cannot be crossed. Becoming a "public figure" does not sanction continual harassment for autographs, pictures, and interviews. Access, in many ways, is still left to the individual—and this is how it should be.

On my view, an important part of a right to privacy is the right to control personal information; "control" in the sense of deciding who has access and to what uses the information can be put; "personal" in the sense of being about some individual as opposed to being about inanimate objects, corporations, institutions, and the like. These are not intended to be precise definitions—rather I am trying to capture the common everyday notion of a privacy interest. The appropriateness of who knows particular facts about an individual is, in an important sense, dependent on certain relationships. The kind of information access between doctor and patient, husband and wife, mother and child, and total strangers, are all appropriately different.[20]

Against this backdrop what sense can be made of the public's "right to know"? A newspaper may publish information about a kidnapping and rescue, but this does not sanction publishing sensitive personal information about the victim. Right-to-know arguments may carry some weight in cases where public funds are being spent or when a politician reverses his stand on a particular issue, but they seem to be suspect when used to justify intrusions. Sissela Bok echoes these concerns when she writes:

> Taken by itself, the notion that the public has a "right to know" is as quixotic from an epistemological as from a moral point of view, and the idea of the public's "right to know the truth" even more so. It would be hard to find a more fitting analogue to Jeremy Bentham's characterization of talk about natural and imprescriptible rights as "rhetorical nonsense—nonsense upon stilts." How can one lay claim to a right to know the truth when even partial knowledge is out of reach concerning most human affairs, and when bias and rationalization and denial skew and limit knowledge still further?
>
> So patently inadequate is the rationale of the public's right to know as a justification for reporters to probe and expose, that although some still intone it ritualistically at the slightest provocation, most now refer to it with a tired irony.[21]

The social and cultural benefits of free speech and free information are generally cited as justification for a free press and the public's right to know. This is why news services can publish photographs and stories that contain sensitive personal information about almost anyone. But computer technology has changed the playing field and such arguments seem to lose force when compared to the overwhelming loss of privacy that we now face. The kinds of continual and systematic invasions by news services, corporations, data mining companies, and other individuals that will be possible in a few short years is quite alarming.

In response to these worries the European Union has taken a strong stand with respect to privacy and information control. Unlike the American economic model where most kinds of information can be bought and sold with no strings attached, the EU model prohibits the unconstrained buying and selling of personal information. Simon Davies of *Wired Magazine* writes:

> Under this regime, known as the European Data Protection Directive, any country that trades personal information with the UK, France, Germany, Spain, Italy, or any of the other 10 EU states will be required to embrace Europe's strict standards for privacy protection. No privacy, no trade. It's that simple.[22]

European citizens have the right to access their data, the right to know where the data originated, the right to have inaccurate information rectified, the right of recourse in the event of unlawful processing, and the right to withhold permission to use their data for direct marketing. Like the moral rights afforded authors and inventors, I applaud the recognition of these privacy rights concerning personal information. It would seem that on two fronts the Europeans are well ahead of their American counterparts.

Conclusion

I think that it is plausible to maintain that information can be owned—including trade secrets, lists of customers, and sensitive personal information. Even so, such rights are not without limitations. I cannot justifiably slash your tires with my knife nor may I publish your medical records on my web site. The proliferation of the Internet and the World Wide Web into everyday life is forcing us to rethink our views about information access and control. Too much restriction or control may be a bad thing, but then again so is too much access. The former leaves us with little to talk about and perhaps an impoverished intellectual and cultural life. The latter offers up sensitive personal information for public consumption and manipulation. Where to draw the line with respect to access and control is a tricky matter. Many net anarchists claim that "information want to be free" and advocate a model of unrestricted access to all kinds of information. In this chapter I have argued otherwise—information, especially sensitive personal information, can be owned and restricted on grounds of property or privacy. And echoing Loren Lomasky if we are to err on the side of too much access or too much privacy, better—far better—the latter.

Notes

1. A longer version of this section appears in my article "Intangible Property: Privacy, Power, and Information Control," *American Philosophical Quarterly* 35 (October 1998). I would like to thank the editors of APQ for allowing me to present this material here.
2. John Perry Barlow, "Coming Into the Country," *Communications of the ACM* 34 (1991): 12-21.
3. This phrase comes from John Perry Barlow, "The Economy of Ideas: Everything You Know About Intellectual Property is Wrong" in *Intellectual Property: Moral, Legal, and International Dilemmas*, edited by A. Moore (Lanham, MD: Rowman & Littlefield, 1997), chapter 15.
4. Kevin Kelly and Gary Wolf, "Push," *Wired Magazine* (March 1997), 14.
5. Deborah Johnson, *Computer Ethics* (Upper Saddle River, NJ: Prentice Hall, 1994), 84.
6. John Locke, *The Second Treatise of Government,* chapter 5, § 33.
7. Frank Easterbrook echoes this view when he writes, ". . . recognizing that the right to exclude others from using your idea is no more a monopoly than is the right to exclude others from using your barn." Frank Easterbrook, "Intellectual Property is Still Property," *Harvard Journal of Law and Public Policy* 13 (1990): 113.
8. The following restrictions may also find purchase in the realm of copyrights, patents, and trade secrets—if an intellectual work contains harmful or private information.
9. The "harm" that I have in mind here is in terms of an individual's level of well-being. Obviously, alternative accounts of bettering and worsening will defend a different standard of harm.
10. Alan Westin, "Privacy in the Modern Democratic State" in D. Johnson and J. Snapper, *Ethical Issues in the Use of Computers* (Belmont, CA: Wadsworth Pub., 1985): 187.
11. W. A. Parent, "Privacy, Morality, and the Law," *Philosophy & Public Affairs* (Fall 1983): 269-88, reprinted in D. Johnson and J. Snapper, *Ethical Issues in the Use of Computers* (Belmont, CA: Wadsworth Pub., 1985): 203 (all page citations refer to the reprint).
12. Dean William Prosser, "Privacy," *California Law Review* 48 (1960): 383, 389, quoted in E. Alderman and C. Kennedy, *The Right to Privacy* (New York: Alfred A. Knopf, 1995), 155-56.
13. C. Rossiter, *Aspects of Liberty* (Ithaca, NY: Cornell University Press, 1958), quoted in Westin, "Privacy in the Modern Democratic State," 188.
14. For more about privacy rights, see Charles Fried, "Privacy," *Yale Law Journal* 77 (1968): 477; A. Westin and M. Baker, *Databanks in a Free Society*, (New York: Quadrangle Press, 1972); and J. Rachels, "Why Privacy is Important," *Philosophy and Public Affairs* 4 (Summer 1975): 323-33.
15. Would I be doing something morally illicit if I put on my new anti-monitoring suit that afforded me complete protection from every surveillance devise except the

human eye?

16. Branscomb, *Who Owns Information?* 9.
17. There are numerous ways to maximize one's control over personal information. Gary Marx lists the following. "1. Don't give out any more information than is necessary. 2. Don't say things over a cellular or cordless phone that you would mind having overheard by strangers. 3. Ask your bank to sign an agreement that it will not release information about your accounts to anyone lacking legal authorization and that in event of legal authorization, it will contact you within two days. 4. Obtain copies of your credit, health, and other records and check for accuracy and currency. 5. If you are refused credit, a job, a loan, or an apartment, ask why. 6. Remember that when you respond to telephone or door-to-door surveys, the information will go into a databank. 7. Realize that when you purchase a product or service and file a warranty card or participate in a rebate program, your name may well be sold to a mailing-list company." Marx, "Privacy and Technology," *Whole Earth Review* (Winter 1991): 91-95. Quoted from Deborah G. Johnson, *Computers Ethics*, 100.
18. John Perry Barlow, "Private Life in Cyberspace."
19. This case is cited in E. Alderman and C. Kennedy's, *The Right to Privacy*, 171.
20. Rachels in "Why Privacy is Important" argues that privacy is valuable because it is necessary for creating and maintaining different kinds of relationships with people.
21. Sissela Bok, *Secrets* (New York: Pantheon, 1982), 254.
22. Simon Davies, "Europe to U.S.: No Privacy, No Trade," *Wired Magazine* (May 1998), 135.

9

Employee Monitoring, Nondisclosure Agreements, and Intangible Property[1]

"Too many employers practice a credo of 'In God we trust others we monitor.'"
—Marlene Piturro, "Electronic Monitoring"[2]

Introduction

Few would deny the profound impact, both positive and negative, that computers and digital technology are having in the modern workplace. Some of the benefits include safer working conditions, increased productivity, and better communication between employees, clients, and companies. The downside of this revolution can be tedious working conditions and the loss of privacy and autonomy. In the workplace there is a basic tension between surveillance technology and privacy. Companies want to monitor employees and reward effort, intelligence, productivity, and success while eliminating laziness, stupidity, theft, and failure. The market demands no less of most businesses. But against this pressure stands the individual within the walls of privacy—walls that protect against invasions into private domains.

Jeremy Bentham once envisioned a prison workhouse that placed overseers in a central tower with glass walled cells and mirrors placed so that inmates could never know if they were being watched.[3] The idea was that "universal transparency" would keep the prisoners on their best behavior. Recent developments in surveillance technology are promising to turn the workplace into the modern equivalent of Bentham's workhouse. There are now computer programs that allow employers to monitor and record the number of keystrokes per minute an employee completes. Employee badges may allow the recording of movements and time spent at different locations

195

while working. There is now the possibility of monitoring voice mail, e-mail, and phone logs—and all without the knowledge or consent of those being watched. There are even global positioning systems that allow companies to track employee movements cross country. While employers have always sought to monitor employees it is arguably the case that digital technology has changed the game, so to speak. For example, there are now computer programs that can search massive e-mail and voice data files for particular words and expressions. We may wonder, in a networked world, when this kind of surveillance technology will be used to monitor all of us? And not by just governments, although this Orwellian nightmare will be possible, but by our employers.

A related set of issues to employee monitoring that also concerns information control and intangible property centers on nondisclosure agreements and trade secrets. Here the worry is that by signing a typical nondisclosure and non-competition agreement an employee might severely restrict future employment opportunities. As controlling information becomes ever more important, there will be strong incentives for companies to protect themselves by requiring these types of agreements—alas, no business wants to train the employees of rivals companies. Intangible property issues come in at two distinct levels. First, trade secrets and nondisclosure agreements grant businesses the right to control certain kinds of information. Second, the creation or refinement of individual talents and capacities coupled with non-competition contracts yields companies a limited control over a different kind of intangible property—here the rights extend to prohibit certain activities of employees or ex-employees.

In this chapter I will first address the tension between evaluative surveillance and privacy against the backdrop of the current explosion of information technology. More specifically, and drawing on the justification of privacy rights offered in chapter 8, I will argue that knowledge of the different kinds of surveillance used at any given company should be made explicit to the employees. Moreover, there will be certain kinds of evaluative monitoring that violate privacy rights and should not be used in most cases. As we shall see, certain jobs may warrant a smaller domain of privacy. We should not conclude, however, that the arguments used in these cases are easily generalized. In the final section, I will take up the issues related to intangible property, employee mobility, and nondisclosure agreements.

Privacy in the Workplace

As noted in chapter 8, a right to privacy can be understood as a right to maintain a certain level of control over the inner spheres of personal information. It is a right to limit public access to the "core self"—personal information that one never discloses—and to information that one discloses only to family and friends. Moreover, rights to privacy may be justified on grounds of autonomy and sovereignty, and are arguably a core human value that should be included in any account of human well-being or flourishing.

If I am correct about all of this, then there is a fairly strong presumption in favor of individual privacy rights—even in the workplace. What justifies a photographer taking pictures of me about the house is my consent. Most would agree that absent such consent a serious violation of privacy would have occurred. Consent is also necessary, I will argue, for employee monitoring. But therein lies the problem. Under what conditions does consent or agreement yield the appropriate sort of permission. Alas the initial bargaining situation must be fair if we are to be morally bound by the outcome.

We are now in a position to consider an individual's right to privacy in the context of a working environment where evaluative surveillance is both necessary and desirable. If pay increases, promotion, profit sharing awards, and incentive pay are to be based on effort, desert, and success, there must be acceptable methods of monitoring employees.

Consider the following case. In January 1990, Alana Shoars, an administrator for the electronic mail system at Epson America Inc., discovered that the company was monitoring the e-mail messages of its employees. She was shown a batch of printouts of employee e-mail messages—messages that she thought were protected through the use of passwords. "I glanced over at some of the printouts, and a lot of warning bells went off in my head. As far as I'd known, as e-mail coordinator, it wasn't possible to do such a thing."[4] Upon criticizing this breach of employee privacy, Ms. Shoars was dismissed from the company for insubordination.[5]

This case represents only the tip of the iceberg with respect to employee monitoring. A survey of companies in *Macworld* concerning electronic monitoring "reported that 21.6 percent of the 301 participating companies admitted searching employee files, including electronic work files (73.8 percent), e-mail (41.5 percent), network messages (27.7 percent) and voice mail (15.4 percent)."[6] And even more alarming, only 30.8 percent of the companies surveyed gave advance warning of the monitoring activities.[7] A more recent study found that 78 percent of large U.S. firms monitor employee communications while working.[8]

In the most general terms, the case of Alana Shoars and e-mail monitoring highlights the tension between rights to control information and individual privacy in the workplace. What was objectionable with Epson America's monitoring was not their wish to control the information that was found on the company's computer network. The objection is that their employees were not notified of the monitoring nor were they notified of the strict company policy forbidding personal use of the network.

Epson argued that the system was company owned and therefore any information found in e-mail accounts, private or otherwise, was justifiably available for inspection. Moreover, it could be argued that notification of surveillance was both unnecessary and unwise from a corporate perspective. If each instance of monitoring was known to an employee, then the data collected would be almost worthless. It would be like telling the fakes to start faking.

Thin Consent

Justifying employee monitoring in light of privacy rights begins with what I call thin consent. A first step in justifying a kind of monitoring is employee notification. The consent takes the following form: if your employment is to continue then you must agree to such-and-so kinds of surveillance. This is appropriately called "thin consent" because it is assumed that jobs are hard to find, the employee in question needs the job, etc. Nevertheless, quitting is a viable option. The force of such agreements or contracts is echoed by Ronald Dworkin:

> If a group contracted in advance that disputes amongst them would be settled in a particular way, the fact of that contract would be a powerful argument that such disputes should be settled in that way when they do arise. The contract would be an argument in itself, independent of the force of the reasons that might have led different people to enter the contract. Ordinarily, for example, each of the parties supposes that a contract

he signs is in his own interest; but if someone has made a mistake in calculating his self-interest, the fact that he did contract is a strong reason for the fairness of holding him nevertheless to the bargain.[9]

An employee cannot consent, even thinly, to a type of monitoring if it is unknown to her. Given a fairly strong presumption in favor of privacy, thin consent would seem obligatory. Here the employee would be notified of each different type of monitoring. Individual acts of surveillance, however, would not require notification—thus slackers would not be notified to stop slacking.

Moreover, a thin consent policy for each different type of surveillance allows companies and businesses to seize the moral high ground in one important respect. There is no sneaking around riffling through office files, midnight program installations, or hidden backdoor keys into e-mail accounts. All of this up front and in the open. Part of what makes this kind of employee monitoring distasteful is the deceit involved. Locked voice-mail accounts, e-mail files, and desk drawers present the air of privacy when these domains are anything but private.

In any case it should be clear that thin consent is not enough to justify the array of monitoring systems that are now possible or will soon be possible—not in every case. When jobs are scarce, unemployment high, and government assistance programs swamped, thin consent becomes thin indeed. In these conditions employees will be virtually forced to relinquish privacy because of the severe consequences if they don't. But notice what happens when we slide to the other extreme. Assume a condition of negative unemployment where there are many more jobs than employees and where changing jobs is relatively easy. In circumstances such as these, thin consent has become quite thick. And if employees were to agree to a certain type of monitoring in these favorable conditions most would think it justified.

As we slide from one extreme to the other—from a pro-business environment (lots of workers and few jobs yields low wage overhead) to a pro-employee environment (lots of jobs and few workers yields high employee compensation)—this method of justification becomes more plausible. What begins looking like a necessary condition ends up looking like a sufficient condition. To determine the exact point where thin consent becomes thick enough to bear the justificatory burden required is a difficult matter. The promise of actual consent depends on the circumstances. Minimally, if the conditions favor the employee then it is plausible to maintain that actual consent would be enough to override a presumption in favor of privacy.

Hypothetical Thick Consent

As noted above, thick consent is possible when employment conditions minimize the costs of finding a comparable job for an employee. Put another way, an employee who doesn't have to work, but agrees to anyway, has given the right kind of consent—assuming of course they have been notified of the different types of monitoring that will occur. What justifies a certain type of surveillance is that it would be agreeable to a worker in a pro-employee environment. If thin consent is obtained and the test of hypothetical thick consent is met, then we have reason to think that a strong presumption in favor of privacy has been justifiably surpassed.

We will also have to assume that the hypothetical worker making the choice is modestly interested in maintaining control over private information. If this constructed individual has nothing to hide and a general attitude of openness, then any type of surveillance will pass the test. And if I am correct about the importance of privacy with respect to sovereignty and autonomy, anyone would be interested in retaining such control. Rawls' notion of placing individuals behind a veil of ignorance may be of some service here.[10] If the individual agreeing did not know whether she was a worker, manager, or owner and if we assume that anyone would be interested in retaining control over private domains, then the correct vantage point for determining binding agreements will have been attained.

The force of hypothetical contracts has been called into question by Dworkin and others—"A hypothetical contract is not simply a pale form of an actual contract; it is no contract at all."[11] Here I agree with Dworkin. The moral bindingness of hypothetical contracts has to do with the reasons for why we would choose to do this or that. Viewing it this way, hypothetical contracts are simply devices that enable us to more clearly understand the reasons, moral or otherwise, for adopting a particular institution or process. Dworkin notes:

> There must be reasons, of course, why I would have agreed if asked in advance, and these may also be reasons why it is fair to enforce these rules against me even if I have not agreed. But my hypothetical consent does not count as a reason, independent of these other reasons, for enforcing the rules against me, as my actual agreement would have.[12]

Thus the test of hypothetical thick consent can be understood as a way of clarifying, and allowing us to arrive at, a position that is fair and sensible. Hereafter, when I talk of hypothetical consent and the moral force of such agreements, be aware that this is simply a tool or device that is notifying us when privacy rights may be justifiably relaxed.

Taking up the Epson case again, we may ask if a policy of e-mail monitoring would satisfy the test of hypothetical thick consent. Here we are to imagine a world where there were numerous jobs like the ones found at Epson and that moving to these other jobs would be relatively easy. Moreover, given that there is no industry-wide interest in monitoring e-mail activity many of these other positions would not include e-mail monitoring. If an employee would not agree under these conditions, then this type of surveillance would fail the test. Had Epson notified its employees of a company e-mail monitoring policy, then those employees who stayed on at Epson would have given thin consent. But we should not rush to judge that such a policy would be automatically justified unless the test hypothetical thick consent is also met. Meeting this latter test in the Epson case seems unlikely.

I take a virtue of hypothetical thick consent to be that satisfaction is determined by imagining a pro-employee situation and then asking what an employee would do in the face of some kind of surveillance. Some may charge that I am stacking the deck, however. Why not imagine a pro-business situation and then ask what an employee would do. We wouldn't have to do much imagining though, and employee consent in such conditions wouldn't justify anything. Moreover, if I am correct in positing privacy rights for each of us, then the deck is already stacked. There is a presumption in favor of individuals having control over personal information—we have privacy rights. Since employee surveillance may cross into private domains, we must consider under what conditions a privacy right may be given up or relaxed. In relatively few cases is thin consent thick enough to handle the justificatory burden. Hence, the use of hypothetical thick consent. We are imagining a case where the bargaining situation favors the employee—and if agreement is offered in these conditions, then we may have binding consent.

I hasten to note that even in a pro-employee environment there would be certain kinds of employee monitoring that would be necessary for any business. Punching a time clock or measuring time spent working, for example, would occur in almost any business or company. Even in a pro-employee market theft would have to be minimized. It is not as if McDonalds would become so desperate for workers that they would leave the register drawers open, allow employees to come and go as they please, and continue to pay wages. The market demands that businesses make a profit or at least break even. Given this, there will be certain kinds of employee monitoring that every business will use.

Moreover, there will be employment specific monitoring as well. For example, trucking companies will have to monitor driving records and ensure that drivers maintain the appropriate skills needed to operate the big rigs. This kind of surveillance may be required by the market or by legislation of one kind or another. There may be laws that require certain licenses that make businesses liable for noncompliance. Absent laws or other government regulation, market efficiency may require certain kinds of monitoring. An example of the latter may be employee time monitoring. The hypothetical or constructed truck driver, no matter where he goes, will be subject to certain kinds of monitoring. So, even in a pro-employee environment certain kinds of surveillance will be justified—those kinds that are necessary for doing business.

If I am correct, thin consent will justify certain kinds of monitoring when employment conditions favor the employee. Absent such conditions actually occurring, we can imagine what an employee would choose if she were in a pro-employee environment. If she would agree to a type of monitoring from this vantage point—either because every business in her field will monitor in the way she is considering or she just simply agrees (maybe because the new monitoring policy will benefit her in some way)—then the monitoring is permitted.

Test Cases and Illustrations

Let us begin with an easy one first. Suppose that one day an employee is approached by his boss and is informed that the company will be moving to a new building. Excited about the new digs, the employee tours the recently constructed office and is quite dismayed. It seems that management has been reading Bentham's *Panopticon* and the site has been built so that employee cubicles can be monitored by an overseer who can't himself be seen. The video cameras found in the new office have been placed so that computer screens can be watched as well as facial expressions, body motions, and the like. The employee complains and asks what conceivable purpose such a system could have at an insurance company. Management replies that only someone with something to hide would object and this system of monitoring will allow hard workers to be recognized and fairly compensated.

We may now ask if such a monitoring system is justified in relation to hypothetical thick consent. I think it is clear that an individual who is modestly interested in protecting privacy and in a pro-employee environment would leave, other things being equal, and find similar employment elsewhere. The "other things being equal" exception is important because if management were to double employee salaries then maybe a deal could be made—no privacy at work for lots of cash.[13] Outside of such offers the presumption in favor of privacy rights would not have been surpassed for this type of surveillance.

Before moving on, I would like to briefly address the kinds of replies that were offered for why employees shouldn't oppose this kind of monitoring. First, that an employee should have nothing to hide is irrelevant. It is her private life that is being monitored and so it is up to her to deny access. Whether or not she has something to hide is nobody's business. We all may have perfectly normal bedroom lives and have nothing to hide in this area. Nevertheless, mounting a company video camera and wake-up siren on the bedroom wall cannot in the least bit be supported by such reasons. Employee benefit is equally, and for the same reasons, dubious.

Consider a different case. Suppose in an effort to eliminate "time theft" a company begins using "active badges" that monitor employee movements while at work. These badges are sophisticated enough to monitor time spent in a specific area. So, employees who linger in the break-room, arrive late, leave early, and stroll the halls, will be discovered and treated accordingly.

Few would deny that time monitoring is a necessary part of any business. Nevertheless, there will be more and less invasive ways to monitor time. Bentham's Panopticon with a time overseer is one of the more invasive methods. Given that there are various less invasive ways to obtain this information about employees, it would seem that a constructed individual interested in maintaining private domains would not agree to this type of surveillance. Thus for most companies such a policy would be unjustified. There may be exceptions, however. For example the U.S. Pentagon, weapons research and development departments, and the like, may have to maintain this level of monitoring to ensure secrecy.[14] Monitoring college professors in this way is clearly unjustifiable.

A final case that I would like to discuss deals with remote computer monitoring. The case is provided by John Whalen:

> A recent ad for Norton-Lambert's Close-Up/LAN software package tempted managers to "look in on Sue's computer screen . . . . Sue doesn't even know you're there!" . . . these "remote monitoring" capabilities, . . . allow network administrators to peek at an employee's screen in real time, scan data files and e-mail at will, tabulate keystroke speed and accuracy, overwrite passwords, and even seize control of a remote workstation. Products like Dynamics Corp.'s Peak and Spy; Microcom Inc.'s LANlord; Novell Inc.'s Net Ware; and Neon Software's NetMinder not only improve communications and productivity, they turn employees' cubicles into covert listening stations.[15]

While this kind of employee monitoring may yield some benefits the preponderance of the evidence would suggest otherwise. Some studies have shown that these monitoring systems produce fear, resentment, and elevate stress levels.[16] Another study concluded that "the introduction of computerized performance monitoring may result in a workplace that is less satisfying to many employees . . . . [and] creates a more competitive environment which may decrease the quality of social relationships."[17]

Putting aside the unsavory consequences, we may ask if such monitoring passes either test under consideration. First, the test of thin consent would not be passed if the employees being monitored were not notified of such practices. Given the absence of a clear pro-employee environment in most industries that would use such surveillance, even if employees were notified the consent would seem too thin. Moreover, remote computer monitoring would fail the test of hypothetical thick consent for most companies. Individuals who did not know if they were the owner, manager, or employee would not agree to such privacy invasions. The presumption in favor of privacy would thus remain intact.

Trade Secrets, Employee Mobility, and Nondisclosure Agreements[18]

Confidentiality agreements have become the norm in our technology and information-based economy. Generally, these agreements require that employees not divulge any company secrets upon termination. The problem is in determining what counts as a protectable company secret and what kind of protection should be adopted. With the modern lapse in company loyalty and the subsequent movement of employees among numerous businesses, confidentiality agreements are becoming more important—here we have a case of an employee's rights to take her skills and capacities and sell them to the highest bidder and a company's right to keep secret vital information or expensively produced procedures. What happens in many cases is that certain applicants are not hired because of potential law suits for trade secret violations. As with the privacy verses monitoring issue, I wonder if there is a strong enough public interest to override or limit the general practice of confidentiality agreements.

To begin with a case, in 1975 Structural Dynamics Research Corporation (SDRC) brought action against three former employees, Kant Kothawala, Karan Surana, and Robert Hildebrand, for unfair competition, misappropriation and misuse of confidential and trade secret material. These three employees left SDRC and formed their own company, Engineering Mechanics Research Corporation (EMRC), and then allegedly used SDRC trade secrets to capture a market share. At issue were two computer programs which tested how physical structures would react to certain forces. These programs were developed and written by Kothawala, Surana, and Hildebrand. But since all three defendants entered into an employee patent and confidential information agreements, the injunction sought by SDRC was granted and the inventors of these programs were not allowed to use them.

In general, the issue this case highlights is that intellectual property rights can interfere with the future job opportunities of employees, especially when certain trade secret and confidentiality agreements are utilized. When an employee agrees not to disclose any of the ideas that she has created or learned while working for some company, the agreement may limit the kinds of work this employee can pursue upon termination. It will most certainly limit the employee's ability to be lured away by a rival company seeking to obtain a competitive advantage. If the contract is made under fair conditions, then the employee can be held to the terms of the agreement. This is precisely what happened in the case of Structural Dynamics Research Corporation (SDRC) verses Engineering Mechanics Research Corporation (EMRC). The employees signed away their rights to use the very computer programs they created.

The messy cases are those in which the employee does not know what she is signing, when she agrees under duress of some sort, or when the contract does not cover certain in-between areas of knowledge. Tom Arnold writes:

> So here we find an area where the common law has fumbled the ball as badly as a hippopotamus playing tidily winks. Even with declaratory judgment procedures, our judicial system does not now afford a clear answer to the right of the former employee in the many in-between areas of know-how necessarily used in new competitive businesses, until *after* the business has committed its capital to some selected design. And even then the answer obtained is not across the full scope of the employee's knowledge but is specific to only the tools litigated—leaving the former employee still in a quandary as to every new tool he designs thereafter.[19]

We may also ask, can an employer obtain an agreement that grants claim trade secret protection to any competitive knowledge that an employee learns or creates on the job? Moreover, there is the following employer related problem:

> it is not the laborer who is critical, and often it is not even the typical research engineer who is the most critical. The man in the young management group with no special technical trade secret as such, is often the man who can hurt you the most by going to the competitor—and this man's know-how is most often totally unprotectable by the law of confidential information.
>
> It does not follow, however, that the employer is helpless to afford itself substantial protection. It can do this by appropriate employment contracts with its critical personnel, including no-competition clauses in appropriate areas for six months, a year or two years, as may be appropriate.[20]

Generally, these cases point to problems about the bindingness and legitimacy of contracts and not to questions of intellectual property ownership. The presumption is that if an employee signs a contract transferring all ownership claims to created or discovered ideas to a company in return for monetary compensation, then the question is not one of whether rights have been generated. The question is one of whether or not the employee, in light of the contract, has any claim to use the ideas in question. The contract, in this case, is not creating rights, it is merely transferring certain rights claims from one party to another. Steadfast or valuable employees may hold out for joint rights (equal rights to use) or even sole ownership upon termination.

It is true that confidential agreements between employee and employer may restrict the future employment opportunities of job seekers. This problem is not germane to trade secrets, however, for companies may require new employees to sign non-competition agreements that prohibit these workers, upon termination, to seek employment with competitors. One justification for such agreements is that they afford companies protection from training the employees of another company. Suppose my company's policy was to lure away trained employees from a rival company with offers of higher earnings—assume these wages were less than the costs of hiring untrained workers, training them, and paying them a competitive salary.

Some individuals object to these kinds of agreements on the grounds that they protect the strong against the weak.[21] Employers are in a position of strength, they can offer a job to anyone they please and if a prospective employee refuses to sign the relevant contract, then someone else will be offered the job. With an army of unemployed seeking jobs, the employer is in a position to require concessions—the strong obtain advantageous agreements at the expense of the weak.

As with employee monitoring, I would agree that the strengths of the bargaining positions of employers and workers is relative to the supply and demand of workers and jobs. Currently, in many parts of the United States there is what economists call negative-employment in certain fields—there are more jobs than workers to fill them. In this case the strength of the relative bargaining positions is clearly on the side of job seekers. Unions along with other market forces may also equalize bargaining positions.

Moreover, it is not obviously the case that in conditions of job scarcity and worker abundance (pro-business environments), confidential information agreements or non-competitive bargains always benefit the strong at the expense of the weak. Consider the following case:

> Imagine three entrepreneurs who wish to expand their highly successful cookie business. A venture capitalist interested in financing the expansion naturally wishes to know the details of the operation—including the prized cookie recipe—before putting up capital. After examining the recipe, however, he decides that it would be more profitable for him to sell the recipe to CookieCo, a multinational food company, and to invest his capital elsewhere.[22]

Without the right to protect the recipe, through a confidential information agreement, the entrepreneurs in this case are likely out of business—especially, if CookieCo can produce and distribute the cookies more cheaply. And more generally, law casebooks are filled with examples of individuals and small companies who have novel ideas that are protected from misappropriation.[23]

As with employee monitoring and privacy, I would argue that nondisclosure agreements and non-competition clauses be justified via the tests of thin and hypothetical thick consent. Here we are asking what an individual would agree to if they didn't know whether they were the owner, manager, or employee. Note that many companies have trade secrets and seek to deter the movement of "home grown" talent and abilities to rival companies as well. Prima facie, it seems the model under consideration would justify these kinds of control within certain obvious limits.

The problems related to the control of information, employee mobility, and contracts are not problems for the Lockean model any more than for alternative arrangements. I do not think a strong enough case has been made to limit intellectual property rights in this area— rights that are protected by trade secrets, confidentiality agreements, and non-competition clauses.

Conclusion

As noted in the opening, high tech surveillance is promising to turn the modern workplace into an Orwellian nightmare achieving Bentham's ideal workhouse for prisoners—"universal transparency." And even if such monitoring somehow produced an overall net increase in utility, it would still be unjustifiable. Sometimes the consequences be damned. Not that I think generally good consequences could be had from such surveillance. Arguably, human beings are the most productive and creative in conditions completely opposite from those found in Bentham's *Panopticon*.

In this chapter I have argued that individuals have rights to privacy that shield us from the prying eyes and ears of neighbors, governments, and corporations—electronic eyes and ears are no more welcome. If we begin with a fairly strong presumption in favor of privacy and test different types of employee monitoring with thin and hypothetical thick consent, many currently used kinds of surveillance will be unjustified. Arguably this consent is necessary and sufficient for overriding or relaxing privacy rights with respect to employee monitoring.[24] Consent of this sort may even serve to justify non-competition clauses and nondisclosure agreements. It is not so clear that trade secrets, confidentiality agreements, and non-com-

petition clauses are damaging enough to justify elimination or radical modification. We will each spend at least a quarter of our lives
and a large part of our most productive years at work. This environment should be constructed to promote creative and productive activity while maintaining the zones of privacy that we all cherish.
Although privacy rights are not absolute, it would seem that in a
networked world filled with devices that may be used to capture
information about each of us we should take privacy invasions—
whether at home, on a public street, or in the workplace—much
more seriously.

Notes

1.   An amended version of this chapter originally appeared in *Business Ethics Quarterly* 10 (July 2000) entitled "Employee Monitoring and Computer Technology:
Evaluative Surveillance v. Privacy."
2.   Marlene Piturro, "Electronic Monitoring," *Information Center* (July 1990), 31 quoted
in Richard Spinello's *Ethical Aspects of Information Technology* (Englewood Cliffs,
NJ: Prentice Hall, 1995), 141.
3.   J. Bentham, *Panopticon* (The Inspection House), originally published in 1791.
4.   IDG Communications, Inc., *Infoworld* (October 22, 1990), quoted in Anne Wells
Branscomb in *Who Owns Information?* (New York: Basic Books, 1994), 92.
5.   Alana Shoars filed a wrongful termination suit. "The lower court agreed with Epson's
lawyer that neither state privacy statutes nor federal statutes address confidentiality
of E-mail in the workplace and dismissed the case." Branscomb, *Who Owns Information?* 93. See *Alana Shoars v. Epson America*, Inc., No. SWC112749 (L.A.
Super. Ct. 1990).
6.   Branscomb, *Who Owns Information?* 93.
7.   "While the courts have ruled that employers cannot monitor their workers' personal
calls, the Electronic Communications Privacy Act of 1986 grants bosses a 'busi-
ness-use exception,' which allows supervisory and quality-control monitoring." J.
Whalen, "You're Not Paranoid: They Really Are Watching You," *Wired Magazine*
(March 1995). See also, *Briggs v. American Filter Co.*, 704 F.2d 577 (11th. Cir.
1983), *Watkins v. L. M. Berry*, 704 F.2d 579 (11th. Cir. 1983), and Hendricks et al.,
Your Right to Privacy, part 2.
8.   Andy Sullivan, "Congress Considers Workplace Privacy Measure," (July 21, 2000)
Internet Report, Technology News, Yahoo http://dailynews.yahoo.com/h/nm/
20000721/wr/congress_privacy_dc_2.html.
9.   Ronald Dworkin, *Taking Rights Seriously* (Cambridge, MA: Harvard University
Press, 1977), reprinted in James Sterba, *Justice: Alternative Political Perspectives*,
3rd ed. (Belmont, CA: Wadsworth Publishing, 1999), 126 (all page references refer
to the reprint).
10.   J. Rawls, *A Theory of Justice* (Cambridge: Harvard University Press, 1971), 136-
42.
11.   Dworkin, *Taking Rights Seriously*, 126-27.
12.   Dworkin, *Taking Rights Seriously*, 127.
13.   Employment agreements grant rights, powers, liberties, and duties to both parties.
Thus an employee may trade privacy for some kind of compensation like time off or

the opportunity to learn. When trade-offs such as these have occurred we may take the obligations, generated by the agreement, as prima facie—alas, the agreement may have been brokered in unfair conditions. If I am correct, fairness of conditions and binding agreements that justifiably relax rights are guaranteed when the tests of thin and hypothetical thick consent are passed.

14. Even in these cases the different types of surveillance used should be made explicit to every employee.

15. J. Whalen, "You're Not Paranoid: They Really Are Watching You," *Wired Magazine* (March 1995).

16. Richard Spinello's, *Ethical Aspects of Information Technology* (Englewood Cliffs, NJ: Prentice Hall, 1995), 128.

17. R. H. Irving, C. A. Higgins, and F. R. Safayeni, "Computerized Performance Monitoring Systems: Use and Abuse," *Communications of the ACM* (August 1986): 800.

18. For more information concerning employer/employee relationships and trade secrets, see *American Cahin & Cable Co., Inc. v. Avery* (Supreme Court of Connecticut, 1964. 143 USPQ 126); *Structural Dynamics Research Corp. v. Engineering Mechanics Research Corp.* (United States District Court of Michigan, 1975. 401 F.Supp. 1102); and *The Anaconda Company v. Metric Tool & Die Company* (United States District Court of Pennsylvania, 1980. 485 F.Supp. 410).

19. Tom Arnold, "Rights in Trade Secrets That Are Not Secret," presented at the Institute of Patent Law 1963.

20. Arnold, "Rights in Trade Secrets That Are Not Secret."

21. Edwin Hettinger, "Justifying Intellectual Property," in *Intellectual Property: Moral, Legal, and International Dilemmas*, edited by A. Moore (Lanham, MD: Rowman & Littlefield, 1997), chapter 1.

22. Lynn Sharp Pain, "Trade Secrets and the Justification of Intellectual Property," in *Intellectual Property: Moral, Legal, and International Dilemmas*, edited by A. Moore (Lanham, MD: Rowman & Littlefield, 1997), chapter 2.

23. For example, see the *Buchwald v. Paramount Pictures Corp.* 13 U.S.P.Q.2d 1497 (Calif. Superior); *Smith v. Dravo Corp.* 203 F.2d 369 U.S. Court of Appeals, 7th Circuit, 1953; and *Hisel v. Chrysler Corp.* U.S.D.C. Missouri, 1951, 94 F.Supp. 996.

24. I take consequentialist concerns to be factored into laws or market demands. That is, hypothetical thick consent includes utility maximization arguments for requiring licenses, safety regulations, and the like.

10

Owning Genetic Information and Gene Enhancement Techniques[1]

"Each new advance in . . . technology . . . disturbs a status quo. It meets resistance
from those whose domain it threatens, but if useful, it begins to be adopted."
—Ithiel de Sola Pool, *Technologies of Freedom*[2]

Introduction

In recent years the ethical issues surrounding genetic enhancement, gene therapy, cloning, and privacy rights have been hotly debated. With the first draft of the human genome completed and the advancement of gene therapy, we stand on the cusp of a brave new world. In the near future it will be possible to alter one's own genetic profile—maybe a change of eye color or a loss of weight. It may also be possible to affect the genetic make-up of future generations. For instance, we may be able to banish diabetes, sickle-cell anemia, and similar diseases from the human genome.

The ethical, political, and social ramifications of this bio-technological movement are profound and have alarmed many. "Messing with the human genome," some claim, "is playing God." Others conjure visions of clone farms, organ banks, and a world where individual distinctiveness has given way to near identical, near perfect, robot-like beings. Some argue that even if good may come from this tampering with nature it will most likely only affect the rich or those who can pay for gene therapy. The general mood of most leaders and scholars with respect to these issues is one of caution.

I have argued that intangible property of this sort can be owned—that the proper subjects of intangible property claims include medical records, genetic profiles, and gene enhancement techniques. Coupled with a right to privacy (see chapter 8) these intangible property rights allow individuals a zone of control that will, in most cases, justifiably exclude governmental or societal invasions into private domains. I will argue that the threshold for overriding privacy rights and intangible property rights is higher, in relation to genetic enhancement techniques and sensitive personal information, than is commonly suggested. Once the bar is raised, so-to-speak, the burden of overriding it is formidable. In the end, I am not so worried about the prospects of a brave new world brought upon us by gene manipulation—I am much more worried when societies, committees, and concerned citizens use the force of government to tell us what we can do to and in our own bodies.

Privacy: Controlling Your Genetic Information

In 1976, John Moore began treatment for cancer at the University of California Medical Center. In the course of study and treatment, his doctors learned that Moore's blood products were special—possibly very valuable:

> They performed many tests without ever telling him of their commercial interest, and took samples of every conceivable bodily fluid, including sperm, blood, and bone marrow aspirate. Eventually, they removed Moore's spleen, a procedure for which there was an arguable medical reason, but only after having first made arrangements to have sections of the spleen taken to a research unit. In 1981, a cell line established from Moore's T-lymphocytes was patented by the University of California, with Moore's doctors listed as the inventors. At no time during this process was Moore told anything about the commercial exploitation of his genetic material. The likely commercial value of the cell line is impossible to predict exactly, but by 1990 the market for such products was estimated to be over $3 billion.[3]

Alarming as this case appears, we can easily imagine cases that are more troubling. What if the tests on Moore's genetic material found, along with certain advantageous traits, defects that would likely cause him to be hospitalized for lengthy periods of time. Upon publishing their findings and maybe patenting certain cell lines, Moore's insurance company drops his policy and other companies refuse coverage. What if Moore's doctors found a genetic marker for homosexuality or a predisposition for diabetes and published this information against his wishes?[4]

The case of John Moore and the patenting of cells produced from his blood-products is interesting because it brings up a number of important issues related to controlling personal information and body rights.[5] At one level this case raises the question of what information doctors should disclose to their patients, especially when the information in question is about the patient. But at a more general level, this case is concerned with the ownership of genetic information and other personal information. Doctor-patient confidentiality agreements are based upon the patient's rights to control certain kinds of sensitive personal information. Binding agreements though, presuppose prior entitlements.

If Moore had agreed to the gathering and disclosure of the genetic information found in his T-lymphocytes, then this case would lose much of its moral impact. What bothers most of us is the deception that occurred—Moore's doctors repeatedly asked for a second signed waiver and Moore repeatedly asked why they wanted such a waiver. Generally we can ask if Moore actually owned the information that was found in his T-lymphocytes. As self-owners it may be the case that we each own and can control our own bodies, capacities, and powers. It does not follow from the notion of "self-ownership" however, that we each own the genetic information found in our cells. Ownership of a token does not entail ownership of a type. In other words, I may own a copy of *The Sun Also Rises* (a token), but this does not mean that I own the intangible work (the plot, characters, theme, and style—or types).

Also, it is not even clear in this case that a privacy interest is at stake. The cell line, or discovered intangible work, established from Moore's T-lymphocytes may contain no personal information at all. And if there is no privacy interest at stake, no information about sexual preferences, possible future ailments, and the like, then it would be difficult to maintain that Moore's privacy was violated. Thus, it could be the case that no prior entitlement claims existed.

A different case, but one that is even more alarming than the Moore case, is what happened in a small village in Greece. In Orchemenos, Greece, there are many individuals who have a gene that causes sickle-shaped red blood cells. The problem is that when two parents both carry the gene their offspring may develop sickle-cell anemia. In an effort to prevent this disease researchers tested everyone in the village so that marriages between gene carriers could be avoided:

> A group of researchers tested the villagers at Orchemenos, assuming that carriers would behave rationally and would pair with noncarriers in order to mix the genes safely and protect the community's children. The noncarriers, however refused to cooperate. Even though the gene is harmless on its own, carriers became stigmatized

and noncarriers refused to marry them. In the end, the carriers became a shunned subclass who were forced to marry among themselves, making the situation even worse that before.[6]

While the researchers goals were noble, they obviously failed to foresee the ramifications of disclosing this kind of personal information. If we are to take privacy rights seriously, there should be general prohibitions against disclosing information of this sort—no matter what the gains in social utility.

Current American practice allows companies and individuals to gather, sell, and buy almost any kind of information including sensitive personal information. Moreover, access to personal information stored on databases held by companies and other citizens is purely voluntary—companies do not have to show you the information that they have gathered about you. And in any case, you have very little control over what can be done with this information. If a company or the government wants to sell this information, there is little that you can do about it.[7]

I think it is plausible to maintain that intangible goods, like genetic enhancement techniques, can be owned and that there is a fairly strong presumption in favor of individual privacy—these claims are argued for at length in Chapters 4-8. These rights, I have argued, are limited by a prohibition of harmful use and a privacy restriction. As noted before the proviso, a no harm no foul rule allows individuals to acquire intangible goods. The harm restriction limits harmful uses of those goods.

A second constraint on what can be done with intangible works has to do with privacy and information control. Without your consent and independent of harm, I may not publish sensitive personal information about you on my Web site, use your image to promote an international product line, or listen in on your phone conversations. The question now becomes when, if ever, can these fairly strong presumptions, or rights, be overridden by other considerations.

Privacy, Property, and Genetic Enhancement Techniques

In this section I will consider several common arguments that purport to show how easily the property and privacy presumptions already established may be undermined. Please note that what follows is not an exhaustive examination of every point and counterpoint that may be offered with respect to these presumptions. My goal is simply to show that privacy rights and intangible property rights, once established, are not so easily swept aside as some might think. Thus many policy decisions that have been recently proposed or enacted—citywide audio and video surveillance, law enforcement DNA sweeps, genetic profiling, and national bans on genetic testing and enhancement of humans, to name a few—will have to be backed by very strong arguments.

Interference with Liberty and Privacy Argument

Let us begin with a fairly simple case. Suppose that Ginger has discovered the genetic markers for diabetes and has developed a gene therapy technique that will correct this defect. In fact her technique will eliminate the gene or combination of genes that cause diabetes in mature cells (somatic cells) as well as cells that may be passed on to one's offspring (germ line cells). Fred, who has been suffering from the complications of diabetes since childhood, contacts Ginger and arranges to have genetic therapy. Moreover, suppose that Fred has privacy rights that allow him a certain kind of control over personal information and his body or its capacities. Fred undergoes the procedure, pays Ginger, and forever alters the genetic profile of his descendants.

Given that Fred and Ginger could be members of any society or culture and assuming that presumptive rights to privacy and intangible property ownership have been established, we have an immediate prima facie case against sweeping governmental or societal interference with this conduct. Ginger's love of science and desire to help others drives her to burn the midnight oil and produce a revolutionary new technique. Fred's right to privacy allows him, within certain constraints, to decide what happens to and in his body. It would seem that there are no grounds for third party interference in this case—nothing that would override the presumptive rights already in place.

Now, if Fred and Ginger had conspired to change his genetic profile in such a way that caused his descendants *to have* childhood diabetes, then surely interference or sanctions are warranted (assuming, of course, that Fred is going to father children). I would hope that such activity would fall under the umbrella of child protection laws. Those individuals who do things that endanger the health and well-being of dependents will have sanctioned interferences with private domains and ownership. A similar example is the individual who is playing Russian roulette with someone who does not care to take part in this activity—surely this would bump against the harm restriction or a similar restriction; the "risk of great harm" restriction.[8]

A few staunch defenders of religious freedom argue that fundamentalists should be able to adhere to certain rules even when doing so will cause a child to die. For example some religious views forbid blood transfusions while others may forbid access to medical doctors altogether. These practices are clear violations of the harm standard, and according to my view may be justifiably prohibited. Moreover, those who disagree with me on this matter and with respect to genetic enhancement seem to stand on shaky ground—they will allow parents to harm their children by adhering to religious principles while forbidding other parents the ability to help their children though genetic enhancement.

Top-down laws that seek to regulate genetic therapy will almost always interfere with individual liberty and privacy. Consider the case where Fred flies off to some foreign country to receive genetic therapy from Ginger. It is difficult to imagine how laws or similar kinds of regulation are going to prohibit this activity without also sanctioning severe violations of liberty and privacy. Is there going to be a national database housing everyone's genetic profile so that individuals can be tested to see if they have been tampering with their genetic make-up? Are we going to prohibit flights to countries where genetic therapy is both legal and safe? Will there be the genome police who investigate and root out those trying to alter their genetic structure?

This is extreme you say? Police agencies in the United Kingdom are already doing DNA sweeps in search of criminals that have left biological evidence at crime scenes. After the sweep the information is housed in a crime agency database so that future crimes may be solved. Iceland's parliament has granted the right to create a national database containing the health records of the entire population to a single private company. Several U.S. cities have floated similar proposals.

Moreover, with better technology and less invasive techniques undergoing genetic therapy may become as simple as getting a shot. Here there is little ground to stand on between draconian laws that clearly cross into private domains and interfere with individual liberty or emasculated regulations that have little force. A ban on genetic testing in the United States will not prevent independent researchers in less regulated countries from this sort of experimentation. And with the possibility of massive profits there will always be companies and universities eager to fund such projects.

While it may be the case that certain types of genetic enhancement are immoral, it does not automatically follow that they should be regulated. There are many actions, both moral and immoral, that fall outside of the domain societal regulation. Lying and helping the poor are two obvious examples.

Certain types of actions should be prohibited on grounds that they present an unjustifiable harm to others—these actions violate the harm restriction. Other actions or policies may be prohibited because they unjustifiably invade private domains. Genetically predisposing your offspring to live in pain or to grow a third arm, causing your child to become afflicted with cancer, poor eyesight, and diabetes, are all actions that warrant prosecution.[9] Moreover, if there is evidence that someone is about to produce these harms then surely intervention is warranted. Put another way, property rights and privacy rights are justifiably overridden in these cases.

None of this, however, sanctions a national database containing individual genetic profiles or outlawing somatic and germ line therapy simpliciter. The norms that guide us as to when and where it is appropriate to interfere with family life should guide us in genetic modification cases as well. If a parent takes action that will result in serious harm to his descendants, then the privacy presumption will have been overridden. Moreover, those who develop and sell such techniques should be liable as well.

In presenting these cases I hope to establish the futility of national, or even international, laws prohibiting gene enhancement in human subjects. Such laws are unenforceable and would almost certainly sanction unjustifiable interferences with individual liberty and privacy. Sending a child to a parochial school is a form of environmental enhancement that many find distasteful. Nevertheless, this activity is generally recognized as falling outside the domain of legitimate government regulation. A father who incessantly pushes his child to become a tennis star may be doing something questionable from a moral point of view. Parents who teach their children to be intolerant or genetically predispose their offspring to grow seven feet tall may also be engaging in immoral behavior. It does not automatically follow that this type of behavior ought to be legally prohibited. We may continue to argue about the ethical status of particular kinds of genetic enhancement as we do about certain kinds of environmental enhancement. Nevertheless, I think that it is important to note the high threshold that must be passed for justifiable interference in private domains.

The Inequality Argument

One argument commonly given against allowing individuals the liberty to undergo genetic enhancement procedures is that such technology is expensive and will only impact the rich. Those with the financial resources will genetically engineer their offspring to eliminate defects while the poor will be left what nature gives them by chance. This inequality in health care will lead to further economic and social inequalities. It may also lead to longer, more healthier lives for some, ultimately creating a class-based society and discrimination against those who are genetically challenged.

This view is subject to several decisive objections. Almost every medical advancement at its beginning was available only to the rich. By refining these advancements and techniques prices dropped which opened up new markets for those less financially fortunate. In the end, procedures that were once cost prohibitive are now available to everyone. There is no reason to think that genetic enhancement procedures won't follow this same course. In fact, our entire market system seems to necessitate this kind of inequality. Most inventors and companies burn the midnight oil and create or discover new and revolutionary medical procedures in order to make a profit. This process requires large up front investments that in turn necessitate higher initial prices when a viable commodity does come to market. Nevertheless, sooner or later the "high priced" market becomes saturated and in order to maintain profits prices are dropped. If this system yields everyone better prospects in the end, the resulting initial inequality of distribution is hardly objectionable.

Moreover, even if gene therapy techniques remain expensive the leveling effect assumed in the inequality argument seems indefensible. Suppose that aspirin-plus is invented and cures with great efficiency headaches and colds. The cost of aspirin-plus, however, is very high—suppose $500 per pill. Are we to prohibit the manufacture and administration of aspirin-plus because it is unfair that some will be able to forgo the suffering bought on by colds and headaches while others will not? This sounds like simple envy and mean spiritedness to me—"if I can't have it, then no one can" or "if I have to suffer, then so does everyone else." Let us dispense with the notion that individuals who hold these sentiments are actually concerned with lessening human suffering.

Now it might be argued that my aspirin-plus case and the social ramifications of allowing genetic enhancement to proliferate are wildly divergent. Curing headaches and colds does not impact an individual's entire life in the way that genetic manipulation does. But here again we bump against other forms of enhancement—replacing a defective liver or heart, teaching your child to read, learning to play chess, going to college, playing sports, nurturing musical abilities, developing the virtue of self-control—that it would seem illicit to legally prohibit even though they each impact an individual's entire life.

Many of these examples are purposely ambiguous in that they may be things we do to ourselves or things that we do to others. Few would deny that parents who create environments that produce these characteristics should be stopped. What if these enhancements could be genetically produced? Why would environmental enhancement or manipulation be permitted yet the genetic-based counterpart be prohibited? One answer is that the former is temporary, ending with the life of the person involved, while the latter will be passed down to all subsequent generations. But this is clearly false given that environmental enhancements may be passed on to one's children and genetic enhancements may be altered with somatic therapy.

One sort of reply to this view is given by the Council for Responsible Genetics which opposes germline modification unconditionally: "The cultural impact of treating humans as biologically perfectible artifacts would be entirely negative. People who fall short of some technically achievable ideal would be 'damaged goods.' And it is clear that the standards for what is genetically desirable will be those of society's economically and politically dominate groups. This will only reinforce prejudices and discrimination in a society where they already exist."[10]

Obviously I disagree. There is no reason to think that gene modification of any sort will necessarily lead to "treating humans as biologically perfectible artifacts" or that those who don't live up to some ideal will be viewed as "damaged goods." Maybe genetically manipulated individuals will be labeled as "unnatural" rather than superior. Moreover, who would know if fairly strong rights to privacy are in place.

Conclusion

If I am correct there is a fairly strong presumption in favor of privacy and intangible property rights that will limit the kinds of legislation that have recently been offered concerning genetic research and gene therapy. Furthermore, the inequality argument fails to justify overriding these rights. While not discussed in relation to controlling sensitive personal information, I think that the social nature of intellectual works argument given in chapter 7 also fails to provide sufficient justification for overriding privacy and intangible property rights. While there is much more to be said concerning these issues, I would urge caution in a different direction and put the burden of proof in a different place. Let property rights and privacy rights stand in the absence of strong overriding reasons. In the end, it seems that we are headed toward a world that includes clone farms, organ banks, and genetic manipulation. If so, let us at least face this future with our basic rights of property and privacy intact.

Notes

1.   A longer version of the is chapter, entitled "Owning Genetic Information and Gene Enhancement Techniques: Why Privacy and Property Rights May Undermine Social Control of the Human Genome," was published in *Bioethics* 14 (Spring 2000).
2.   Ithiel de Sola Pool, *Technologies of Freedom* (Cambridge, MA: Belknap Press, 1983), 7.
3.   James Boyle, *Shamans, Software, and Spleens: Law and the Construction of the Information Society* (Cambridge, MA: Harvard University Press, 1996), 22. The prediction of market value comes from Beverly Merz, "Biotechnology; Spleen-Rights," *The Economist* 30 (August 11, 1990). *Moore v. Regents of the University of California* 793 P.2d 479 (Cal. 1990), *cert denied*, 499 U.S. 936 (1991). See also, *Miles, Inc. v. Scripts Clinic and Research Foundation*, 810 F. Supp. 1091 (S.D. Cal. 1993).
4.   The Patients Bill of Rights, currently being discussed in Congress, would limit these kinds of activities. Also being discussed, maybe as part of the Patients Bill of Rights, is a Genetic Non-discrimination in Health Insurance and Employment provision. In 1996 the Health Insurance Portability and Accountability Act was passed. Also, there are currently a number of state Acts that protect genetic privacy. For example, see Oregon Law No. 276 (formerly Senate Bill No. 276).
5.   "The 1990 Moore decision held that the removal of a person's cells and bodily

tissues extinguishes a patient's property interest in his cells and genetic material . . . the California Supreme Court left the final disposition of such involved policy matters to the legislature." Michael Lin, "Conferring A Federal Property Right in Genetic Material: Stepping into the Future with the Genetic Privacy Act," *American Journal of Law and Medicine* (Spring 1996): 109.

6.   The example comes from Charles Platt "Evolution Revolution," *Wired* (Jan. 1997).
7.   For example, the United States Postal Service sells your change of address to marketing companies who then send you mountains of junk mail. The USPS gets paid by the junk mailers for the change of address and the junk mail. See Anne Wells Branscomb in *Who Owns Information?* (New York: Basic Books, 1994), 9.
8.   Suppose X is a hermit and has no contact with others—he builds traps all over his property so that those who come onto his land after his death will be killed. This is a private matter and one where X is simply doing what he wants with his property. Nevertheless, given the likelihood that someone will be killed or suffer serious harm due to the traps that X set, clearly a violation of the harm restriction has occurred.
9.   If it is possible to modify mature cells (somatic gene therapy), then may be possible to correct the defects that have been foisted on children by "troubled" parents.
10. Council For Responsible Genetics, Human Genetics Committee (Fall, 1992). T. Beauchamp and L. Waters, *Bioethics*, 4th ed. (Belmont. CA: Wadsworth, 1994), p. 671

11

Information Control and Public Policy:
The Encryption Debate

"... trusting the government with your privacy is like trusting a Peeping Tom with your window blinds."
—John Perry Barlow, "Introduction to PGP"[1]

"Regulated [weak] encryption would provide considerably greater security and privacy than no encryption .... We must balance our competing interests in a way that ensures effective law enforcement and intelligence gathering."
—Dorothy Denning, "To Tap or Not to Tap"[2]

Introduction

The tension between privacy and surveillance or public account-ability has long been an area of intense philosophical and political debate. Many defend the view that upstanding and good citizens should not fear robust government surveillance because they have nothing to hide—hiding from public scrutiny is the domain crimi-nals or those with suspect moral characters. On the other side of the "nothing to hide" view are defenders of privacy rights that limit in-vasions into private domains. There has always been a tenuous bal-ance between individual privacy and public accountability. Searches and seizures may be conducted in private domains but only if cer-tain conditions are met. Moreover, the Privacy Act of 1974 "regu-lates virtually all government handling of personal data."[3]

This balance, however tenuous, is being threatened by the ever increasing flow of data streams across electronic networks. The data that flows across computer networks, satellite transmissions, televi-sion broadcasts, and cellular phones could be about financial trans-actions, voting trends, or personal medical records. The ones and zeros that make up digital information streams transfer content almost flawlessly—any content. An e-mail message could contain sensitive personal information or plans for criminal activity.

In this final chapter I will consider a number of issues related to governmental and societal control of information. More specifically, I will focus on the question of when rights to control certain kinds of information may be justifiably overridden in the name of public security. For example, the wiretap laws of 1968 give certain government agencies limited authority to conduct wire surveillance. In a digitally networked world, however, encoding programs allow individuals to encrypt information so that no one (in theory) could ever view this information without a pass key. If digital cell phones, e-mail messages, electronic transfers, and the like are encrypted with unbreakable codes, then governments will have a difficult time spying on and catching criminals.

Moreover, if money, sales, and services can all be hidden through the use of encryption software, then governments may have a difficult time collecting taxes. For example if financial advice is sold and the transfer of funds encrypted, then it would be virtually impossible for any government to discover this transaction and levy a tax. Business conducted over secure lines, whether a computer network or a cellular phone transmission, may become impossible to trace. Financial privacy guaranteed through the use of strong encryption software could have a profound impact on governmental redistributive models.[4]

Nevertheless, I will argue that a government mandated standard of weak èncryption is not justified—security arguments are not forceful enough to override individual privacy rights. In fact, security arguments actually cut the other direction. It is only through the use of strong encryption that we can obtain an appropriate level of security against industrial espionage, unwarranted invasions into private domains, and information warfare or terrorism.

Cryptography and Government Access to Information

A prominent view in the encryption verses privacy debate is that good upstanding citizens should have nothing to hide. Why, they ask, should you be worried about government agents poking around your hard drive, reading your e-mail, or looking at your financial records? Only criminals should be worried about such surveillance.

Generally, I am dumbfounded by the naiveté exhibited in these views. As if our government, or other governments, would never use such power immorally or illegally. One of the major battles fought over the U.S government's weak encryption scheme (Clipper) was a provision that what would have allowed ill-gotten information to hold up in court. "noncompliance with these procedures [failure to get a warrant or subpoena] shall not provide the basis for any motion to suppress or any other objection . . ."[5] The Fourth Amendment, protecting citizens from "unreasonable searches and seizures," and the decades of supporting case law allowing the suppression of information or evidence that was unjustifiably obtained is quietly swept aside.[6]

To take another example, in the 1950s the United States government sponsored a coup d'état in Guatemala to overthrow a democratic government that had initiated land reform policies. Information control was essential to the overthrow. By restricting access to the area and planting certain stories and rumors government officials were able to convince the American public that we were behind the overthrow of a communist dictator.[7]

It would be quite naive of us to think that big brother has not already compiled databases on many of us along with algorithms, called "spiders," to search for certain patterns that point toward criminal activity. Keeping records of citizens has been, and continues to be, a way for governments to maintain control over their populations:

> Behind a locked door on the second floor of the Beijing Engineering Design Institute is a small room stacked with files from floor to ceiling.
> There is a file here on each of the institute's 600 employees, and although they are never allowed to peek inside, they live their lives with their files looming over them.
> As part of China's complex system of social control and surveillance, the authorities keep a dangan, or file, on virtually everyone except peasants. Indeed, most Chinese have two dangan: one at their workplace and another in their local police station. . . . A file is opened on each urban citizen as he or she enters elementary school, and it shadows the person through school to college and employment.
> Particularly for officials, students, professors, and Communist Party members, the dangan contain political evaluations that affect career prospects and permission to leave the country.[8]

Currently, under the Privacy Act of 1974, U.S. citizens can view their government files although such requests take years and much of the information is blacked out due to national security provisions. The Privacy Act requires that federal agencies:

1. Permit an individual to determine what records pertaining to him are collected maintained, used, or disseminated;

2. Permit an individual to prevent records pertaining to him obtained by such agencies for a particular purpose from being used or made available for another purpose without his consent;

3. Permit an individual to gain access to information pertaining to him in federal agency records, to have a copy made of all or any portion thereof, and to correct or amend such records;

4. Collect, maintain, use, or disseminate any record of identifiable personal information in a manner that assures that such action is for a necessary lawful purpose, that the information is current and accurate for its intended use, and that adequate safeguards are provided to prevent misuse of such information;

5. Permit exemptions from the requirements with respect to records provided in the act only in those cases where there is an important public policy need for such exemption as has been determined by specific statutory authority; and,

6. Be subject to civil suit for any damages which occur as a result of willful or intentional action which violates any individual rights under the Act.[9]

In reviewing these provisions, it is quite alarming to see how little control individuals have over their own personal information. Government agencies are limited in what they can do with personal information and individuals may request that inaccurate information be corrected, but this hardly constitutes control in any robust sense.

Moreover, data sharing by different government agencies threatens the creation of a de facto national database on most Americans. Consider the following examples given by Carl Hausman.[10] Kentucky has a law that allows for the suspension of a student's drivers license if that student cuts class. In Detroit, reporters for various news organizations were tracing the strands of a major web of organized crime by recording license plate numbers on autos parked outside a reputed mobster's home. In Los Angeles, a disturbed young man who doted on an actress spotted her at the wheel of her auto, hired a private investigator to run her plate number through a data base, and learned that her address was in the Fairfax neighborhood of Los Angeles. The obsessed fan shot actress Rebecca Schaeffer to death as she opened her front door. When school reports, driving histories, criminal files, library records, income statements, and the like, all become connected there is the danger of bureaucrats allowing this information to be used in suspect ways.[11]

Wire Tapping and Electronic Searches

In *Olmstead v. United States* (1928)[12] the court ruled that the Fourth Amendment against unreasonable searches and seizures applied to physical things like houses, notebooks, and receipts, but not to electronic communications. Thirty-nine years later the Supreme Court, in *Katz v. United States*,[13] overturned the *Olmstead* decision affirming that privacy interests may be found in personal communications as well as "persons, houses, papers, and effects." More recently, Digital Telephony (1994) was signed into law. This law allows the FBI and other law enforcement agencies to eavesdrop on conversations by simply flipping a (digital) switch at headquarters. Moreover, the cost of ensuring this ability may fall on the phone companies. In the end though, law enforcement walked away with much less they would have liked:

> The Electronic Frontier Foundation led a powerful opposition, backed by AT&T, DEC, Lotus, Microsoft, and Sun Microsystems, which were able to effectively remove on-line information providers from the legislation. The final version . . . also required law enforcement agencies to obtain a court order to obtain telephone transactional information—as opposed to a mere subpoena which was previously required.[14]

But now the stage is set for the encryption debate. If phone and other electronic transmissions are protected with strong encryption, then whether or not law enforcement can jack in is irrelevant.

Encryption

Phil Zimmerman, in 1992, developed an encryption program that was, in large part, built on the work of others. Along with what is now known as public-key cryptography, new encryption algorithms had been developed by a company called RSA (named after the founders and MIT scientists, Rivest, Shamir, and Aldeman). Private/Public key encryption works the following way. Each individual gets a private key that no one else has access to. Everyone also gets a public key that is widely accessible—maybe posted on a Web page. If Fred wants to send a secret e-mail to Ginger, he types it up, encrypts it with Ginger's public key, and sends it to her. She then decrypts it with her private key. Public keys can encrypt messages but not decrypt them. Private keys can un-encrypt messages but not encrypt them. Simple, but brilliant![15] The system RSA developed was powerful and the encryption algorithms were eventually patented.[16] Zimmerman, not wanting such important privacy tools to be monopolized by a single company or government, copied RSA's encryption algorithms and produced a PC encryption program called PGP—which stands for Pretty Good Privacy. In terms of protection, PGP is a remarkable program that affords the user virtually unbreakable encryption power along with an authentication system that leaves a digital signature which cannot be falsified. PGP was then placed on the internet and downloaded by thousands of individuals in numerous countries.[17]

RSA cried foul and sued Zimmerman while the National Security Agency (NSA) questioned him and hinted that use of encryption tools might be unlawful under an Arms Regulation law.[18] It seems that cryptographic tools are listed as national security threats right along side of tanks, biological weapons, and nuclear warheads. The National Security Agency's position is that the widespread use of encryption software will allow criminals a sanctuary to exchange information necessary for the completion of illegal activities.

The battle lines over the general use of encryption technology have already been drawn. On one side are the cypherpunks and net-anarchists who champion complete privacy secured by unbreakable encryption algorithms—odd that many of these same individuals also champion the claim that "information wants to be free." These individuals claim that governments have no business reading the e-mail messages that flow between individuals on the internet or nosing around on network servers looking for incriminating discourse. This is not to deny that governments have a legitimate role to play in protecting individuals against criminal activity. In the most general terms, what many net-anarchists are against is government interference with thought—the thoughts of millions of individuals flowing in bit streams around the globe. Allowing governments to govern thoughts and ideas is quite alarming, for crime, it is argued, is about action, not thought.

Many different arguments are given in support of this view ranging from privacy right arguments to John Stuart Mill's argument for the freedom of thought and expression. Putting aside arguments based on privacy rights (see chapter 8), Mill argues that allowing complete freedom of thought and expression has certain benefits.

> the peculiar evil of silencing the expression of an opinion is that it is robbing the human race, posterity as well as the existing generation—those who dissent from the opinion,

still more than those who hold it. If the opinion is right, they are deprived of the opportunity of exchanging error for truth; if wrong, they lose, what is almost as great a benefit, the clearer perception and livelier impression of truth produced by its collision with error.[19]

The problem, frequently cited by the opposition, is that other concerns such as national security or pursuing and stopping criminal activity may overbalance the benefits gained by complete freedom of expression and thought. More importantly, those against the proliferation of strong encryption programs do not want to censure thought or expression, they merely want to monitor them. If terrorists and criminals are allowed a sanctuary where information can be disseminated without risk of interception, then our national security may be compromised. The wiretap statutes of 1968 and 1978 allow government agencies to monitor communications so long as a court order is secured. The idea is to expand this kind of monitoring into computer environments.

What the NSA and other government agencies propose is the use of Clipper (also known as Slipjack) encryption which would require a key escrow system.[20] The idea is that government agencies could access encrypted data with a court order by obtaining a copy of the encryption key which would be stored at some secure site. Moreover, this strategy not only works for computer networks, but it also works for cordless transmissions such as cellular phone operation, pagers, satellite transmissions, and the like. Current technology leaves cellular phone conversations unprotected and easily intercepted by anyone with the appropriate scanning device. Under Digital Telephony, the government's telephone equivalent of Clipper, all phone transmissions will be encrypted. Like Clipper, however, there will be a backdoor key that the government can use to listen in.

The insidious element in this debate about privacy guaranteed by strong encryption and the government's ability to pursue and catch criminals is that policy seems to be driving the debate. The NSA and other government officials propose some new key escrow encryption scheme and then try to get it adopted as an industry standard. If all, or most, of our e-mail software, telephone communications, and other transmissions are protected by some "built in" version of Clipper, then one side has won by default.

Cypherpunks and net-anarchists typically respond by claiming that new technology coupled with government monitoring through the use of "back-door" encryption keys will allow invasions of privacy unparalleled in history. John Perry Barlow, a co-founder of the Electronic Frontier Foundation, writes:

> I'm willing to take my chances with the few terrorists and drug lords there are out there rather than trusting government with the kind of almost unlimited surveillance power which Clipper and Digital Telephony would give them. It's a tough choice. But when you look at the evil perpetrated by government over this century in the name of stopping crime, it far exceeds that done by other organized criminals.[21]

Moreover, like the NSA's strategy of winning by default, those who defend strong privacy rights have used this method themselves. Zimmerman's creation of PGP and subsequent dispersal can be viewed as nothing more than an attempt to win by default. No matter what conclusions are reached in the debate about information ownership, privacy, and government access, the cat is already out of the bag, so-to-speak. PGP is available, and barring making its use illegal, it or similar encryption software will be used. Only stupid criminals or those individuals who do not care if the government has access to their personal information will use Clipper when more secure encryption is available.

Controlling Information—Some Final Thoughts

Putting aside questions about what will actually occur concerning encryption technology, we may ask what should be the case. As I have argued, it seems plausible to maintain that individuals have, or should have, control of their own personal information. Consider the following example. Suppose that in a few years a new frequency is discovered and a system developed that allows others to monitor your thoughts without your knowledge. Rather than listening to your words with microphones, recording your movements with remote video cameras, or accessing your hard drive with a back door encryption key, suppose the government could obtain a court order and plug into your very thoughts. Advocates of law enforcement may charge that this is going too far, but there is little difference between this case and the digital profiling that will be possible in a few short years. It seems that digital technology has put us on a very slippery slope indeed, and do we really want governments, the most coercive and oppressive institutions in history, to have this kind of power? Consider the following argument given by Ron Rivest, a developer of RSA:

Given the small number of currently available wiretaps per year (under 1000) and the ease of using alternative encryption or superencryption it seems plausible to me that law enforcement could expect at most ten "successful" Clipper wiretaps per year. This is a pretty marginal basis for claiming that Clipper will "block crime."[22]

Rivest raises two important points. First, on average there are less than 1,000 legitimately conducted wiretaps per year in the United States. Second, under the current proposal, the use of Clipper is voluntary. This makes the law enforcement argument very suspicious. Are there numerous *illegal* wiretaps that strong encryption will block? Is the plan to *outlaw* strong encryption after Clipper or some other weak encryption standard becomes the norm?[23]

Furthermore, consider how easily the "security" argument can be stood on its head. National security for government agencies, companies, and individuals actually *requires* strong encryption. With the growing number of attacks on computer networks it is strong encryption, not weak encryption, that will protect us from information war, industrial espionage, and other unwarranted invasions of private domains. Both the French and Soviets have admitted to "tapping in" and collecting valuable information on U.S. companies— information that was then used to gain a competitive advantage.[24] A report from the CSIS Task Force on Information Warfare & Security notes that "Cyber terrorists could overload phone lines . . . disrupt air traffic control . . . scramble software used by major financial institutions, hospitals, and other emergency services . . . or sabotage the New York Stock Exchange."[25] With all of this at stake we may wonder why the FBI and other law enforcement agencies insist on weak encryption.

As noted in chapter 8, there used to be domains of a person's life that were totally inaccessible. A person's home and bedroom, notebook and hard drive, were all sanctuaries against the prying eyes and ears of others. What is alarming is that digital technology is sweeping these domains away. Allowing government restricted access to private phone conversations may have a cost, in terms of privacy, that we are each willing to tolerate, but few would feel comfortable with allowing the government to freely monitor our motions, speech, and expressions—and fewer still would defend government access to our thoughts.

What grounds these sentiments is the plausible intuition that individuals have rights to control personal information. Would I be doing something morally illicit if I put on my new anti-monitoring suit that afforded me complete protection from every surveillance devise except the human eye? It is not as if we have a choice between a ring of Gyges problem and a breakdown of privacy. Criminals will still be caught and certain kinds of surveillance will always be available. For example, "bugs" may still be placed and informants paid. Given this, and my view that individuals have rights to control personal information, I would advocate strong privacy protection—let us make government surveillance of private citizens fairly difficult and costly.

To put the point another way, I do not think that there is a strong enough "public interest" argument on the side of law enforcement to warrant this level of access. It is not as if old fashioned bugging won't work anymore or that physical surveillance will become impossible. There will still be government informants who will gladly hand over incriminating evidence in exchange for immunity from prosecution. Moreover, technological advances will allow law enforcement to keep pace with even the most thrifty of criminals.[26]

If I am correct about all of this, one commonly used "public interest" argument given for limiting privacy rights and intangible property rights has been undermined. It is also far from true to claim that the prevalence of strong encryption technology will lead to disaster. While I do not adhere to the view that "rights hold, though the heavens may fall," in this final chapter I have argued that the "public interest" arguments of law enforcement do not even come close to meeting the threshold for violating rights. The heavens are far from falling.

Conclusions

Robert A. Heinlein, author of *Stranger in a Strange Land* as well as countless other science fiction stories, once claimed that "The sole thing achieved by any privacy law is to make the bugs smaller."[27] Heinlein may be correct, but that travesties will happen does not sanction them—and maybe we will invent bugs to root out and foil other bugs.

It is also most certainly the case that intellectual and intangible works of all sorts will be copied, pirated, and distributed against the wishes of their creators. That this is happening, and will continue to happen, does not justify these activities. There is also no sanctuary in numbers—millions of intellectual property pirates does not justify theft any more than millions of pickpockets.

I have argued in this volume that individuals can unilaterally generate rights to control intellectual works, and at a higher level, that a Lockean model of intangible property is justified. Key features of this model include: deontic-based intellectual property rights that stand independent of utilitarian incentives-based (value maximization) rights; the elimination of the free use zones of "fair use" and "first sale"; a contractual approach for controlling intellectual works after embodiment or sale; and the inclusion of creator's rights within the domain of protection.

I have also argued for individual privacy rights or rights to control sensitive personal information. The explosion of digital technology has made possible severe violations of individual privacy by corporations, news agencies, and the government. In light of these technological changes I am willing to add another exception—a privacy exception—to free speech. The First Amendment should be thought of as a guarantee that protects more abstract political and philosophical kinds of speech and not expressions that contain sensitive personal information about ordinary private citizens. Putting aside the obvious exceptions, there are certain things that are no one else's business.

The cases discussed in these final chapters indicate just how high the stakes actually are. Falling under the domain of intangible property is information of all kinds, including sensitive personal information that may be found in the bedroom, workplace, or hard drive. Those who claim that "information wants to be fee" and advocate universal access cannot maintain this position. Neither can those who defend an exceptionless view of free speech.

It is often said that information is power—and this claim seems true to me. Controlling information, as well as other kinds of intangible and physical property, yields sovereign and autonomous beings the freedom to pursue lifelong goals and projects and order their lives as they see fit.

Notes

1.   John Perry Barlow, "Introduction to PGP," *PGP Guide*.
2.   Dorothy Denning, "To Tap or Not to Tap," *Communications of the ACM* (March 1993), reprinted in M. Erman, M. Williams, and M. Shauf, *Computers, Ethics, and Society* (New York: Oxford University Press, 1997), 262 (all page numbers refer to the reprint).

3.   E. Hendricks, T. Hayden, J. Novik, *Your Right to Privacy* (Carbondale, Ill: Southern
      Illinois University Press, 1990), 3.
4.   In *U.S. v. Miller,* 425 U.S. 435 (1976), the court held that individuals do not have
      a right to privacy in bank records. This, and *California Bankers Ass'n. v. Shultz,* 416
      U.S. 21 (1974), led to several other cases undermining what might generally be
      called "financial privacy." See also *Smith v. Maryland,* 442 U.S. 735 (1979); *Whalen
      v. Roe,* 429 U.S. 589 (1977); and *California v. Greenwood,* 486 U.S. 35 (1988).
5.   Clipper Proposal, cited in J. Wallace and M. Mangan, *Sex, Laws, and Cyberspace:
      Freedom and Censorship on the Frontiers of the Online Revolution* (New York:
      Henry Holt Publishers, 1997), 55.
6.   More recently a debate has raged over the use of Carnivor—a method used by the
      FBI to monitor e-mail and other electronic communications. "It is the electronic
      equivalent of listening to everybody's phone calls to see if it's the phone call you
      should be monitoring." Mark Rasch cited in "Carnivor Eats Your Privacy, Wired
      News Report (July 11, 2000), html://www.wired.com/news/poltics/
      0,1283,37503,00.html.
7.   For a somewhat disheartening account of the many illicit government invasions into
      private domains, see Ellen Alderman and Caroline Kennedy, *The Right to Privacy*
      (New York: Alfred Knopf Press, 1995).
8.   Nicholas D. Kristof, "For Chinese, Lives in Files, Perpetually Open and Over-
      head," *International Herald Tribune*, March 19, 1992, 5, quoted by Anne Wells
      Branscomb in *Who Owns Information?* 16.
9.   U.S. Congress, Office of Technology Assessment, *Federal Government Informa-
      tion Technology: Electronic Record Systems and Individual Privacy*, OTA-CIT-296
      (Washington, DC: U.S. Government Printing Office, June 1986), quoted in Deborah
      G. Johnson, *Computers Ethics*, 96. For more about current laws and regulations
      protecting privacy rights, see Evan Hendricks, Trudy Hayden, and Jack Novik,
      Your Right to Privacy (Carbondale, Ill: Southern Illinois University Press, 1990),
      and Fred H. Cate, *Privacy in the Information Age* (Washington DC: Brookings
      Institute Press, 1997).
10.   Carl Hausman, "Information Age Ethics: Privacy Ground Rules for Navigating in
      Cyberspace," *Journal of Mass Media Ethics* (1994): 135-44.
11.   See generally, John Shattuck, "Computer Matching is a Serious Threat to Individual
      Rights," *Communications of the ACM* 6 (1984): 537-45; and Richard P. Kusserow,
      "The Government Needs Computer Matching to Root Out Waste and Fraud," *Com-
      munications of the ACM* 6 (1984): 546-52.
12.   *Olmstead v. United States* 227 U.S. 438 (1928).
13.   *Katz v. United States* 389 U.S. 347 (1967). See also, *Berger v. New York* 388 U.S.
      41 (1967).
14.   J. Wallace and M. Mangan, *Sex, Laws, and Cyberspace,* 54.
15.   The creators are Whitfield Diffie and Martin Hellman.
16.   "To give an idea of the strength of RSA, consider a challenge the team printed in the
      August 1977 issue of Scientific American. It was an encrypted sentence coded in the
      form of a 129-digit number. The team offers $100, but the world's cryptographers
      sat stumped for 17 years. In the Spring of 1994 an international team of 600
      cryptographers and computer scientists from 24 countries took 8 months and 1600
      workstations to factor the number and crack the code: 'The magic words are squea-
      mish ossifrage.'" J. Wallace and M. Mangan, *Sex, Laws, and Cyberspace,* 46.
17.   DES, another powerful encryption standard developed by IBM and adopted by the
      NSA, is tightly controlled. Recently DES has been cracked in under 24 hours

making it virtually obsolete.

18. See Title 22, Section 2778 of the Federal Criminal Code.

19. John Stuart Mill, *On Liberty*, chapter II, Of the Liberty of Thought and Discussion.

20. The original Clipper system, which was based on a hardware chip failed for lack of market support, design flaws, and sustained criticism. In 1995 the government came up with what some have called Clipper II. This was a software solution and conceded that key escrow agencies need not be associated with the government. Once again there was no market support and 1996, in a draft of a white paper, a third proposal was made—Clipper III. This latest government sponsored encryption scheme is merely Clipper II repackaged. All versions of Clipper allow government agencies access to encrypted information through the use of a second encryption key.

21. John Perry Barlow, "Barlow v. Denning Transcript," (March 10, 1994 online debate between John Perry Barlow and Dr. Dorothy Denning, over the Clipper Chip scheme).

22. Ron Rivest, "A Reply to Dorothy Denning," in *Newsday* editorial (February 25, 1995).

23. Recently the United States and thirty-three other countries signed the Wassenaar Arrangement agreeing to limit strong encryption exports.

24. J. Wallace and M. Mangan, *Sex, Laws, and Cyberspace,* 51.

25. Cited in Christopher Jones, "Averting an Electronic Waterloo" *Wired Magazine* Online News Flash (February 1999).

26. One example that comes to mind is the new technology that can capture an image from a computer screen at a distance. With the appropriate warrant, law enforcement officials can sit nearby and capture information before it is encrypted.

27. Quoted in David Brin's, "The Transparent Society," *Wired Magazine*, December 1996.

Bibliography

Ackerman, Bruce A. *Economic Foundations of Property Law.* Boston Little Brown 1975.

Adelstein, Richard P., and Steven I. Peretz. "The Competition of Technologies in Markets for Ideas: Copyright and Fair Use in Evolutionary Perspective. *International Review of Law and Economics* 5 (1985).

Adler, R. G. "Biotechnology as an Intellectual Property." *Science* 224 (1984): 357-63.

Alderman, Ellen, and Caroline Kennedy. *The Right to Privacy.* Knopf Press, New York, 1995.

Allan, Steven. "New Technology and the Law of Copyright." *U.C.L.A. Law Review* 15 (1968): 993-1028.

Anderson and Hill. "The Evolution of Property Rights: A Study of the American West." *Journal of Law & Economics* 18 (1975).

Ayres, R. "Technological Protection and Piracy: Some Implications for Policy." *Technological Forecasting and Social Change* 30 (1986).

Arnold, N. Scott. "Economists and Philosophers as Critics of the Free Enterprise System." *The Monist* 73 (October 1990): 621-41.

Austin, J. L. "Agathon and Eudaimonia in the Ethics of Aristotle." *Aristotle: A Collection of Critical Essays*, edited by M. E. Moravcsik. Garden City, NY: Anchor Books, 1967, 261-96.

Barlow, John Perry. "The Economy of Ideas: Everything You Know About Intellectual Property is Wrong." *Intellectual Property: Moral, Legal, and International Dilemmas*, edited by A. Moore. Lanham, MD.: Rowman and Littlefield, 1997.

Becker, Lawrence C. *Property Rights: Philosophic Foundations.* London: Routledge and Kegan Paul, 1977.

_____. "Deserving To Own Intellectual Property." *Chicago-Kent Law Review* 68 (1993): 609-29.

Bender, David. "Licensing Trade Secrets Including Software." *Harvard Business Review* (November/December 1968).

_____. "Software Protection; The 1985 Perspective." *Western New England Law Review* 7 (1985): 405-58.

Benko, Robert P. *Protecting Intellectual Property Rights.* Washington, DC: American Enterprise Institute for Public Policy Research, 1987.

Bibas, Steven A. "A Contractual Approach to Data Privacy." *Harvard Journal of Law and Public Policy* 17 (Spring 1994): 591-605.

Boonin, Leonard G. "The University, Scientific Research, and the Ownership of Knowledge." In *Owning Scientific and Technical Information*, edited by V. Weil and J. Snapper. New Brunswick and London: Rutgers University Press, 1989.

Boyle, James. *Shamans, Software, and Spleens*. Cambridge, MA: Harvard University Press, 1996.

Brandt, Richard B. *A Theory of the Good and the Right*. Oxford: Oxford University Press, 1979.

Branscomb, Anne W. *Who Owns Information*. New York: Basic Books, 1994.

Bringsjord, Seinfer. "In Defense of Copying." *Public Affairs Quarterly* 3 (1989): 1-9.

Buchanan, Allen. *Ethics, Efficiency, and the Market*. Totowa, NJ: Rowman & Littlefield Publishers, 1985.

Bugbee, Bruce. *Genesis of American Patent and Copyright Law*. Washington, DC: Public Affairs Press, 1967.

Carey, David. *The Ethics of Software Ownership*. Ph.D. Dissertation at Pittsburgh University, 1988.

Cate, Fred H. *Privacy in the Information Age*. Washington, DC: Bookings Institute Press, 1997.

Child, James W. "The Moral Foundations of Intangible Property." *Intellectual Property: Moral, Legal, and International Dilemmas*, edited by A. Moore. Lanham, MD: Rowman and Littlefield, 1997.

Clark, A. *The Movement for International Copyright in Nineteenth Century America*. Westport, CT: Greenwood Press, 1973.

Cleveland, H. "Can Intellectual Property Be Protected." *Change*, May/June 1989, 10-11.

Cohen, G. A. "Self-Ownership, World-Ownership, and Equality." *Justice and Equality Here and Now*, edited by F. S. Lucash. Ithaca, NY: Cornell University Press, 1983.

Croskery, Patrick. "The Intellectual Property Literature: A Structured Approach." *Owning Scientific and Technical Information*, edited by V. Weil and J. Snapper. New Brunswick and London: Rutgers University Press, 1989.

_____. "A Selected Annotated Bibliography of the Intellectual Property Literature." *Owning Scientific and Technical Information*, edited by V. Weil and J. Snapper. New Brunswick and London: Rutgers University Press, 1989.

_____. "Institutional Utilitarianism and Intellectual Property." *Chicago-Kent Law Review* 68 (1993): 631-57.

D'Arcy, Eric. *Human Acts*. Oxford, MA: Oxford University Press, 1963.

DaSilva, R. J. "Droit Moral and the Amoral Copyright: A Comparison of Artists' Rights in France and the U.S." *Bulletin of the Copyright Society of the USA* 28 (1980): 1-58.

Davidson, D. M. "Common Law, Uncommon Software." *University of Pittsburgh Law Review* 47 (1986): 1037-117.

Davis, Michael. "Patents, Natural Rights, and Property." *Owning Scientific and Technical Information*, edited by V. Weil and J. Snapper. New Brunswick and London: Rutgers University Press, 1989.

Denning, Dorothy. "To Tap or Not to Tap." *Communications of the ACM* (March 1993). Reprinted in M. Erman, M. Williams, and M. Shauf, *Computers, Ethics, and Society* (New York: Oxford University Press, 1997), 247-263.

Dworkin, R. *Taking Rights Seriously.* Cambridge: Cambridge University Press, 1980.

Easterbrook, Frank H. "Intellectual Property is Still Property." *Harvard Journal of Law and Public Policy* 13 (1990): 108-18.

Epstein, Richard A. "On the Optimal Mix of Private and Common Property." *Social Philosophy and Policy* 11 (Summer 1994).

Erman, M., M. Williams, and M. Shauf. *Computers, Ethics, and Society.* New York: Oxford University Press, 1997.

Feinberg, Joel. "The Forms and Limits of Utilitarianism." *Philosophical Review* (1967).

————. "The Nature and Value of Rights." *Journal of Value Inquiry* 4 (1970): 243-57.

————. *Doing And Deserving.* Princeton, NJ: Princeton University Press, 1970.

————. "Grounds for Coercion: Hard Cases for the Harm Principle." *Social and Political Philosophy*, edited by E. Smith and H. G. Blocker. Englewood Cliffs, NJ: Prentice Hall, 1994, 268-81.

————. "The Rights of Animals and Unborn Generations." *Social and Political Philosophy*, edited by E. Smith and H. G. Blocker. Englewood Cliffs, NJ: Prentice Hall, 1994, 364-75.

————. "Wrongful Life and the Counterfactual Element in Harming." *Social Philosophy and Policy* 4.

Fenrich, William J. "Common Law Protection of Individuals' Rights in Personal Information." *Fordham Law Review* 65 (December 1996): 951-1004.

Filmer, Robert. *Patriarcha and Other Writings*, Cambridge (England) New York: Cambridge University Press, 1991, edited by J. Sommerville, 1991.

Fish, Stanley. *There's No Such Thing as Free Speech.* New York: Oxford University Press, Princeton University Press, 1994.

Finnis, John. *Natural Law and Natural Rights.* Oxford: Clarendon Press, 1980.

Fishkin, James S. "Liberty versus Equal Opportunity." *Social and Political Philosophy*, edited by E. Smith and H. G. Blocker. Englewood Cliffs, NJ: Prentice Hall, 1994, 413-19.

Flew, Antony. "Libertarians Versus Egalitarians." *The Libertarian Reader*, edited by Tibor Machan. Rowman and Littlefield Press, 1982, 252-63.

Forester, Tom, and Perry Morrison. *Computer Ethics: Cautionary Tales and Ethical Dilemmas in Computing.* 2nd ed. Cambridge, MA: MIT Press, 1990.

Foster, Frank H., and Robert L. Shook. *Patents, Copyrights, & Trademarks.* 2d ed. New York: John Wiley & Sons, Inc., 1993.

Frey, R. G. "Rights, Interests, Desires and Beliefs." *Social and Political Philosophy*, edited by E. Smith and H. G. Blocker. Englewood Cliffs, NJ: Prentice Hall Inc., 1994.

_____. "Act-Utilitarianism, Consequentialism, and Moral Rights." *Utility and Rights*, edited by R. G. Frey. Minneapolis: University of Minnesota Press, 1984.

Friedman, David. "A Positive Account of Property Rights." *Social Philosophy and Policy* 11 (Summer 1994).

Friedman, Milton. *Capitalism & Freedom*. Chicago: University of Chicago Press, 1962.

_____. "Freedom Under Capitalism." *The Libertarian Reader*. Edited by Tibor Machan. Totowa, NJ: Rowman and Littlefield Press, 1982, 76-85.

Gadbaw, M. R., and T. J. Richards, eds. *Intellectual Property Rights: Global Consensus, Global Conflicts?* Boulder, CO: Westview Press, 1988.

Gauthier, David. *Morals by Agreement*. Oxford: Clarendon Press, 1986.

George, Henry. *The Land Question*. New York: Doubleday, Doran, and Co., 1930.

Gibbard, Allan. "Natural Property Rights." *Nous* 10 (1976): 77-88.

Gilbert, S. W., and P. Lyman. "Intellectual Property in the Information Age: Issues Beyond Copyright Law." *Change*, May/June 1989, 23-28.

Givens, Beth. *The Privacy Rights Handbook*. Avon Books, 1997.

Goldberg, Morton, and John Berleigh. "Copyright Protection for Computer Programs: Is the Sky Falling?" American Intellectual Property Law Association, New York: Computer Law Association, 1989.

Gordon, Wendy J. "Property Right in Self Expression: Equality and Individualism in the Natural Law of Intellectual Property." *Yale Law Journal* 102 (1993): 1533-609.

_____. "Assertive Modesty: An Economics of Intangibles." *Columbia Law Review* 94 (1994): 2579-93.

Greenberg, Dan. "Radin on Personhood and Rent Control." *The Monist* 73 (October 1990): 642-59.

Griffin, James. "Towards a Substantive Theory of Rights." *Utility and Rights*, edited by R. G. Frey. University of Minnesota Press, 1984, 137-60.

Griffin, James. *Well-Being*. Oxford: Clarendon Press, 1986.

Grunebaum, James O. "Ownership as Theft." *The Monist* 73 (October 1990): 544-63.

Gurnsey, John. *Copyright Theft*. London: Association for Information Management, 1995.

Halpern, Sheldon W. *The Law of Defamation, Privacy, Publicity, and Moral Right*. 3rd ed. Columbus, OH: JPM Books, 1995.

_____, and Shipley, David E., and Howard B. Abrams. *Copyright: Cases and Materials*. St. Paul, MN: West Publishing Co., 1992.

Hanser, Matthew. "Harming Future People." *Philosophy and Public Affairs* 19 (Winter 1990).

Hardie, W. F. R. "The Final Good in Aristotle's Ethics." *Aristotle: A Collection of Critical Essays*, edited by M. E. Moravcsik, Garden City, NY: Anchor Books, 297-322.

_____. *Aristotle's Ethical Theory*. 2nd ed. Oxford: Clarendon Press, 1980.

Hardin, Garrett. "The Tragedy of the Commons." *Science* 162 (1968): 1243-48.

Hardin, Russell. "Valuing Intellectual Property." *Chicago-Kent Law Review* 68 (1993): 659-74.

Harris, Amy M. "The Proposed UCC Article 2B," *Intellectual Property Update* (1998): 5.

Hart, H. L. A. "Are There Any Natural Rights." *Rights*, edited by David Lyons. Belmont, CA: Wadsworth Pub., 1979.

_____. *The Concept Of Law*. Oxford: Oxford University Press, 1961.

Hayek, Frederick A. *The Constitution of Liberty*. Chicago: University of Chicago Press, 1960.

Hegel, G. *Philosophy of Right*. translated by T. M. Knox. Oxford: Clarendon Press, 1967.

Held, Virginia. "John Locke on Robert Nozick." *Social Research* 43 (Spring 1976): 169-95.

Hendricks, Evan, Trudy Hayden, and Jack Novik. *Your Right to Privacy*. 2nd ed. Carbondale, Ill: Southern Illinois University Press, 1990.

Hettinger, Edwin C. "Justifying Intellectual Property." *Intellectual Property: Moral, Legal, and International Dilemmas*, edited by A. Moore. Lanham, MD: Rowman and Littlefield, 1997.

Heyman, H. G., and Robert Bloom. *Opportunity Cost In Finance Accounting*. New York: Quorum Books, 1990.

Hill, Christopher S. "Desert and Moral Arbitrariness of the Natural Lottery." In *Philosophical Forum,* XVI (1987): 207-22.

Hohfeld, Wesley N. *Fundamental Legal Conceptions*. New Haven, CT: Yale University Press, 1923.

Holcombe and Meiners, "Market Arrangements Versus Government Protection of Innovative Activity." *Social Science Review* 5 (1983).

Honoré, A. M. "Ownership." *Oxford Essays In Jurisprudence*, edited by A. D. Guest. Oxford: Clarendon Press, 1961.

Hooker, Brad. "Ross-style Pluralism versus Rule-consequentialism." In *Mind* 420 (1996): 531-52.

_____. "Reply to Stratton-Lake." *Mind* 106 (1997): 759-60.

Horowitz, Irving Louis. *Communicating Ideas*. New York: Oxford University Press, 1986.

_____. "Privacy, Publicity, and Networking." Paper delivered at a research conference on privacy. Rutgers University, April 14, 1999.

Hospers, John. *Libertarianism*. Los Angeles: Nash Press 1971.

Howard, Philip K. *The Death of Common Sense: How Law is Suffocating America*. New York: Warner Books, 1994.

Hubin, D. Clayton. "Justice and Future Generations." In *Philosophy And Public Affairs* (1976): 70-83.

_____, and Mark B. Lambeth. "Providing For Rights." *Dialogue* (1986).

Hughes, Justin. "The Philosophy Of Intellectual Property." In *Intellectual Property: Moral, Legal, and International Dilemmas*, edited by A. Moore. Lanham, MD: Rowman and Littlefield, 1997.

Hume, David. *A Treatise of Human Nature*, edited by L. A. Selby Bigge, Oxford: Oxford University Press, 1978.

_____. *Inquiries Concerning The Human Understanding And Concerning The Principles of Morals,* edited by L. A. Selby-Bigge. Oxford: Clarendon, 1972.

Husak, Douglas. "Why There Are No Human Rights." *Social and Political Philosophy*, edited by E. Smith and H. G. Blocker, Englewood Cliffs, NJ: Prentice Hall Inc. 1994, 328-36.

Johnson, Deborah, and John W. Snapper. *Ethical Issues in the Use of Computers.* Wadsworth Press, 1985.

Johnson, Deborah. *Computer Ethics.* Englewood Cliffs, NJ: Prentice Hall, 1985.

_____, and Helen Nissenbaum. *Computers, Ethics, and Social Values.* Englewood Cliffs, NJ: Prentice Hall, 1995.

Johnston, Donald F. *Copyright Handbook.* New York: Columbia University Press, 1967.

Kahin, Brian. "Software Patents: Franchising the Information Structure." *Change*, May/June 1989, 24-25.

Kant, I. *Foundations of the Metaphysics of Morals.* Translation by Lewis M. Beck. Indianapolis, IN: Bobbs-Merrill, 1969

_____, I. *Critique of Practical Reason.*

Karjala, Dennis. "Misappropriation as a Third Intellectual Property Paradigm." *Columbia Law Review* 94 (December 1994): 2595-609.

Katz M. "The Doctrine of Moral Rights and American Copyright Law—A Proposal." *South California Law Review* 24 (1951).

Kenny, A. P. "Aristotle on Happiness."*The Anatomy of the Soul*, Oxford: Blackwell, 1973.

_____. "Happiness." *Proceedings of the Aristotelian Society* LXVI (1965-1966): 93-102.

Kitagawa, Zentaro. "Comment on a Manifesto Concerning the Legal Protection of Computer Programs." In *Columbia Law Review* 94 (December 1994): 2611-629.

Kleinig, J. "The Concept of Desert." In *American Philosophical Quarterly,* 1971.

Kohler, Heinz. *Scarcity And Freedom.* Lexington, MA: Heath and Company, 1977.

Kuflik, Arthur. "The Moral Foundations of Intellectual Property Rights." *Owning Scientific and Technical Information*, edited by V. Weil and J. Snapper. New Brunswick and London: Rutgers University Press, 1989.

Kvart, Igal. *A Theory of Counterfactuals.* Indianapolis, IN: Hackett Publishing Co., 1986.

Kwall R. "Copyright and the Moral Right: Is an American Marriage Possible?" *Vanderbilt Law Review* 38 (1985): 1-100.

Lawson, Gary. "Proving Ownership." *Social Philosophy and Policy* 11 (Summer 1994).

Levin, Michael E. "Equality Of Opportunity." *The Philosophical Quarterly* (1981).

_____. "Opportunity - Right!" *The Philosophical Quarterly*, 1892.

Levy, Steven. *Hackers: Heroes of the Computer Revolution.* New York: Dell Publishing Co., 1984.

Lewis, David. "Probabilities of Conditionals and Conditional Probability."*Ifs*, edited by W. L. Harper, et al. Boston, MA: D. Reidel, 1981, 129-50.

Lieberstein, Stanley H. *Who Owns What Is in Your Head?: Trade Secrets and the Mobile Employee*. New York: Hawthorne Books, 1979.

Lindy, Alexander. *Plagiarism and Originality*. New York: Harper, 1952.

Locke, John. *Two Treatises of Government*, edited by Peter Laslett. New York: New American Library, 1965.

Lomasky, Loren E. *Persons, Rights, and the Moral Community*. New York and Oxford: Oxford University Press, 1987.

_____, and Gerald F. Gaus. "Are Property Rights Problematic." *The Monist* 73 (October 1990): 483-503.

Lyons, David. *Rights*. Belmont, CA: Wadsworth, 1979.

_____. *Forms and Limits of Utilitarianism*. Oxford: Clarendon Press, 1965.

Machan, Tibor. "A Justification Of Private Property." *The Personalist,* 1972.

_____. "The Justification Of Property Rights Again." *The Personalist,* 1973.

_____. "Some Recent Work in Human Rights Theory." *Philosophical Quarterly* 17 (1980): 103-15.

_____. "Dissolving the Problem of Public Goods: Financing Government Without Coercive Measures." *The Libertarian Reader*, edited by Tibor Machan. Lanham, MD: Rowman and Littlefield Press, 1982, 201-10.

Machlup, F. *Production and Distribution of Knowledge in the United States*. Princeton, NJ: Princeton University Press, 1962.

_____, and Penrose. "The Patent Controversy in the Nineteenth Century." *Journal of Economic History* 10 (1950): 1-29.

Mack, Eric. "Individualism, Rights, and the Open Society." *The Libertarian Reader*, edited by Tibor Machan. Lanham, MD.: Rowman and Littlefield Press, 1982, 3-15.

_____. "Moral Individualism: Agent-Relativity And Deontic Restraints." *Social Philosophy & Policy* 7.

_____. "Gauthier on Rights and Economic Rent." *Social Philosophy and Policy* 6.

_____. "Distributive Justice and the Tensions of Lockeanism." *Social Philosophy & Policy* 1 (Autumn 1983): 132-50.

_____. "Self-Ownership and the Right of Property." *The Monist* 73 (October 1990): 519-43.

Mackaay, Ejan. "Economic Incentives in Markets for Information and Innovation." *Harvard Journal of Law and Public Policy* 13 (Summer 1990): 867-910.

MacPherson, C. B. *The Political Theory of Possessive Individualism*. Oxford: Clarendon Press, 1962.

Mangan, Mark, and Jonathan Wallace. *Sex, Laws, and CyberSpace: Freedom and Censorship on the Frontiers of the Online Revolution*. New York: Herry Holt and Company, 1997.

Marx, Karl, and Friedrich Engels. *The Marx-Engels Reader,* edited by Robert Tucker. 2nd ed., 1978.

McCloskey, H. J. "Respect for Human Moral Rights versus Maximizing Good." *Utility and Rights*, edited by R. G. Frey. University of Minnesota Press, 1984, 121-36.

_____. "Rights." *Social and Political Philosophy*, edited by E. Smith and H. G. Blocker, Englewood Cliffs, NJ: Prentice Hall Inc., 1994, 321-28.

McDowell, John. "The Role of Eudaimonia in Aristotle's Ethics." In A.O. 1980.

McMullin, E. "Openness and Secrecy in Science: Some Notes on Early History." *Science, Technology, and Human Values* 10 (1985): 14-23.

Meiners, Roger, and Robert Staaf. "Patents, Copyrights, and Trademarks: Property or Monopoly." *Harvard Journal of Law and Public Policy* 13 (Summer 1990): 911-948.

Mill, John Stuart. *Utilitarianism.* In *J. S. Mill, Utilitarianism and Other Writings*, edited by M. Warnock. Cleveland: World Pub. 1962, New York, 1962.

_____. *On Liberty.* 1859.

Miller, Arthur R., and Michael H. Davis. *Intellectual Property - Patents, Trademarks, and Copyright.* St. Paul, MN: West Publishing Co., 1983.

Miller, Fred D. "Aristotle on Property Rights." *Aristotle's Ethics, Essays in Ancient Greek Philosophy*, edited by John P. Anton and Anthony Preus. Albany State University Press of New York, 1991.

_____. "The Natural Right to Private Property." *The Libertarian Reader*, edited by Tibor Machan. Totowa, NJ: Rowman and Littlefield Press, 1982, 275-87.

Mises, Ludwig Von. "Market Versus Bureaucratic Planning." *The Libertarian Reader*, edited by Tibor Machan. Lanham, MD: Rowman and Littlefield Press, 1982, 147-63.

Moore, Adam D. "Employee Monitoring and Computer Technology: Evaluative Surveillance v. Privacy." *Business Ethics Quarterly* 10 (July 2000).

_____. "Owning Genetic Information and Gene Enhancement Techniques: Why Privacy and Property May Undermine Social Control of the Human Genome." *Bioethics* 14 (Spring 2000).

_____. "Privacy and the Encryption Debate," in *Knowledge, Technology, and Policy* 12 (Winter 2000).

_____. "Intangible Property: Privacy, Power, and Information Control." *American Philosophical Quarterly* 35 (October 1998).

_____. "A Lockean Theory of Intellectual Property." *Hamline Law Review* 21 (Fall 1997): 65-108.

_____. *Intellectual Property: Moral, Legal, and International Dilemmas.* Edited by A. Moore. Lanham, MD: Rowman and Littlefield, 1997.

_____. "Introduction to Intellectual Property." *Intellectual Property: Moral, Legal, and International Dilemmas*, edited by A. Moore. Lanham, MD: Rowman and Littlefield, 1997.

_____. "Toward A Lockean Theory of Intellectual Property." *Intellectual Property: Moral, Legal, and International Dilemmas*, edited by A. Moore. Lanham, MD: Rowman and Littlefield, 1997.

Munzer, Stephen R. *A Theory of Property.* Cambridge: Cambridge University Press, 1990.

Nance, Dale A. "Forward: Owning Ideas." *Harvard Journal of Law and Public Policy* 13 (Summer 1990): 757-74.

Narveson, Jan. "Contractarian Rights." *Utility and Rights*, edited by R. G. Frey. Minneapolis, MN: University of Minnesota Press, 1984, 161-74.

National Assembly of France 1791. "Declaration of the Rights of Man and of Citizens." In *Social and Political Philosophy*, edited by E. Smith and H. G. Blocker. Englewood Cliffs, NJ: Prentice Hall, 1994, 317-18.

Nelkin, D. *Science as Intellectual Property.* New York: Macmillan, 1984.

Nickle, J. "Recent Work On The Concept of Rights." *The American Philosophical Quarterly* (1980).

Nimmer, "Does Copyright Abridge the First Amendment Guarantees of Free Speech and Press?" *U.C.L.A. Law Review* 17 (1970).

Nozick, Robert. *Anarchy, State, and Utopia.* New York: Basic Books, 1974.

_____."Coercion." *Philosophy, Science and Method,* edited by Morgenbesser et al. New York: St. Martin's Press, 1969, 440-72.

Oakley, Robert L. "UCC Article 2B: Some Preliminary Comments on a New Issue for the Library Community." Presented at the Annual Meeting of the Association of Research Libraries, October 16, 1997.

O'Nell, John. "Property in Science and the Market." *The Monist* 73 (October 1990): 601-20.

Pain, Lynn Sharp. "Trade Secrets and the Justification of Intellectual Property: A Comment on Hettinger." *Intellectual Property: Moral, Legal, and International Dilemmas,* edited by A. Moore. Lanham, MD: Rowman and Littlefield, 1997.

Palmer, Tom G. "Are Patents and Copyrights Morally Justified? The Philosophy of Property Rights and Ideal Objects." *Harvard Journal of Law and Public Policy* 13 (Summer 1990): 817-66.

_____. "Intellectual Property: A Non-Posnerian Law and Economics Approach." *Intellectual Property: Moral, Legal, and International Dilemmas,* edited by A. Moore. Lanham, MD: Rowman and Littlefield, 1997.

Patterson, L. R. "Free Speech, Copyright, and Fair Use." *Vanderbilt Law Review* 40 (1987): 1-66.

Pennock, J. R., and J. W. Chapman, eds. *Property: Nomos XXII.* New York: New York University Press, 1980.

_____. *Privacy.* Nomos XIII. Atherton Press, New York, 1971.

Plant, A. *The Economic Theory Concerning Patents for Inventions.* 1934.

_____. "The Economic Aspects of Copyright in Books." *Selected Economic Essays and Addresses,* 1934.

Pool, Ithiel de Sola. *Technologies of Freedom.* Cambridge, MA: Harvard University Press, 1983.

Posner, Richard A. *Economic Analysis of Law.* Boston: Little, Brown and Co., 1972.

_____. "Privacy, Secrecy, and Reputation." *Buffalo Law Review* 28 (Winter 1979): 1-56.

_____. "The Right of Privacy." *Georgia Law Review* 12 (Spring 1978): 393-422.

_____. *The Economics of Justice.* Cambridge. MA: Harvard University Press, 1981.

_____, and William Landes. "An Economic Analysis of Copyright Law." *Journal of Legal Studies* 17 (June 1989).

Prescott, P. "The Origins of Copyright: A Debunking View." *European Intellectual Property Review* 11 (1989): 453-55.

Prichard, H. A. "The Meaning of Agathon in the Ethics of Aristotle." *Aristotle: A Collection of Critical Essays*, edited by M. E. Moravcsik. Garden City, NY: Anchor Books, 1967, 241-60.

Proudhon, P. J. *What is Property? An Inquiry into the Principles of Right and of Government*, trans. by D. Kelly and B. Smith. New York: Cambridge University Press, 1994.

Rainbolt, George. "Rights as Normative Constraints." *Philosophy and Phenomenological Research*, 1993.

Rand, Ayn. "Copyrights and Patents." *Capitalism: The Unknown Ideal*. New York: Signet Books, 1967.

Rawls, John. *A Theory of Justice*. Cambridge, MA: Harvard University Press, 1971.

_____. "Two Concepts of Rules." *Philosophical Review* 64 (1955): 3-32.

Rashdall, Hastings. "The Philosophical Theory Of Property." *Property*. London: Macmillan, 1915.

Raz, Joseph. "Right-Based Moralities." In *Utility and Rights*, edited by R. G. Frey. Minneapolis, MN:University of Minnesota Press, 1984, 42-60.

Robertson, John. "Opportunity Rights?" *The Philosophical Quarterly*, 1982.

Roeder, M. A. "The Doctrine of Moral Rights: A Study in the Law of Artists, Authors and Creators." *Harvard Law Review* 53 (1940): 554-78.

Rose, Lance. *Net Law.* New York: McGraw-Hill, 1995.

Rothbard, Murry N. *The Ethics of Liberty*. Atlantic Highlands, NJ: Humanities Press 1982.

Rothfeder, Jeffrey. *Privacy for Sale: How Computerization Has Made Everyone's Private Life and Open Secret.* Simon and Schuster, 1992.

Ryan, Alan. "Utility and Ownership." *Utility and Rights*, edited by R. G. Frey. Minneapolis: University of Minnesota Press, 1984, 175-95.

_____. "Self-Ownership, Autonomy, and Property Rights." *Social Philosophy and Policy* 11 (Summer 1994).

Samuelson, P. "Creating a New Kind of Intellectual Property: Applying the Lessons of the Chip Law to Computer Programs." *Minnesota Law Review* 70 (1985): 471-531.

_____. "Why the Look and Feel of Software User Interfaces Should Not Be Protected by Copyright Law." *Communications of the ACM* 32, (1989) 563-72.

_____, R. Davis, M. Kapor, and J. H. Reichman. "A Manifesto Concerning the Legal Protection of Computer Programs." *Columbia Law Review* 94 (December 1994): 2308-429.

Sandel, Michael. *Liberalism and the Limits of Justice*. Cambridge: Cambridge University Press, 1982.

Sanford, Bruce W. *Libel and Privacy*. Englewood Cliffs, NJ: Prentice Hall, 1996.

Sartorius, Rolf. "Persons and Property." *Utility and Rights*, edited by R. G. Frey.

Minneapolis: University of Minnesota Press, 1984,196-214.

Scheffler, Samuel. "Natural Rights, Equality and the Minimal State." *Canadian Journal of Philosophy* (1976): 59-75.

Schmidtz, David. "When Is Original Appropriation Required?" *The Monist* 73 (October 1990): 504-18.

_____. "Choosing Ends." *Ethics* 104 (January 1994): 226-51.

_____. "The Institution of Property." *Social Philosophy and Policy* 11 (Summer 1994).

Schoeman, Ferdinand D, ed. *Philosophical Dimensions of Privacy: An Anthology.* Cambridge University Press, 1984.

_____. *Privacy and Social Freedom.* New York: Cambridge University Press, 1992.

Shue, Henry. "Basic Rights." *Social and Political Philosophy*, edited by E. Smith and H. G. Blocker, Englewood Cliffs, NJ: Prentice Hall Inc. 1994, 350-356.

Simmons, A. J. *The Lockean Theory of Rights.* Princeton University Press, 1992.

_____. "Original Acquisition Justifications of Property." *Social Philosophy and Policy*, 1994.

Smart, J. J. C. "Extreme and Restricted Utilitarianism." *Philosophical Quarterly* 6 (1956): 344-54.

Spinello, Richard A. *Ethical Aspects of Information Technology.* Englewood Cliffs, NJ: Prentice Hall, 1995.

_____. *Case Studies in Information and Computer Ethics.* Englewood Cliffs, NJ: Prentice Hall, 1997.

Spooner, Lysander. *The Law of Intellectual Property.* Weston, MA: M & S Press, 1971 (Originally published in 1855).

Stallman, R. "The GNU Manifesto." *GNU EMacs Manual.* Free Software Foundation, 1986.

_____. "Why Software Should Be Free." *Intellectual Property: Moral, Legal, and International Dilemmas*, edited by A. Moore. Lanham, MD: Rowman and Littlefield, 1997.

Stalnaker, Robert C. "Probability and Conditionals." *Ifs*, edited by W. L. Harper et al. Boston, MA: D. Reidel Publishing Co., 1981, 107-47.

Steering Committee for Intellectual Property Issues in Software, *Intellectual Property Issues in Software.* Washington, DC: National Academy Press, 1991.

Steiner, Hillel. "The Natural Right To The Means Of Production." *Philosophical Quarterly* (1977): 41-49.

Stillman, "Property, Freedom, and Individuality in Hegel's and Marx's Political Thoughts." *Property, Nomos XXII*, edited by J. Pennock & J. Chapman, New York: New York University Press, 1980.

Stratton-Lake, Philip. "Can Hooker's Rule-Consequentialist Principle Justify Ross's Prima Facie Duties?" *Mind* 106 (1997): 751-58.

Strong, William S. *The Copyright Book: A Practical Guide.* 3d ed., Cambridge, MA: MIT Press, 1990.

Sumner, L. W. "Rights Denaturalized." *Utility and Rights*, edited by R. G. Frey. Minneapolis, MN: University of Minnesota Press, 1984, 20-41.

United Nations. "Universal Declaration of Human Rights." *Social and Political Philosophy*, edited by E. Smith and H. G. Blocker, Englewood Cliffs, NJ: Prentice Hall Inc. 1994, 318-21.

U.S. Patent and Trademark Office. "Patentable Subject Matter: Mathematical Algorithms and Computer Programs." *Official Gazette*, September 1989.

Waldron, Jeremy. "Enough And As Good For Others." *Philosophical Quarterly* 29 (1979).

_____. "The Advantages and Difficulties of the Humean Theory of Property." *Social Philosophy and Policy* 11 (Summer 1994).

_____. "From Authors To Copiers: Individual Rights and Social Values In Intellectual Property." *Chicago-Kent Law Review* 68 (1993): 841-87.

Weil, V., and J. Snapper, eds. *Owning Scientific and Technical Information*. New Brunswick and London: Rutgers University Press, 1989.

Wellman, Carl. "A New Conception of Human Rights." In *Human Rights*, edited by E. Kamenka and A. Tay. London: Edward Arnold, 1978.

Whalen, John. "You're Not Paranoid: They Really are Watching You." *Wired Magazine* (March 1995).

Wiggins, David. "Claims of Needs." In *Morality and Objectivity*, edited by T. Honderich. London: Routledge and Kegan Paul, 1985.

Williams, Bernard. "A Critique of Utilitarianism." *Utilitarianism: For and Against,* edited by J. Smart and B. Williams. Cambridge: Cambridge University Press, 1973.

Winter, Sidney G. "Patents in Complex Contexts: Incentives and Effectiveness." *Owning Scientific and Technical Information*. New Brunswick and London: Rutgers University Press, 1989.

Wolf, Clark. "Contemporary Property Rights, Lockean Provisos, and the Interests of Future Generations." *Ethics* 105 (July 1995): 791-818.

Worlock, D. "The Challenge of Network Publishing." *Online Information 92.* 16th International Online Information Meeting, London, December 1992. Oxford: Learned Information, 1992.

Young, Robert. "Dispensing With Moral Rights." *Political Theory* (February, 1978): 63-74.

Index